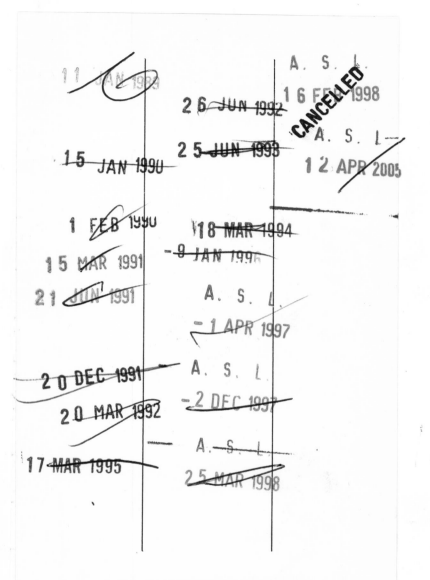

The Post-Imperial Presidency

The Post-Imperial Presidency

Edited by
Vincent Davis

PRAEGER SPECIAL STUDIES • PRAEGER SCIENTIFIC

Library of Congress Catalog Number: 79-67064

Library of Congress Cataloging in Publication Data
Main entry under title:

The Post-imperial Presidency.

    A selection of articles taken from Society magazine.
    CONTENTS: Allison, G. The advantages of a Presidential Executive
Cabinet (EXCAB).—Jewell, M.E. The selection process and the
President.—Korb, L.J. The evolving relationship between the White House
and the Department of Defense in the post-imperial Presidency. [etc.]
    1. Presidents—United States—Addresses, essays, lectures.   I. Davis,
Vincent. II. Society.
JK516.P6   353.03'13   79-67064
ISBN 0-03-055741-0

Published in 1980 by Praeger Publishers
CBS Educational and Professional Publishing
A Division of CBS, Inc.
521 Fifth Avenue, New York, New York 10017 U.S.A.

© 1980 by Transaction, Inc.

0123456789 056 987654321

Printed in the United States of America
H 7999 |5

Contents

Editor's Foreword

Vincent Davis

At the end of 1978, Irving Louis Horowitz, president of Transaction Publications, Inc., and editor in chief of its magazine *Society*, invited me to serve as the editor for a book of collected essays built around six pieces in the November-December 1978 issue of the periodical. Those six pieces, including one of my own, appeared in *Society* under the special theme "The Post-Imperial Presidency," and Horowitz proposed that the anticipated book might carry the same name.

At the beginning of 1979, I accepted the Horowitz suggestion, and the book in hand is the result. I should add, however, that—as much as I appreciated the warm encouragement accompanying the invitation—I did not accept the proposal entirely without misgivings. First, a publication timetable had already been set which allowed only a few months for adding several more contributing authors. This necessarily meant finding good people with significant ideas already formed, and perhaps already expressed in some earlier variation, because no worthy observer-writer on the U.S. political scene was likely to be sitting around in January 1979 with a surplus of time in which to start from scratch cranking out fresh thoughts for a May 1979 deadline. On the other hand, this requirement gave us precisely one of the main things that we sought: Carefully considered viewpoints expressed in readable essays, largely devoid of footnotes and the other trappings so essential to basic research reports, but unnecessary from mature scholars asked to draw on their experience and expertise in providing insightful judgments and speculations.

We think that we did in fact achieve this goal. Although one or two of the essays, including my own, may appear in some respects dated because they were written a year or more earlier, all of the essays deal with questions that remain widely shared by almost all professional observers of the U.S. presidential scene as the United States prepared to enter the decade of the 1980s.

Even the Wildavsky essay, which at first glance might appear so preoccupied with reflections on *The Memoirs* of Richard M. Nixon that subsequent presidential developments were slighted, focuses on an issue of great continuing interest to many behavioral-quantitative as well as traditional-historical observers of the presidency: To what extent are styles in presidential rhetoric a valid indicator of a mindset on the part of the chief executive which can severely restrict the options that get considered while prefiguring the options most likely to get chosen for implementation?

Some of our authors have gone beyond raising questions to the point of suggesting answers for perceived problems. It is probably not surprising that these answers are not uniform, nor, for that matter, are the precise questions chosen for emphasis. What may be surprising, however, is that a group of observers, each working entirely independently of one another, seem to reflect considerable consensus on the broader questions, and on assumptions underlying those wide issues.

The first premise that appears widespread among our authors is that the United States, and indeed the entire world, is undergoing a complex set of massive and profound changes as the decade of the 1970s gives way to the 1980s—changes that can be suggested in general terms, but that are not clearly understood yet by anyone. This may be little more than the current conventional wisdom among scholarly specialists and other professional observers but, if this is what it is, it has been reaffirmed in the essays in this book.

A second premise that appears as a relatively general consensus among our authors is, in contrast, a kind of refutation of the conventional wisdom that many seem to associate with the title of this book. A term such as "post-imperial presidency"—or "post-anything"—seems to suggest a linear theory of history, as if a national society had experienced some unique stage in its development which was then left forever behind as the society moved into a new stage. Our authors, on the whole, do not accept this notion. If there was in fact a recent era when the U.S. presidency could have been accurately described as in some respects "imperial"—and not all of our authors would go this far—they seem to be saying that important components of the era were not entirely unprecedented in American political history, and might reappear (some would argue *should* reappear, although with improvements). While some readers might conclude that this second premise is an unencouraging portent when viewed alongside the first premise or, more bluntly, might say that our authors have described Rome burning while they suggested that a little more fiddling around with Nero would be quite appropriate, our authors on the whole are a bit more sanguine.

In other words, our authors, while expressing pessimism if not alarm on various points and considerations, have looked at American political institutions, and are relatively optimistic. The conclusion seems to be that adaptability has proven one of the system's great virtues, often under great stress, and that this adaptive quality is likely to be evident again, even if painfully slow, with some organizational and procedural tinkering here and there. A rough balance has been maintained between continuity and change, and no author here has been willing to state flatly that the United States has reached the end of the road. Problems, yes, enormous problems, and challenges, but with adequate adaptive capabilities.

In seeking additional contributors for this book, I took note of the fact that all of those who had written the original *Society* essays were political scientists. Thus, I thought it would be useful to get at least one or two people from other backgrounds—ideally, a seasoned journalist with good credentials as a participant-observer around the White House, an economist with a blend of the theoretical and the practical from a policy-oriented perspective sharpened by experience in or near Washington, and perhaps even a longtime bureaucrat with the judgments of a governmental insider. I was more than a little successful in signing up George Reedy in the category of experienced journalist, and in getting Ronald Krieger as an economist with richly diversified experience. Moreover, I was able to add three more political scientists with widely respected reputations—Graham Allison, Lawrence Korb, and Malcolm Jewell—to add to the distinguished political scientists who contributed the earlier magazine essays. Two of those original essayists requested and obtained my permission to expand on their earlier words—an opportunity that the others might have welcomed if the possibility had been more widely advertised, but that in any case accounts for the fact that the pieces in this book by Lawrence Dodd and Martin Levin are longer than their previous versions.

Where I failed was in obtaining a full-scale essay from a longtime bureaucrat, but it is a failure that I can partially remedy here by quoting at some length from a letter addressed to me by a friend who learned of this project. This person is Scott Breckinridge, a learned scholarly sort of man who retired in early 1979 after more than thirty years in an executive branch agency mainly working in Washington, and often in assignments that required close and frequent dealings with elected members of the legislative branch. Moreover, Breckinridge's brother served several recent terms in the U.S. House of Representatives, and a forebear once served as the U.S. vice president. Scott Breckinridge's comments are interesting in part because—although he was trained as a lawyer, and was never much in touch with the political science literature on the subject at hand—his observations in key respects coincide with the findings of our primary contributors. The following are the excerpts from his letter:

> From the New Deal through World War II and the ensuing Cold War, the requirements for effective organization of national resources created a centralized federal system and machinery. The public, and its elected representatives, have

come to look to the center for answers to an entire range of issues that traditionally were handled largely locally or on a regional basis for the first 150 years [of our national experience]. Whether really needed or merely accumulated, the fact is that there is a machinery that should have great strengths in addressing problems comprehensively (regardless of whether any particular person might opt philosophically for more decentralization). The availability of capability does contribute to expectations of performance. And the Congress continually piles new programs and bureaucracies on those already existing.

It was the exaggerations and aberrations arising from the unique personalities of Johnson and Nixon that have crystalized popular feeling about the power of the presidency. It wasn't that we should not have tried in Vietnam, but that we did it badly under LBJ that resulted in social fragmentation and demoralization. It is not that Nixon did things so different from his predecessors, but that he carried them to extremes that gave his administration the tone that the public rejected. It was not so much a basic concern over imbalance between the Congress and the presidency that really focused the new thinking, as it was the eccentricities of the residents at 1600 Pennsylvania Avenue during those years.

I, for one, believe that the trend towards centralization is a product of the more general evolution of our society toward bigness, reinforced by the facilities of communication and transportation unique in the last several decades. This bigness and centralization in the federal structure have been most evident in the executive branch, with the president at its head. The initiatives of the United States as a world leader have merely created additional pressures for growth of executive power.

Congress, which continues to write legislation creating further bigness in government, really has created its own Frankenstein. The creature thus brought into existence provides the Congress with a subject for criticism that distracts attention away from its own failures; if it wishes to reduce the bigness, it has to prove it by stopping its own habit of creating more of it.

It was the Congress that went along with—to say nothing of encouraging—the proliferation of programs that were known as Johnson's Great Society. And even those in Congress who then began to worry about too strong a presidency under LBJ added to these programs, their costs, and the size of the bureaucracies that serve them during the Nixon regime.

At present I see the Congress as reaching rather blindly for tools to strengthen its ability to intervene in proper areas of executive branch performance, albeit in the name of recreating an appropriate balance. Because the Congress is a disparate gaggle of uncoordinated egos, it cannot speak institutionally except in the most simplistic manner on complex major issues. Congress runs its own affairs so badly that its claims as an expert critic of management in the executive branch must be considered as something of an anomaly. As a result, it strikes at the symptoms rather than the basic problems. The ultimate consequence is further confusion about the degree of independence that the executive branch possesses to exercise its responsibilities.

The president continues to need an array of authorities, under the system that now exists, for addressing and resolving problems. While the president must work with the Congress, the Congress must also find a way to work with the president.

The congressional attempt to exercise its control over the budget as a way to manage things in detail may satisfy the image that Congressmen have of themselves, but it also frequently demonstrates a one-dimensional approach to complex problems that should be embarrassing to them if viewed outside the forum of political rhetoric.

I view the concept of an ''imperial presidency'' as serving unfortunately to distort the picture. I see the ineptness (or absence) of leadership in Congress, and its inability to perceive and articulate complex problems and solutions, as being just as dangerous as the threat of overweening executive power. I cannot focus on the presidency apart from our overall governmental/political system, wherein the real question is whether we can long continue to govern ourselves.

Mr. Breckinridge concluded by conceding that his rhetoric in this letter might have been ''a bit high flown,'' and some might think that his long years in an executive branch agency provoked him to deal too severely with the Congress here. But his final question, in one variation or another, is doubtless the ultimate question that animated the contributing authors of all of the essays here. It is the perennial question of the American nation-state, no less pressing after 200-plus years of history: Can we govern ourselves and, if so, precisely how?

*   *   *

I want to thank my old friend Irv Horowitz for giving me this opportunity, all of the contributors who made it possible, and all of my campus coworkers and family members for resisting what must have been a temptation to say, ''The old fool has done it again—taken on yet one more commitment for which he really doesn't have the time, leave aside the ability.''

Vincent Davis
Patterson School of Diplomacy
University of Kentucky
May 31, 1979

The Selection Process and the Presidency

Malcolm E. Jewell

In recent years the debate over the presidency has focused on a variety of problems and conflicts. Does the president have too much power, or too little? Has he become too isolated and too dependent on a small group of White House advisers? Has the country been hurt more by cases of presidential domination of Congress or by deadlock between the two branches of government? Some presidents have been accused of being so absorbed in foreign policy issues that they ignored pressing domestic problems; other are said to have come to the presidency without enough experience to handle foreign policy. Some observers believe that we must analyze the character of candidates more carefully before choosing a president; others believe that the voters must learn more about the candidates' stand on issues.

There is no single cause for the problems afflicting the presidency, and consequently no single cure. We might, however, understand better what has been happening to the presidency if we look more carefully at the process used to select the chief executive. The procedures for recruiting, nominating, and electing a president are changing, and these changes affect the kind of man we elect and his preparation for the job.

Why Do We Sometimes Nominate the Wrong Candidate?

Our method of nominating presidential candidates is a confusing mixture of primaries, state conventions, polls, and exhausting campaigns from New Hampshire to California, culminating in a national convention that may be more disruptive than unifying. The Constitution is silent on the process of recruiting and nominating presidential and vice-presidential candidates except for stipulating natural-born citizenship and age minimum; federal laws on this matter deal mainly with campaign financing and vote fraud; state laws are a

1

crazy patchwork quilt. No rational political scientist or founding father, starting from scratch, would have devised such a system, but in recent years our conventional wisdom has generally held that the system works as well as any alternative. We have been told that it tests the intellectual, physical, and political strength of candidates and that it usually produces the nominee who has the best chance to win the presidential election.

The nomination of Barry Goldwater in 1964 and George McGovern in 1972, however, raised serious questions about that premise. Both won convincing first ballot victories in the national convention, but both were defeated by overwhelming margins in the November election because they lost the support of millions of voters in their own parties. In both cases it seems certain that the party did not nominate its strongest candidate.

Some critics of the nominating process blame the increasing use of primaries and would prefer to return to state conventions for the choice of delegates to national conventions. But Barry Goldwater's support came mostly from state conventions. Other critics urge adoption of a nationwide primary or a series of regional primaries, but George McGovern's nomination was achieved principally through the primaries in a year when there were more presidential primaries than ever before in our history. The primary system exaggerated McGovern's popularity in the party because a large proportion of Democrats failed to vote in the primaries, and because primaries do not give voters a chance to show second or third choices, and therefore failed to show how many of those voting for other candidates would be unwilling to support McGovern in November.

In 1976 the turnout in primaries was higher than ever before (but still less than one-third of that in the presidential election). The Democrats may have nominated their strongest candidate; at least they chose one who could win. But the Republicans nearly nominated a candidate, Reagan, who could appeal to only one segment of his party (like Goldwater and McGovern); one reason was the greater participation of right-wing activists in conventions and primary elections.

The argument here is that the problems of presidential selection are fundamental ones that cannot be solved by tinkering with the nominating machinery, whether conventions or primaries. Our present practices not only fail to assure nomination of the strongest candidate, but they also fail to produce presidents who have demonstrated that they are well prepared for that office. The basic problem is that we have failed to develop any logical, systematic process of screening and training presidential candidates. Our selection procedures place a higher premium on the ability to campaign than the ability to govern. A presidential success story must include a person who is actually three different persons, or, at least, one who has three different sets of skills and talents that do not necessarily overlap: (1) first, the person who can get the party nomination;

(2) second, the one who can get elected by the nation; (3) finally, the person who can successfully deal with the issues that he must confront when he assumes the job in the White House.

Where Do We Find Presidential Candidates?

For a number of years, both parties turned almost automatically for nominees to governors, particularly those from the large, competitive states that were most crucial in the electoral college. From 1928 through 1956 seven of the ten nonincumbents nominated by the major parties were governors. Since 1956 the only governor nominated by either party has been Jimmy Carter; the only other governors seriously considered for nomination have been Rockefeller of New York, Wallace of Alabama, and Reagan and Brown of California. Increasingly we look to Washington rather than to state government for the solution to pressing domestic problems. Governors who want to inaugurate significant new programs find it necessary to raise new taxes, a course of action that leaves them vulnerable to political attack and often defeat. The tenure of most governors is too short to gain national visibility; certainly Carter's four year term in Georgia had little impact on the national political scene. Perhaps most important, governors have absolutely no chance to establish a record of experience in international affairs, in an age when most voters perceive this to be the most important responsibility of the president.

Not since 1928 has either party nominated a cabinet member to be president. Cabinet positions have declined in importance with the growth of the White House staff. Presidents seem less inclined than in the past to select cabinet members because of their political stature. Members now hold cabinet positions for rather brief periods, an average of three years since World War Two. Those with political ambitions leave at the first opportunity to run for governor or senator, while others return to Wall Street, universities or corporations.

In recent years the parties have turned increasingly to the Senate for their candidates. In addition to Kennedy, Goldwater, and McGovern, who were nominated, a large number of senators have been serious contenders for the nomination, including Johnson, Humphrey, and Symington in 1960, Robert Kennedy and McCarthy in 1968, Muskie, Jackson, and Humphrey again in 1972, and Jackson, Bayh, and Church in 1976. There are several reasons for the growing importance of senators. They have visibility in the national media, they deal with national issues, they have longer tenure than governors and cabinet members and so become better known, and they have the opportunity to play some role in foreign affairs—at least to the extent of having a legitimate arena for expressing views on foreign policy.

There are, of course, one hundred senators. What determines which ones become serious presidential candidates? Is is not committee leadership. The seniority system still prevents many senators from becoming chairmen or ranking minority members until they are too old to be seriously considered as presidential candidates. (The major exceptions seem to be senators like Frank Church and Edward Kennedy who were first elected when relatively young.) Although party leadership is not based heavily on seniority, leadership positions are seldom stepping stones to presidential nominations. Recent exceptions are Robert Taft and Lyndon Johnson, who both held top leadership positions and gained reputations as effective leaders before seeking the presidential nomination. The point is that a record of leadership or committee responsibility in the Senate is not considered to be a prerequisite for serious consideration as a presidential candidate. Humphrey, Muskie, and Jackson may be cited as men with strong records of accomplishment in the Senate prior to their seeking the nomination. On the other hand, Estes Kefauver's accomplishments were limited to some highly publicized committee hearings. McCarthy, McGovern, and John Kennedy are examples of members who exercised relatively little influence within the Senate and lacked major records of accomplishment, while Robert Kennedy owed almost none of his political standing to his relatively brief term in the Senate. On the Republican side, Barry Goldwater's senatorial reputation was primarily that of an outspoken, ideological conservative.

What separates most of these men who sought the presidency from their senatorial colleagues is almost entirely the simple fact that they decided to become active candidates and had the resources necessary to sustain their campaigns long enough to gain visibility and credibility as presidential candidates. It has become common practice for candidates to begin their intensive campaigns for the nomination at least two years before the November election; the year prior to the election year itself is perhaps the most important period during which contacts and organizational machinery must be established in most of the states, media attention must be sought, and money must be raised. The growth in the number of primaries has escalated the costs in time, effort, and resources. Senators engaged in such intensive campaigning have been forced to neglect most of their senatorial responsibilities for months on end. In the 1976 campaign both Jackson and Bayh were handicapped by their reluctance to leave Washington and become full-time campaigners.

One of Jimmy Carter's major assets in 1975 and 1976 was that he was unemployed and was able to devote full time to the presidential campaign. As Carter said, "I will spend 250 days on the road in 1975; no one else will do that much. I have nothing to do but campaign." During that same time Jerry Brown was beginning his gubernatorial term and had to spend most of his time in Sacramento building a record and an image; as a result of his late entry into the campaign, his victories in state primaries had little impact on the outcome.

One new trend in the presidential selection process has been the emergence of the vice president as a serious candidate. It has been common for a vice president who succeeded to the presidency through the death of an incumbent to seek election to a full term. But not since John C. Breckinridge in 1860 had any other vice president (or former vice president) been nominated for president by a major party until Richard Nixon ran in 1960. In the 1968 race two vice presidents were nominated by the major parties, and, until his fall from power, Spiro Agnew was leading in polls for the 1976 Republican nomination. Recent doubts about the careless way in which some vice-presidential nominees have been selected and the ambiguous and powerless character of the office itself, however, raise some questions about whether this trend toward the vice president as a potential candidate is one that will, or should, continue.

There is no well defined pattern of leadership succession in either the administration or opposition party that leads to presidential nomination. Rarely does a president groom a member of his administration for the nomination. Leading members of the House rarely become candidates. The Senate now provides a breeding ground for candidates, but they seldom come from its leadership. The governorship is declining as a route to the presidential nomination. Senators or governors emerge as serious presidential candidates less because of their record of accomplishment than because of their skills at image-building and their willingness to neglect their jobs in prolonged and expensive pursuits of the presidential nomination.

In recent years there has been an increase in the number of political amateurs who have run, often successfully, for high political office such as governor or senator. The list includes astronauts (John Glenn), movie stars (Ronald Reagan), and athletes (Jack Kemp and Bill Bradley), as well as the more familiar categories of business and professional people. The growing importance of the media and the ability of candidates with access to lots of money to gain name recognition through the media have contributed to this trend. There is no evidence yet, however, that one can become a plausible candidate for president without some significant experience in government, usually in an elected office. Wendell Willkie was the last businessman to be nominated for president, almost forty years ago. Although Dwight Eisenhower was a popular hero who have never held elective office, he had extensive experience in governmental administration as a general.

The System of State Conventions and Primaries

The route to the presidential nomination requires success in both state conventions and primaries. It used to be possible to win the nomination by concentrating on the convention states because they were in a large majority. Humphrey followed this route entirely in 1968, and Goldwater's greatest success came in convention states in 1964. It used to be true that most state conventions were controlled by party organizations, but in recent years there have been many examples of state conventions being captured by the supporters of a candidate; the examples of Goldwater in 1964 and McGovern in 1972 are familiar. The McGovern reforms in the Democratic party have made state Democratic conventions more vulnerable to such organized assaults. But the result of more democratic procedures and broader participation in choosing delegates to state conventions is an increase in the number of activists who are involved. It does not by any means guarantee that the delegates selected at a convention will be representative of the preferences of the state party's voters.

Because almost two-thirds of the states now use presidential primaries, a candidate must campaign in them, but must also choose with care and foresight which ones to enter and which to avoid. To run a successful race in a series of primaries requires enormous resources: money, volunteers, staff, time, and tactical skill. Because the primaries are spread out over a period of more than three months, and the results are reported in depth by the media, a candidate must not only win substantial numbers of votes and delegates to appear successful, but must win more votes than he is expected to and must increase, rather than decrease, his percentage of the vote as the campaign moves from state to state. As soon as the candidate begins to falter, his sources of funds start to dry up and his volunteers desert him. The key to primary success is momentum. In 1976 Jimmy Carter demonstrated his success by: first, winning more votes than anyone expected in the first caucuses and primaries; second, entering and winning most primaries during the middle part of the campaign; and third, establishing such a large lead in committed delegates that he was able to survive some defeats in the last few primaries.

It is true that primary campaigns demonstrate something about the relative ability of candidates to win support from the voters—an essential characteristic for the party's nominee. But the demonstration may be deceptive. Goldwater defeated Rockefeller in the 1964 California primary, but he lost the state by more than a million in the November election. John Kennedy was thought to have proven, by his West Virginia primary victory in 1960, that his Catholic religion would not be a serious liability in heavily Protestant states, but in fact it was such a liability in the general election. McGovern's surprising strength in the 1972 primaries did not accurately foreshadow his weakness as a candidate in the November election, when he won a smaller proportion of the two-party vote than any Democratic candidate in a century.

There are several reasons why the primaries may provide a poor measure of candidates' potential voting strength in the fall election. Not all candidates run in all primaries. The turnout of voters is relatively low, frequently a third or less of the party's voters who will go to the polls in November. In some states members of the other party may vote in a presidential primary, but in most states the primary offers no real measure of a candidate's ability to attract votes from outside his own party. The primary measures only the first choices of voters and provides no clue to the breadth of support a candidate has. Voters in a primary are never asked: which of these candidates would you be willing to vote for if he were nominated? McGovern and Wallace won substantially more primary votes in 1972 than any other Democratic candidate, but neither could have been elected because of the adamant opposition of substantial numbers of Democrats and independents. There is reason to believe that those voters with strong ideological commitments are disproportionately likely to vote in primary elections.

One final point about primaries deserves to be emphasized. We know little about what factors influence the choice of voters in presidential primaries, but there is evidence that voters are often poorly informed about the views on issues of those candidates who have only recently become household words. For example, polls have shown that Eugene McCarthy won more votes from hawks than from doves (regarding Vietnam) in the 1968 New Hampshire primary. There is evidence that voters' perceptions of McGovern were not clearly formed early in the campaign, and that many of them began to perceive him as a radical only after most of the primary elections were over. It is not true that most voters do not care about the issue orientation of candidates. It is true that voters are likely to develop perceptions about issue positions rather slowly, only after they have become familiar with the candidate's image and style.

The lack of voter familiarity with the issue positions of relatively new candidates is partly the fault of the media, which tend to report more about the candidate's personality and style and to devote excessive amounts of time and space to reports and predictions about the outcome of primaries. It is sometimes the fault of candidates who, like Jimmy Carter, talk about trusting the American people and not lying to them, rather than confronting the often difficult and divisive issues of the time. It is now possible in the early primaries for relatively unknown candidates who have strong organizations, plenty of funds, shrewd advisers, and appealing campaign styles to defeat candidates whose record of service and stands on major issues are much better known. Consequently, as the primary campaign progresses, voters are more often forced to make choices among candidates whose record and issue orientation are not clear to them. As the voters become more familiar with the candidates and issues during the fall campaign, they may become disillusioned with the candidate whose fresh style and image were so appealing early in the primary campaign.

What Are the Consequences of the Selection Process for the Presidency?

The presidential selection process not only makes possible the nomination of candidates like Goldwater and McGovern who cannot be elected. It also facilitates the election of a president, like John Kennedy or Jimmy Carter, who has not held major administrative or legislative posts in the national government (or even governed a major state) and thus must acquire on-the-job training as president. A candidate who has been elected president has demonstrated his ability to organize and finance a prolonged campaign for the nomination and election, his skill in putting together a winning coalition, and his personal ability to win the trust and confidence of millions of voters. But he has not demonstrated that he has administrative skills, that he understands the complex processes of government, or that he can exercise good judgment. Even if he is talented and experienced, with a good grasp of the nation's problem, he may be ill-prepared for the presidency because he has devoted almost all of his time and attention for more than a year to campaigning.

A new president does not necessarily come into office with a clear understanding of the major policies that he wants to follow. In theory, the campaign should not only give a candidate an opportunity to develop and articulate his policies, but force him to do so. In practice, this is not always the case. During a campaign, priority is usually given to developing a candidate's image. Modern techniques for using the media, particularly television, emphasize brief commercials based on cliches rather than long speeches. The speeches that a candidate gives have become increasingly general, and some candidates have developed the practice of repeating the same speech, with minor variations, from coast to coast. This does not mean that there are not substantive differences between the positions taken by candidates, which voters should be able to recognize. But the issues that generate most controversy during a campaign are often trivial or of temporary importance.

The nature of campaigns does not force the candidate to develop policies in enough detail and with enough pertinence to acual problems so that he knows what his program is going to be when he takes office. When he is elected, he has to turn to the interest groups that supported him, or set up special task forces, in order to develop policies for his administration.

Jimmy Carter came to Washington in 1977 knowing very little about how the national government operates and apparently convinced that the Congress was simply a larger version of the Georgia legislature. Although it is difficult to recall any new president in the last half century who was less familiar with national government, most recent presidents have been poorly prepared for the job. No president since Hoover has had major civilian administrative experience in the national government, although Eisenhower's military experience should have familiarized him with many aspects of government. Two recent presidents, Johnson and Ford, had held major congressional leadership posts, though these experiences did not lead to consistent success in legislative-executive relations. Neither John Kennedy nor Richard Nixon, whose congressional experience had been in nonleadership roles, demonstrated a deep understanding of the intricacies of the legislative process when they were in the White House. While an apprenticeship as vice president might appear to be excellent training for the presidency, the curious nature of that position makes it an imperfect training ground. If both Lyndon Johnson and Richard Nixon came to the presidency relatively well prepared, it is not clear that the vice-presidency contributed much to that preparation. Johnson's training ground was the Senate, while Nixon's was the national political arena.

Perhaps the most serious difficulty that a winning presidential candidate faces is that of staffing his administration. There is a tendency for the new president to pick as his closest advisers and members of his White House staff persons whose major qualification is that they have demonstrated skill as campaigners—as political tacticians, advance men, and advertising specialists. Among President Kennedy's closest advisers were several men whose experience had been primarily in the area of campaign politics—Lawrence O'Brien and Kenneth O'Donnell, for example. Three of President Nixon's closest advisers were H.R. Haldeman, an advertising man who served as an advance man in the 1956 and 1960 campaigns and ran the 1962 gubernatorial campaign; John Ehrlichman, a lawyer active in the 1960, 1962, and 1968 campaigns; and John Mitchell, a lawyer specializing in municipal bonds who served as campaign manager in 1968. Jimmy Carter's closest advisers had served him as governor in Georgia, but men such as Hamilton Jordan and Jody Powell had got their start as campaign advisers in 1970 and had proven themselves in the 1976 presidential campaign. The question is not whether these men were competent, but whether their friendship and loyalty to the president precluded their giving him an objective report on unpleasant facts, and whether they understood the processes of national government and national problems well enough to advise the president and to negotiate with other political groups and leaders.

The difficulty faced by the new president in staffing his administration is not limited to the White House staff, but extends to members of the cabinet and the other top administrative positions. John Kennedy summarized the problem when he said: "For the last four years, I spent so much time getting to know people who could help me get elected president that I didn't have time to get to know people who could help me, after I was elected, to be a good president."[1] The new president needs a pool of talent from which to choose his cabinet members and other top advisers. Ideally these should be persons who have been associated with the president and share his views on major policy issues, who are familiar with both the executive and legislative processes in Washington, and who have enough stature to add political strength to his administration.

If we read accounts of how recent presidents have chosen their top administrators and advisers, we are struck by the difficulties they have had. There is, of course, a large pool of talent, much of it to be found in research centers and institutes, universities, corporations, and law firms in the Northeast, whose members are characterized by experience in government, a diversity of skills, and often ambition. But these are not individuals well known to the president;

they do not share his confidence and perhaps not even his views. Presidents seem to have given little or no thought to filling cabinet posts until they were elected. Although the most important members have been chosen after considerable thought, some cabinet posts seem to have been filled casually and almost accidentally.

The president often must seek cabinet members from beyond the range of his acquaintances. President Kennedy had never met either Robert McNamara or Dean Rusk before bringing them to Washington for an interview and selection to the cabinet. President Carter has had only the most casual contact with many of those whom he appointed to his cabinet. New presidents appear to give little thought to the policy implications of major appointments, even in such fields as foreign affairs. John Kennedy's appointment of Dean Rusk, instead of Adlai Stevenson or William Fulbright, had important policy consequences that seem to have been ignored during the selection process. Carter's choice of Vance and Brzezinski does not seem to reflect a concern about implementing a clear, consistent position on foreign policy. Richard Nixon apparently did not recognize that Walter Hickel and George Romney were likely to become advocates within the cabinet of policies that were contrary to his own.

The president has a great deal of freedom in choosing his cabinet. Unlike the British prime minister, he does not need to include certain members because of their political strength or the strength of interests that they represent. It is difficult to find an example of a cabinet member who was included because he was too powerful politically to be excluded, although Eisenhower's choice of John Foster Dulles as secretary of state satisfied the conservative-nationalism wing of the Republican party. On the contrary, there are recent examples of individuals who have been excluded because they were politically powerful and might constitute threats to the president. President Nixon made it clear that he did not want Nelson Rockefeller in his cabinet, and President Kennedy resisted great pressures to appoint Adlai Stevenson to his cabinet.

In summary, the president's cabinet usually consists of individuals most of whom are not well known to him and have not been associated with his campaign, are not known to be committed to his program, are seldom very familiar with the executive and legislative processes, and do not have significant political stature or power as individuals. Perhaps because of this, recent presidents have made less use of the cabinet than did their predecessors, and have relied more heavily on the White House staff. The president starts his administration with a small staff of persons who are loyal to him and have proven their skill in campaigns but know little about government, and an assortment of cabinet members, few of whom he knows well and few of whom are familiar with the intricacies of national government and politics. Over a period of years, most presidents come to rely heavily on those persons from both groups who have the skill and knowledge to master the process of government. But the period of learning and transition often proves to be difficult and costly for the new administration.

The Personal Basis of Presidential Power

One consequence of the growing importance of presidential primaries and the decline of traditional party organizations is that winning the nomination is a personal achievement, based on campaign skills and resources. The presidential nominee does not owe his nomination to any particular political leaders or organizations. Moreover, victory in the presidential election is based increasingly on the ability of the candidate to put together a winning coalition; it is based less on traditional party strength. This is because of the importance of television and the replacement of established party organizations by ad hoc groups of workers committed to one candidate. It is also because fewer voters owe allegiance to a party or vote in accord with party loyalty than in the past. The victories of Eisenhower and Nixon were personal victories, because they had to overcome the Democratic advantage in party identification; and Lyndon Johnson's landslide victory in 1964 was obviously a personal victory. Even Carter's narrow victory was a personal one in the sense that his coalition was distinct from those of recent Democratic candidates.

It is also significant that presidential and congressional elections are becoming increasingly independent. Congressional candidates win because of their own skills in developing a political base, and incumbents remain in office by keeping in touch with their constituents and providing services for the district, as well as staying in tune with the dominant interests and ideology of the district. Many Congressmen represent safe districts, while those from more marginal districts learn how to develop political security by serving the needs and interest of their constituents. Just as the President is less dependent on his party for election, the Congressman has become more independent of both partisan trends and presidential coat-tails in winning election.

One reason for the independence of Congressmen and their reluctance to follow presidential leadership is a recognition that their past and future elections depend much less on presidential coat-tails than on their own efforts. Nevertheless, the size of the president's electoral margin may have an important effect on his success, particularly in his relations with Congress. Congressmen seem to believe that a presidential landslide election is an indication of public support for the president's programs, at least in broad terms. Lyndon Johnson's landslide victory in 1964 not only led to larger Democratic margins in Congress but also created an atmosphere of support for the president's programs during the next two years. On the other hand, John Kennedy was very conscious of the narrow margin of his victory in 1960; he believed it seriously reduced his effectiveness and limited the scope of what he could accomplish both in legislative matters and foreign affairs. He talked about programs that he could not initiate until he had won a larger margin in 1964.

Because the political base of presidential power is so personal, the president does not feel responsible to broader elements in either the national party or the congressional party. There is no one who can call him to account if he abuses his power or ignores the opinions of others, short of the draconian and therefore rarely used impeachment process. A landslide victory, such as Johnson won in 1964 and Nixon won in 1972, may tempt the president to act arrogantly. But if the president's electoral margin is narrow or he suffers from other political liabilities, he tends to be unable to draw political strength from his party, and may in fact look upon strong leaders in his party as rivals rather than sources of strength.

If a president's political base is highly personal, he may place undue emphasis on the results of public opinion polls. One recalls President Johnson carrying poll summaries in his pocket and showing them to anyone who raised questions about his policies. Of course, poll findings can sometimes be an asset rather than a liability. But, as a broad generalization, most presidents in recent decades have tended to experience declines more often than increases in public support as reflected in the polls, once the steadily shorter postelection "honeymoon" is over and the new president begins to cope with the nearly intractable problems of contemporary America. Moreover, the poll-indicated increases in public support tend to be momentary jumps associated with specific events, but jumps that quickly fall back again into the overall pattern of declining or erratic support.

Conclusions and Suggestions

The central argument here has been that a variety of political trends in the United States have tended to weaken the processes of presidential recruitment and selection. In some cases the result has been the nomination by parties of weaker rather than stronger candidates. Even the winning presidential candidates have been hampered, once they assumed the presidency, by the narrow base of their political power and the shortage of political skills and knowledge, possessed by them and by their closest associates and appointees.

Recent presidents have fallen short of the qualifications that ideally a president should have, including:

1. the ability to articulate policies and to lead public opinion;
2. the political skills needed for bargaining with congressional and interest group leaders;
3. administrative experience and effective managerial skills for harnessing and guiding the massive federal bureaucracy;
4. a familiarity both with the political process in Washington and with the vast array of issues—national and international—that confront a president.

Where would we find candidates who could approximate these ideal requirements? The unfortunate answer is: in no single place. Members of Congress, particularly experienced senators, may have several of these qualities, but generally lack administrative experience. Governors, even in large states, lack familiarity with both the political process and the issues of national government. Cabinet officers and private sector executives often lack the political skills necessary for dealing with both public opinion and political leaders. Most certainly, we can say that we will not find the ideal president among those whose strongest claim to fame is their ability to win in the early party caucuses and primaries.

The problem of recruiting better qualified presidents has two aspects: one is to develop practices and procedures that might produce more candidates with a better blend of political and administrative skills and experience; the second is to enhance the possibility that such candidates will be nominated, rather than those who have the time, resources, and skills needed to win primaries.

To begin with the second part of the problem, we must recognize that most of the rules and procedures now guiding the nominating process were adopted by national party organizations and by the various states. Nevertheless, it would be possible for the Congress to pre-empt this field by passing legislation establishing a national primary or regional primaries, and the Congress can also influence the presidential selection process through its regulation of campaign financing and the federal funding of campaigns. Whether any particular plan adopted by Congress to regulate and/or fund the selection process would achieve the desired results is, of course, open to question. There is no way of assuring that voters will choose experienced, skillful leaders if they are disillusioned with Washington politicians and prefer outsiders. Moreover, it seems impossible as well as undesirable to turn back the clock, reverse the steps taken to open up the nominating process, and return control over that process to state political leaders.

The single feature of the nominating process that most handicaps established political leaders is the long and extensive campaign, in both primary and caucus states, that has become necessary to win the nomination. The effect is to require office holders to neglect their jobs to campaign personally across the country. A logical goal of reform might be to impose some kinds of restrictions on the length of the campaign. One cannot, of course, forbid prospective candidates from attracting public attention months and years before the election. However, the primary calendar might be shortened, as the Democratic party is attempting to do; the geographic pattern of primaries might be rationalized through a regional primary system; and the laws regulating campaign funding of presidential candidacies might be changed to discourage early full-scale, expensive campaigns.

The problem of developing and recruiting potential candidates who have a broader range of skills and experience does not lend itself to any single solution.

The challenge is to create circumstances in which persons with potential presidential aspirations could acquire both legislative-political and executive-managerial skills in significant national and international responsibilities at the federal level, and also utilize the talents of the most able governors who may lack federal experience. This suggests the need to facilitate greater mobility among branches and levels of government.

It is already true that governors often move into federal positions, either Senate seats or cabinet positions. It is somewhat less common for members of either branch of Congress to accept cabinet positions, for the obvious reason that they may be unable to regain their congressional seat and they will lose their seniority. This latter factor may become less of a deterrent as the importance of seniority gradually declines in Congress. If members of Congress, particularly those with previous executive experience in the states, are among the most promising presidential candidates, the question is whether the most able members of Congress have enough opportunity to assume leadership positions there.

Until recently, the answer was clearly negative, in large part because of the seniority system. In recent years a series of factors have increased the prospects that a talented, experienced, and ambitious member of Congress, particularly in the Senate can, within a few years, gain leadership positions that will provide the responsibility, experience, and publicity needed by a presidential candidate. One new factor has been the weakening of the seniority system of selecting chairmen, particularly in the House; closely related has been the growing importance of subcommittee chairmanships in both houses. A substantial increase in voluntary retirements has also reduced the waiting time for more junior members.

The most logical place to look for presidential candidates might be in the party leadership of both houses; in fact, this has seldom been a source of presidential recruitment, as we noted earlier. In the House, leaders are chosen in large part because of seniority, or more specifically their place on the ladder of succession. In both houses, leaders tend to be chosen because of their skills in legislative compromise and alliance-building with little regard to other skills needed to win, or succeed in, the White House. In order to enhance the prospects of congressional leaders to become effective presidential candidates, there must be a change in congressional norms for electing leaders, which cannot be dictated from outside the Congress.

A final source of presidential candidates is the vice presidency. The first question is whether a vice president can be chosen who has many of the qualities required of a president. Recent experience suggests that there is a trend in that direction, and that presidential candidates are giving more thought to the selection process. The second questions is whether the role of the incumbent vice president can be enhanced to groom that person more effectively as a prospective presidential candidate (as well as a possible president by succession in midterm). The factors making it difficult if not impossible for a president to give substantial responsibilities to the vice president are too well known to need repeating here. However, if the vice president were not publicly elected but were appointed by the president, subject to senatorial confirmation and to dismissal by him like a cabinet member, it is possible that the choice would be made more carefully and that the president would be more willing to grant him broad responsibilities. A president could, if he chose, announce his proposed choice at the start of the campaign. The experience in the selection of Nelson Rockefeller and Gerald Ford as vice presidents suggests that such an appointment is much more carefully undertaken and reviewed than the choice of a running mate at a national convention. If, as has sometimes happened in recent years, one of our most skillful and experienced leaders is chosen as vice president, there ought to be some way to make that office more significant and to use the vice president's talents better.

Anyone who proposes structural reforms in the political system should be aware not only that they are difficult to effect but that they often have unintended consequences. But the point of this paper is that there have been important structural changes as well as political trends in our presidential selection system in recent years, and that many of them have undermined the presidency. Those who propose, or oppose, future changes ought to give serious thought to the probable effects of change on the nature of the presidency and the political system as a whole.

Note

1. Kennedy P. O'Donnell, David F. Powers, and Joe McCarthy, *Johnny, We Hardly Knew Ye* (New York: Pocket Books, 1973), p. 270.

Citizen Participation in the Presidential Process

Richard Rose

The ideal of citizen participation is most nearly approached in national elections, when every citizen is eligible to vote, and most citizens do. But voting is only a means to the end of governance. Voting is politically important when related to the choices that citizens have in an election, and the influence that votes have upon determining who governs.

Viewing the political participation of Americans in a comparative perspective can show whether citizen participation in the United States is relatively high or low. It also emphasizes the extent to which American institutions for citizen participation—elections, parties, and forms of government—are *different* from those common to the great majority of Western nations that enjoy free elections and a developed modern economy. Such differences may be interpreted as positive evidence of America's uniqueness, or alternatively, make one wonder why the United States should be out of step with the rest of the world.

Who Votes?

In every Western nation, the right to vote is granted to every adult, man or woman, who is a resident citizen. The chief practical implication of this definition of the right to vote is the exclusion of resident noncitizens, who now constitute a visible minority of *gastarbeiter* (guestworkers) in nearly every European country, but a relatively small proportion of the total electorate, of the order of 2 to 5 percent. Only in Switzerland, are *gastarbeiter* and other resident aliens a substantial proportion of the total population; 59.5 percent of the Swiss population is eligible to vote, compared to 67.3 percent in neighboring Austria and 70.0 percent in America. In Europe today the ineligibility of residents to vote is important only in the context of the direct elections to the European

Parliament in 1979. The five million or more citizens of one member-state of the European community living in another member-state remain citizens of the community, but will not be eligible to vote in their country of residence in the 1979 European parliamentary election.

In virtually every Western nation, the government is responsible for ensuring that persons eligible to vote are actually registered to vote, a prerequisite for participation in national elections. Voting registration is carried out in an annual nationwide census-type canvass undertaken by public officials, or registration records are updated regularly with information about the movement of citizens from one residence to another. The United States is unusual in following the obsolete English practice of placing upon the individual citizen the burden of registering to vote, a practice abandoned in Britain with the adoption of universal suffrage in 1918. Since then, the British government has required local government officials to compile annually the list of voters in each parliamentary constituency. In Canada, where distances are as great as America and population far sparser, an enumeration of eligible voters is carried out specially before each general election.

The absence of any statutory requirement in America to compile an accurate register of eligible voters for generations facilitated the denial of the vote to southern blacks and to many southern whites. Today, it still effectively disfranchises tens of millions of Americans because they have not or cannot register sufficiently far in advance of the date of an election.

The result is that the turnout of voters in the American presidential election—the most widely publicized free election in the Western world—is far below the level of participation in almost any other Western country. In countries where voting is compulsory, such as Australia, Belgium, and Italy, turnout is consistently above 90 percent, and in Western nations without compulsory voting, turnout is usually above 80 percent (see Table 1). In the United States, turnout at the five presidential elections since 1960 has averaged 59.1 percent of the estimated eligible electorate.

The question that European experience raises is: Should the American federal government compile or compel the 50 states to compile a register of voters? The practical effect of doing so is certain: it would significantly increase voter participation. The argument for doing so is an argument of principle: the right to vote should be positively facilitated by government action, in an age when the government is active in doing so much else for citizens. The arguments against are couched in practical language, emphasizing the administrative obstacles in compiling a uniform register, and the added complications of federalism.

How Much Voting?

While the United States lags far behind other Western nations in the proportion of its citizens voting at national elections, it is far ahead of any other Western

TABLE 1
Voting Turnout in Western Nations since 1960

Country	Number of Elections	Highest Turnout %	Average Turnout %
Australia	8	95.5	95.0
Italy	4	93.2	93.0
Austria	5	93.8	92.9
Belgium	6	95.1	91.8
Iceland	4	91.4	91.0
Luxembourg	3	90.6	89.8
Germany	5	91.1	88.6
Sweden	7	91.7	88.3
New Zealand	6	90.5	88.2
Netherlands	5	95.1	88.1
Denmark	8	89.3	87.8
Norway	5	85.4	82.3
Finland	5	85.1	81.5
France	4	80.9	77.7
Canada	6	80.3	76.7
Britain	5	78.9	75.4
Ireland	5	76.9	75.1
Switzerland	4	64.5	59.4
United States	5	62.8	59.1

Source: Calculated from data in T.T. Mackie and Richard Rose, *The International Almanac of Electoral History* (New York: Free Press, 1974).

---

nation in the *number of votes* cast by the average citizen in a given four-year period.

The first reason for this is federalism. Americans typically vote in at least four jurisdictions—federal, state, county, and town elections. This four-layer system of government is not usually found in Europe.

The second reason is the separation of powers. Americans are unique in being able to vote for both legislative representatives and executive leaders at all levels from city council members and mayor to congressmen and president. In a parliamentary system, individuals vote only for legislative respresentatives; those elected choose the prime minister and cabinet.

A third reason is the long ballot. When Americans vote, they vote for many executive offices from dog-catcher or coroner to governor and president. By comparison, parliamentary regimes do not allow citizens to vote for any incumbent of an executive office. France is unique in Western Europe in having a powerful directly elected president. Countries with figurehead presidents often still choose the president indirectly (e.g. Italy) or without a contest (e.g. Ireland), and only a few by popular election (e.g. Finland and Austria).

America is also distinctive in that some of its judges, and in some cases, police commissioners or sheriffs, are subject to direct election.

Fourth, there are many special purpose jurisdictions—school boards, sewer districts, etc.—which are directly elected. In Europe, such bodies almost invariably are appointed by the government of the day, or do not exist at all. For example, education is often a branch of central government; its officials are no more subject to direct election than would be military commanders.

Fifth, many Americans are able to enact or repudiate legislation through referenda on legislation and some taxes affecting current or capital expenditure. The principle of the referendum is not unique to America, and at the national level, is it most important in Switzerland. But state and local governments do use the autonomy of federalism to hold more such ballots collectively in a given year than does the whole of Europe put together. The recall of elected officeholders is another distinctive American institution, but rarely used and hardly needed if terms of office can be as brief as two years.

Sixth, primary elections in which all registered electors have the right to cast a ballot to choose among a party's potential candidates are unique to America. In continental Europe, the mechanics of proportional representation "slate-making" normally compel centralized decision making by party committees determining the party's candidates for safe and hopeless seats. Voters have a limited opportunity to alter party endorsements. Primaries at multiple levels of government can double many of the opportunities to vote described above. In southern states where a run-off election is prescribed when no candidate secures half the vote in the first primary contest, it can treble an individual's opportunity to vote.

Such a contrast might first lead an American to ask: Why do Europeans have so few opportunities to vote? The answers are several: the heritage of aristocratic rather than populist decision making; the belief in the efficacy and impartiality of civil servants as executive agents of government; and reliance upon parties to organize and direct government through parliamentary institutions. A European who enquired about the advantages and disadvantages of the American system of multiple voting would first of all be met with answers emphasizing the principle of direct determination of issues by citizens (e.g., bond issues or school tax referenda) and, the superiority of decision making by elected representatives. A European might wonder whether something was not lost by reducing the standing of experts and civil servants, and by the disintegration of parties.

How Competitive Are Elections?

A vote without a choice is useless. In a state with one party and only one candidate for each office, the act of voting registers a government's ability to mobilize its subjects, and not the free choice of citizens. In fact, elections with absolutely no choice are relatively rare in the world. But it is equally the case that elections that are truly free and competitive are in the minority.

American voters are offered less choice than voters in any other Western nation, for consistently only two parties have a chance of winning congressional seats or the White House, and there is far less variation in party labels at the state level in America than, say, in neighboring Canada. In 1977 in Denmark 11 different parties won election to the 175-seat Folketing, and in the Netherlands, 11 parties won seats in the 150-seat Tweede Kamer.

American voters are also greatly restricted in the ideological range and variety of parties. There are some differences between the median Republican and the median Democrat, and differences *within* each party that can show up in primary contests. But there are no more (and quite possibly less) than the spectrum of choice within the anti-Socialist coalition that governs Sweden today. A typical European voter may easily be offered a choice between a conservative, agrarian, and middle-of-the-road liberal party on one side of the political spectrum, and a socialist and communist party on the other. In addition, Christian and nationalist parties might also win seats in the national legislature and sometimes other parties as well.

As previously noted, American voters are distinctive because they vote for *governments that compete* against one another to control policies, and to evade the responsibility of financing them. An American would be in a small minority if he or she was out of sympathy with all major elected officials at all levels of government affecting himself, and unable to share any sympathy with a faction or tendency in the dominant party of a one-party area.

At the level of the presidency, American voters have demonstrated the effectiveness of competition by a readiness to turn one party out, and put its opponents in. In four of the eight presidential elections since 1945, the incumbent party has lost the election. Only Dwight D. Eisenhower has served two full elected terms of office, and President Carter's four predecessors were all unable to serve as long as they had originally wished. In Europe, by contrast, one party can rule indefinitely by itself or in coalition. In Sweden, the Social Democrats governed for 44 years from 1932 to 1976, and in Italy, the Christian Democrats have governed for 32 years without a break since 1946. A man such as Robert Menzies, Liberal leader in Australia, was prime minister there for 18 years.

In the United States, competition is effectively guaranteed by primary elections offering voters in a one-party area the chance to choose between different standard-bearers. Primary elections may turn more on questions of personality than issues, but a voter does have the opportunity at this stage to register an effective protest against an incumbent representative, even if in a one-party area. In Europe only the Republic of Ireland gives voters a similar opportunity, for the single-transferable-vote feature of its proportional representation system requires each voter to rank candidates in order of preference. In a constituency returning, say, four representatives to the Dail, Fianna Fail might be sure of winning two seats; it would leave the voters to decide which two of the three candidates it nominated would be its winners by the way in which they ordered their first, second, and third preferences.

There is no agreed or simple answer to the chicken-and-egg question: Do American voters have a restricted choice between non-socialist parties because no bloc of voters favors socialist or social democratic type programs, because political leaders are opposed to such ideologies, or because parties are prepared to adopt socialist type policies on an ad hoc basis, without becoming members of the Socialist International? There is evidence to support a qualified yes to all three of these propositions. An American might note that, in the absence of primaries, competition within European elections is normally restricted to choices between parties, and not between individual candidates. Moreover, there may well be such a thing as "too much" choice, as in the celebrated polarized pluralism of Italian politics, which has kept one party in government with no alteration in office, for fear of too great a change if the pendulum swung to the Communist party of Italy. Polarization in France has excluded Socialists as well as Communists from office for more than 20 years.

How Representative Are the Results?

Proportional representation is the usual means by which voters choose their representatives in free competitive elections. While the particular methods of allocating seats in proportion to votes are many, all have one thing in common: the desire to apportion seats in the national Parliament in close approximation to a party's share of the total national vote. In the extreme case of the Netherlands, a party need win less than one percent of the vote (0.67 percent, to be precise) in order to be given a seat in the Tweede Kamer. Proportional representation does not cause a multiplicity of parties; for example, the Federal Republic of Germany has proportional representation, and only three parties are represented in the Bundestag. It simply assures a party with, say 10 percent of the national vote, that it will win something like 10 percent of the seats in the national legislature.

By comparison, the first-past-the-post electoral system used in America, Britain, Canada, and New Zealand is a system of *dis*proportional representation. The single-member constituency produces a winner-take-all contest; the candidate with the most votes—whether more *or* less than a 50.1 percent absolute majority—is the sole victor. Proportional representation has multi-member constituencies returning anything from three to 150 members; seats are allocated to parties in proportion to the votes received in the constituency. The United States requires a presidential candidate to win a majority of electoral college votes, but in 1948, 1960, and 1968, presidents have not won a majority of the popular vote. In a parliamentary system with a first-past-the-post ballot it is even a more unusual for a party that takes half the seats also to win half the popular vote. This has not happened in Britain since 1935, in Canada since 1945, and not since 1951 in New Zealand. In the extreme case of Britain in 1974, in February the Labour party under Harold Wilson won office with 37.2 percent of the popular vote, slightly less than George McGovern polled when being routed in the 1972 American presidential ballot. In October 1974 the Labour party won an absolute majority of seats in the House of Commons with 39.3 percent of the popular vote, only 0.8 percent more than Barry Goldwater polled in losing nearly every state in America in the 1964 presidential contest.

The great anomaly in the American electoral system today is that the judicially mandated concern with the apportionment of voters to equalize constituencies is not matched by a similar concern about apportioning seats according to votes. A black man's vote in a predominantly white district in Mississippi has no more value than a white person's vote in Harlem. The courts, and with them, eminent American political scientists, have shown no intellectual or practical interest in proportional representations' ability to ensure that voters in a minority can secure *some* representation, as is possible in a multimember proportional representation district. In the Deep South, blacks and whites may achieve equality in registration, but if the black minority is evenly spread throughout a state, then the 65 or 76 percent of the electorate that is white can determine 100 percent of the state's congressional representation, and the black minority vote may be of no value. Under proportional representation, blacks might select three or four congressmen in a 12-seat multimember district. Their representatives would remain a minority—but a minority in proportion to their electoral strength, rather than a voiceless minority.

The characteristic British defense of the first-past-the-post ballot is that it makes for strong and effective single-party government. Historically this has been regarded as far preferable to coalition government, or government by a party needing a few third-party votes in Parliament to pass legislation. The political crisis of 1974 in Britain has led a number of British political scientists to question whether the conventional adversary contest between two parties alternating in office is desirable. Moreover, the surge of nationalist parties in Scotland and Quebec raises the spectre of the government of a part of a country demanding complete independence because it has won a majority of seats in a provincial assembly—but only two-fifths of the popular vote.

One American defense of the first-past-the-post ballot is practical: the impossibility of electing a president, governor or mayor by anything other than a winner-take-all decision. Senate elections could not be held by proportional representation, without abandoning the allocation of two representatives per state. In the House, proportional representation would be meaningless in the 15 states with only one or two representatives. In the six largest states, each returning 20 or more representatives, it would destroy any link between individual members and a congressional district. The second defense is empirical: the clustering of population (especially blacks) does provide some representation for the country's largest and most important minority. In the mosiac of American society, national minorities can often be local majorities. A third point is that of principal: proportional representation could encourage the fragmentation of parties along socially divisive lines—whether racial, regional, religious, or ideological. It can be argued that the only thing that holds the loose coalition of Democrats and Republicans together is the *necessity* for unity in elections fought on the first-past-the-post basis.

How Responsible Is Government?

The overwhelming mass of citizens can only participate vicariously in government, by electing representatives to act on their behalf. A government in which everyone was forced to participate would be totalitarian, if effective, and pandemonium if not centrally directed. In some circumstances, increasing participation can be inefficient because of extra time required for deliberations, or even counterproductive, insofar as participants lack the expertise to make decisions in their long-term interests.

The European ideal of government emphasizes centralized decision-making by party leaders rather than popular participation. The determination of the policies of government is meant to be in the hands of a cabinet which controls both legislature and executive, united by party loyalties and discipline. The governing party defines programs by recognized and accepted procedures that tend to support the domination of a small group of technical experts and brokers of votes within annual party congresses. Government decisions are not subject to judicial negation, and in most European countries they are also not hamstrung by complexities of federalism. In such circumstances, an individual can vote for or against a party according to an overall assessment of the state of the country.

In practice, most European countries depart from this simple ideal of party government, because coalition government is usual. In nine of 14 European countries, coalition government is almost invariably the rule, and in six—Denmark, Finland, the Netherlands, Belgium, Switzerland, and Iceland—no one party is ever in a majority by itself. In France, the personal appeal of the president (especially since de Gaulle's demise) cannot manufacture a majority for his party in the National Assembly. Only Germany and Italy have coalition governments with one party as a dominant partner. Three countries appear to be in transition—Norway and Sweden moving toward coalition government as the norm, and Austria away from it. Only in Britain and Ireland is single-party government without coalition normal. Within Britain, the Conservative and Labour parties are each coalitions of interest, held together by a desire for office, and, the same is true, *mutatis mutandis*, of Fianna Fail in Ireland. Single-party governments do not consist of a set of politicians banded together because of agreement upon basic principles and immediate programs of government; they are a coalition of politicians united by a mutual desire to share in office.

In Washington, government can be described as a coalition between parts of the executive branch and Congress, cutting across party lines and differing from issue to issue, rather than from general election to general election. It is hard for an individual to elect a representative to represent accurately his whole bundle of interests, for one candidate may reflect accurately the voter's domestic political views, and the other his views on international security. In Europe, such a voter might have four parties to choose from, and thus have a much higher probability of one party agreeing with both major concerns. But the greater multiplicity of parties also makes for a greater probability of coalition government. Instead of coalitions occurring separately on domestic and foreign policy bills in Congress, they must last the duration of a Parliament. A voter's policy preferences are as likely to be completely, half-way, or not at all represented under one system as the other.

The fundamental contrast between European and American institutions of representative government is that the American system makes government responsible for *doing less* in society. The Founding Fathers built a system of checks and balances into national government, as well as dispersing power through a federal system. The difficulty of assembling winning coalitions in a political system in which party and governmental fragmentation mirror each other reduces the things that government can do. For better or worse—and judgment is a matter of political values—American government does less for an to its citizens than its European counterparts. For example, the proportion of the gross national product spent by government is much lower in America than in almost any other Western nation.

If one fears a "too powerful" government and has confidence in pluralistic and individualistic social institutions, this emphasis upon individual and group responsibility is desirable. If one believes government is a postive and benign influence, which can better provide for the public interest than social pluralism, then a more powerful government, subject to fewer constraints because of popular election and fragmented institutions, is desirable.

Is Voting Enough?

While popular participation in free elections is a necessary condition of what we mean by democracy, it is not the only attribute of what may be regarded as good government in the Western world. There are some who argue that elected representatives should be socially as well as politically representative of the electorate—that is, a legislature should have the same proportion of manual workers, women, or racial or religious minorities as are in the electorate as a whole. Another critique of voting is that elected officials are no longer able to make the major decisions needed in a complex postindustrial society.

The early introduction of white male suffrage in America prior to industrialization meant that there was not a long struggle to achieve suffrage for propertyless manual workers and farmers, as occurred in nearly every European society prior to 1918. Early Socialist and Communist parties sought to demonstrate that they were the party of the newly enfranchised working class by nominating and electing manual workers to Parliament. By contrast, the American Congress has long been dominated by lawyer legislators, though an American law degree could be obtained without facing many social barriers once widespread in Europe. Congressmen, whatever their social origins, are at least middle class, and a significant minority are rich or of high social status as well. Ironically, the postwar social revolution in European education and social status has led to the "bourgeosification" of political leadership on the Left. Many so-called "workers" parties cannot criticize opponents on class grounds, if their leaders too—e.g., Olaf Palme in Sweden, Enrico Berlinguer in Italy, and Francois Mitterand in France—are university graduates.

The heterogeneity of American society is such that historically social differences could not be reduced to two groups, except in the division of black and white in the South. American parties have encouraged participation by consciously emphasizing the need for social representation within a party—the "balanced ticket"—and, at local electoral levels, organizing a national minority into a dominant or decisive voting bloc. Because of persistent discrimination against blacks in the Democratic party in the Deep South, (and because of the tactical interests of would-be presidential nominees), the Democratic party took the lead after 1968 in trying to impose standards of social representativeness upon the selection of elected delegates to its presidential nominating convention. But the resulting innovations of the McGovern-Fraser Commission produced a dilemma. In the words of a political science member of that commission, Austin Ranney: "Representation of biological characteristics was at odds with the commission's other objectives of open access and representation of preferences. The party could provide for a fair fight or it could provide for a guaranteed result, but it could not provide for both." Both American and European experience have demonstrated that making elected representiatives socially representative is difficult, and may even be contrary to other requirements of free elections.

In contemporary postindustrial society, government responsibility for the management of the economy makes it depend upon what happens in the market place, as well as at the polling place. People can vote with their feet or their pocketbooks, as well by putting an X on a ballot paper. Nineteenth-century liberal philosophers were concerned with individuals securing their wants in both domains, and securing them through their own choices. In late twentieth-century Western societies, however, big decisions are made by large organizations—business corporations and labor unions, as well as government agencies. The interdependence of each group upon others to achieve prosperity or avoid depression has drawn their leaders together in tripartite "corporate" bodies to deliberate upon such problems as wage and price controls, and inflation and unemployment.

There is a good common-sense reason for the growth of trilateral deliberations about the economy: business, unions, and government each have some powers important in the economy, yet each is affected by what the others do. Yet these deliberations also raise basic political questions. Neither unions nor business corporations can claim to represent the whole of a society, as a government can. This is particularly the case in the United States, where the proportion of the labor force belonging to trade unions (22 percent) is one-half or one-third the proportion in European countries. Peak business organizations are even harder to assimilate to the institutions of democratic elections, for their constituent parts may be trade associations or corporations. When shareholders vote, they do not do so on the basis of equal votes for all shareholders; votes are distributed in proportion to shareownership.

The growing importance of these trilateral relationships raises questions about the extent to which more attention ought to be directed, in both America and Europe, to mechanisms for protecting or advancing rank-and-file influence in both unions and business corporations. These organizations have been subject to far less scrutiny than have government institutions and are far more likely to "misrepresent" those in whose name they claim to speak, because of tendencies to oligarchy in any large organization. Failure to make corporate leaders responsive to followers could lead to the growth of civic indifference neutralizing government's authority.

To compare American and European provisions for popular participation in government is to test one reality against another. An American cannot dismiss as "impossible" institutions of government that palpably *do* work in Europe, just as a European cannot scoff at American innovations unknown on his side of the Atlantic. Such comparisons avoid the mistake of judging reality by ideals unattainable even in an ancient Greek polis, where slaves and nonvoters were even more numerous than in Thomas Jefferson's Virginia.

It is easy and tempting to explain the different and often unique attributes of the American system by reference to history, especially that which is institutionalized as the very framework of government by the Constitution. Yet there are issues raised by comparison that can be acted upon as well as thought about by Americans. The foregoing discussion highlights the following:

- Is there a need for American government to attain midtwentieth century standards of electoral administration, by making government responsible for voter registration?
- At state and local government level, where constitutions can be periodically revised, what are the relative merits of electing a single chief executive, as against voting separately on a long ballot slate of executive officeholders?
- Would it be desirable, through legislation or by measures initiated within parties, to encourage more *or* less concern with the development of distinctive programs and policies?
- Under what circumstances if any, (e.g., radically evenly balanced or highly imbalanced cities) would proportional representation provide a more desirable council of elected representatives?
- If coalitions are inevitable in any large party, including nominally ideological European parties, what are the variety or types of coalition that would best suit American conditions?
- To what extent do new trends in the economy mark a turning away from decision making in the electoral market place to decision making in the economic market place? If so, what alternations—in terms of participation in union or business organizations, as well as government—are desirable or practicable?

The Presidency, and Questions About National Unity

George E. Reedy

At the end of the decade of the 1970s, any effort to analyze the future of the presidency can be nothing but crystal-gazing. The office is caught in fundamental social changes, nationally and internationally, which are too massive to permit a careful scrutiny of all possible causes and consequences. That the office will continue to occupy a central role in the American society and political system, barring a major upheaval, is a reasonably good guess. But the extent of the president's powers, the manner in which they will be used, and the efficacy of the White House as a symbol of national unity and commitment are questions which cannot be readily answered. The last question may well be the most important.

Unfortunately, far too little attention has been focused on the essential role played by the presidency in holding the nation together. We live in a management-oriented age in which people tend to regard government as an exercise in administration. The need for a symbol of public identification has received short shrift in academic studies. The president's ceremonial duties have generally been treated as a secondary aspect of the White House office and, in fact, there have been numerous proposals to relegate all of them to the vice president. This approach is much too simplistic. It assumes that problems can be solved solely through the application of rational thought and sufficient resources—a very dubious assumption.

Naturally, a combination of rationality and resources is one element in achieving social solutions. But it is only one, and not the most important, element in the equation. First, there must be some means by which people can identify themselves as members of a group who will act in concert. Second, the unifying force must have sufficient potency to keep the group together even when many of the individuals within it disagree with the course of action that has been adopted. Intellectual debate, as academics will attest, has a tendency

29

to widen rather than narrow differences. Ranks are closed only in response to symbols, and, in the United States, the most important such symbol has been the presidency itself.

In many respects, this has been an unfortunate reality. An effective symbol of unity should be removed from the partisan arenas where people invariably divide into ideological groupings that can come to detest each other passionately. The president is not aloof from political combat. On the contrary, he is the nation's principal politician. He is responsible for devising programs, for persuading Americans to follow his lead in fields where opinion is sharply divided, for enforcing laws which are rarely noncontroversial. Above all, he has the responsibility for finding a proper balance between the many factions that compete for resources and for prestigious positions in the body politic. Even the most skillful of chief executives could not possibly discharge these functions without sowing seeds of discord and, on the record, they all have.

Nevertheless, the presidency as an office has succeeded remarkably well as a national symbol. It got off to a good start with George Washington who, whatever else may have been his merits or demerits, projected a picture of a man well above partisan squabbles. Actually, it was not too difficult to sustain a dignified posture in the early days of the Republic as government was largely the creature of ''gentlemen.'' Of course, there were some fights with nasty overtones, such as the dispute between Jefferson and Hamilton. But the passionate debates that have characterized most of our history did not crop up immediately. When they did, the presidency proved capable of holding the nation together except for the tragic period of the Civil War.

Of course, it was never the presidency alone that sustained unity. There was a whole complex of forces at work, the most important being a tradition of accommodation and a flexibility that held out hope for the future to groups at the bottom of the social ladder. Nevertheless, the presidency has been the symbol of that complex, and the strength of the nation has usually varied directly with the esteem in which the office was held. It is difficult to ascribe to sheer coincidence the lowly state of the White House in the 1850s, and the outbreak of the Civil War. It is not necessary to claim that one caused the other in order to realize that they were connected.

The presidential mystique has been so strong that it even survived unpopular presidents. In Washington, there is a widely held belief that a highly popular and respected Republican senator lost his opportunity to secure the presidential nomination by making a slighting remark concerning Harry S Truman at a point when the Truman political stock was low. It was not even a public remark, but one made by the senator at a Gridiron Club banquet where statements are supposedly off-the-record. It was heard by newspaper publishers, however, and notwithstanding the fact that most of them were Republicans (and anti-Truman), they were offended by a slur against even an incumbent president whom they did not like. Consequently, to the extent that newspaper people figure in processes that can enhance or diminish a prospective candidate's image, that senator's name became blurred in political speculation.

The strength of the symbol is difficult, perhaps impossible, to measure. It is an intangible which makes its presence felt but only in forms that are not quantifiable. It is visible insofar as men imitate the president and women imitate the First Lady. It can affect the economic life of the nation by setting new styles. It manifests itself in the strongest possible form when people sense international trouble and instinctively draw around the chief executive. One of the more cynical observations of the political "pros" on the Washington scene is that nothing repairs low presidential ratings quite so quickly as a foreign crisis.

The question at the approach of the decade of the 1980s is whether this presidential mystique has been injured and, if so, can it (or should it) be restored? It is a good question to which, so far, only simplistic answers have been forthcoming.

It is almost axiomatic in "pop" political analysis to assume that sharply adverse public reaction to the combination of the Vietnam War and the Watergate events shook the presidency so strongly that the prestige of the office was partially destroyed, perhaps irreparably. It is not too difficult to conclude, certainly, that the prestige was damaged. This is quickly apparent in the inability of the three presidents starting with Nixon to serve as models of conduct and attire. Earlier, huge numbers of American men switched to small cigarette holders, and Scotties became very popular dogs, in emulation of Franklin Delano Roosevelt. Harry S Truman led the American male into the era of loud sport shirts. John F. Kennedy was the inspiration for the cult of youth. Lyndon B. Johnson made tostadas, tacos, and burritos fast-food items peddled by nationwide chains. No one, however, can point to any lasting impact upon life styles by Presidents Nixon, Ford or Carter. This is not to contend that such matters are in themselves of great importance. But they are indicators of that intangible national mood toward the presidency, and should be noted as such.

Of more immediate importance is the newfound willingness of Congress to enter the field of foreign policy—an area in which presidents have reigned virtually unhampered since the late 1940s, and some might even say since the very early 1940s. The significance of this has not been fully appreciated in the popular literature. With few exceptions, representatives and senators have a positive antipathy to international affairs. This is an arena in which politically *they cannot win*. To support a president in a foreign policy initiative which is successful merely means that the legislator escapes opprobrium. The credit goes to the White House. On the other hand, support of a president in an unsuccessful foreign policy initiative is not at all disastrous. The legislator can always tell his constituents that he had qualms, but felt his duty to be that of supporting the commander-in-chief. However, to oppose a president in a successful foreign policy initiative means to wind up looking ridiculous, and to oppose a president in an unsuccessful foreign policy initiative is to give the president an opportunity to blame the failure on the opposition. It is a "heads, I stay where I am—tails, I lose" proposition and few practical men wish to call it "tails."

Therefore, when the Congress passes such measures as the War Powers Act, blocks even the most innocuous intervention in Africa, and launches deep probes into the Central Intelligence Agency, it is a safe bet that the members are being prodded by their constituents. In the past, the voters have generally signalled "hands off foreign policy" to their Congressmen. It was the domain of the president—so much so that legislative opposition to a war as unpopular as the one in Vietnam was met with reprisal at the polls. As institutions, the House and the Senate are equipped with astonishingly tenacious memories. One of the most persistent is the ludicrous posture in which legislators found themselves in the late spring of 1939 when they turned down President Roosevelt's request to revise the Neutrality Acts. One of the more prominent senators, William Borah of Idaho, explained his opposition to Mr. Roosevelt on the grounds that he had better sources of information than the president and he knew that there would be no war in Europe the coming autumn. This happened less than three months before the Nazi invasion of Poland.

In the forty years that followed, there were many fierce debates on foreign policy issues. Before the U.S. entry into World War II, they included such matters as the Lend Lease Bill, the revision of the Neutrality Acts, and Selective Service. After the war, they included President Truman's Point IV program, and the question of adherence to NATO. As a journalist, I covered all of these events and it became apparent very early that no matter how passionate the opposition, the outcome was inevitable. Every single one of those contentious measures rested upon a presidential initiative and, while that was not enough to secure silence, it was enough to assure assent—usually by lopsided majorities.

There is no reason to belabor the point that in the contemporary political climate leading into the 1980s, presidential prestige is insufficient to carry a controversial proposal. President Carter, as of summer 1979, had been very careful not to submit himself to any "no quarter" showdown with the Congress. It could be doubted whether his efforts to nail down an enduring peace in the Middle East would result in any such test. Speculations suggested that he might eventually find himself forced into such a face-off with Congress in connection with the efforts to secure endorsement of the SALT II treaty package. The prospects were not particularly bright as of the time of this writing. Congressional assertions in foreign policy matters, as noted earlier in this essay, were not harbingers of legislative acquiescence.

The reasons for this state of affairs are worth reviewing. There can be no doubt that the Vietnam War and the Watergate events, in combination, tarred the office of the presidency. Lyndon Johnson emerged as a man who appeared to be rash in regard to human lives, and devious in gaining his points. Richard Nixon projected an image of a man who was not at all scrupulous in the methods that he was willing to employ to retain power. In both cases, the acts were commited by the men, but they necessarily eroded confidence in the White House itself.

It seems a bit simplistic, however, to trace everything that followed to the Vietnam War and to Watergate. The presidency has survived scandals of great magnitude in the past. The land-grant steals, "Teapot Dome," and the "five percenters" faded into the history books with the election of new presidents. We are in mid-1979 two chief executives removed from Richard M. Nixon, and yet the public mood of suspicion toward the White House, if not toward all of the federal government and perhaps other layers of government, remains unmistakably in the air. It may well be that the Vietnam War and Watergate merely served as catalysts to bring together strong currents of suspicion that were already at work but which had not previously surfaced.

There is a peculiarly rhythmic nature to the history of American foreign policy that may be worth further stress at this point, in connection with our efforts to gain a better understanding of some costs attached to the eroding stature of the office of the presidency. Foreign policy is inherently a matter that is primarily in the domain of the president, as opposed to the Congress. Some commentators have depicted the relationship between the president and the Congress as a struggle to run the country, but to me this is not a very accurate description, at least in foreign policy matters. In many if not most contexts, there are clearly adversarial aspects in the executive-legislative relationship, but the president and the Congress ultimately serve different roles. They cannot assume each other's duties successfully. If one of them is dominant over the other, it does not mean that the dominant element can play its own role as well as the role of the other. What it is more likely to mean is that *nobody* will perform the role and the tasks that the dominated element should be doing. If the president dominates the Congress, then some important congressional roles will not be performed; and if the Congress dominates the president, then critical executive tasks will go undone.

Congress is ideally suited to serving as the vehicle through which the people of the United States resolve their political differences. It is a slow-moving vehicle—a fact which causes considerable disgruntlement in the executive agencies. The Congress is also inefficient in output if this is measured in terms of the number of laws enacted each year. But, despite these shortcomings (and not everyone would agree that a relatively small number of annual enactments is a shortcoming), the Congress still remains the best structure for obtaining political agreement. Moreover, once that agreement is obtained in the form of Congressional legislation, the American people can be relied on to abide by the laws. On the other hand, the House and the Senate are not "action bodies." Neither of them is equipped to run the country and, when they are dominant, as they were in the last part of the nineteenth century and the early part of the twentieth, foreign policy becomes chaotic.

In contrast, the presidency is ideally suited to serving as an "action agency." The president has all of the reigns of power in his hands. He is commander-in-chief of the armed forces, and the boss of all American diplomats everywhere. There are no real restraints on him other than the boundaries set by the Congress through the authorization and appropriation process. In periods when policy is clear, these boundaries have ordinarily been very liberal. The problem is that the president has no real means of resolving disagreements between contesting political forces. He cannot, as does the House and Senate, debate and work out a compromise, simply because he has no one on his level with whom he must compromise other than himself. When he is dominant over the Congress, it does not mean that he is doing the legislative work. It merely means that he is operating without the necessary political base and, sooner or later, will find that he lacks sufficient support to continue.

In practice, this has meant episodic, and passionate, debates on the part of Congress, but with the president operating foreign policy virtually unchecked during the intervals between such debates. It has actually worked quite well. Once the Congress had reached a firm decision to resist the Axis powers, Roosevelt encountered little further difficulty from the legislative branch. And once Congress had registered approval of communist "containment" (largely through the debate on NATO) a series of presidents discovered that they could do just about anything that they wanted to do. They were even capable of putting the nation into two large (although undeclared) wars in which congressional consent was not obtained but only inferred from legislative inaction or indirect action.

It eventually became clear that the mandate of communist containment had been stretched by presidents beyond viable limits. It first started to come apart during the Korean War when it slowly dawned upon the American people that their sons and daughters were fighting not to win but for something called the *status quo ante*—to restore the situation that existed before the fighting started. It was not a very inspiring goal. Fortunately, it was achieved and we were able to pull back from Korea before morale had deteriorated to a dangerous point. But it left the nation in an angry mood. Fighting just to stay in the same place was a new experience for a people who had been taught (however erroneously) that their previous military efforts had all led to victory. They did not like the new situation in which a clearly visible triumph was not automatic—indeed, not even the apparent goal.

The Vietnam War was the final straw. Unlike Korea, Vietnam did not have front lines, and the American people were even deprived of maps showing that they were staying in one place. It was a seemingly endless conflict in which there was no real possibility of obtaining victory. The best hope was to punish North Vietnam sufficiently that its leaders would make a "deal." Very few men can be found who are willing to die to "make a deal," and Americans are no exception. The inevitable public reaction was not only disillusionment with the war but a loss of confidence in the leadership that was willing to prosecute it. Since this leadership includes both a Democratic and a Republican president, there was a tendency to think of the situation in terms of "national" rather than "partisan" leadership.

The simple reality was that the containment doctrine, which had apparently served so well in the late 1940s, had become an anachronism within a few years. It was based upon certain balances of power which favored the United States, and those balances did not last very long. The communist sector had succeeded in mobilizing forces which made the costs, in both blood and treasure, prohibitive. Human beings at any time have a tendency to see the world as it existed ten years earlier. The United States leaders looked at Vietnam in the mid-1950s and thought they saw post-World War II Greece of the mid-1940s where containment doctrines had appeared to work beautifully. The American leaders failed to realize that the two situations were not only in different parts of the globe but within different historical moments.

In retrospect, however, it is not at all surprising that Congress waited so long to inject itself into foreign policy matters. The members had merely been following the tradition laid down during the administration of Franklin D. Roosevelt—"leave the president alone in foreign policy matters. He is the only one we've got!" But when the congressional reaction finally came, it overstepped all previous bounds. It would have been unthinkable for the Congress to approve a War Powers Act in the 1950s and early 1960s and, as for the legislative investigation of the CIA, it had been impossible to secure even a legislative review of its budget before the mid-1970s.

Unfortunately, the limits of congressional action in the field of foreign policy were all negative. Congress can forbid and even exhort. But it cannot *do*. It can examine a list of options coming to it from the outside, and select one of them as a mandate for congressional action. But it cannot make its selection effective. Only the president can turn a mandate into action.

The end of the 1970s marked a time when Americans were living between the death of an outmoded and largely discredited mandate, but before the birth of a new one. The latter had yet to take shape. As of 1979, the Congress had not even been presented with the kind of issue out of which mandates arise. We were floundering as we approached the 1980s, and more time was likely to elapse before we once again would find our feet planted on firm foreign policy ground.

Under these circumstances, it was not possible to make any reasonable judgments on the quality of a leader. This became painfully evident to me whenever I tried to assess the conduct of President Carter. Perhaps he was or could be, or was not and could not be, a strong and able man. I could not resolve the issue, because leadership can be exercised only when there is a coherent body of followers ready to hand. I did not believe in the summer of 1979, as these words were written, that the American people were sufficiently united to provide that body. Mr. Carter found himself in the position of having to make bricks without straw, and I could only speculate how well he might have performed had the straw been available.

As a corollary, this situation also obscured efforts to examine the office of the presidency. The office is bigger than any of its occupants, but it can only be seen through its occupants. Even those whom we have generally acknowledged to be among our strongest leaders, Jackson, Lincoln, the two Roosevelts, would doubtless have appeared rather helpless if they had found themselves in the situation of President Carter. There was not sufficient unity among the constituencies at the end of the 1970s.

In this context, the old distinction between "foreign" and "domestic" policy had become meaningless. The major "domestic" issues facing President Carter as the decade rushed to a painful close—energy and inflation—could have been called "domestic" only by ignoring realities. Both were inextricably bound up with America's position in the world, and neither was going to be solved within the domestic boundaries of the United States. It may well be the case, as many have suggested, that the globe is now so "interdependent" that this description of the context of the energy and inflation issues will apply in the future to *all* issues big enough to affect the presidency.

Where this leaves the presidency in the 1980s is anyone's guess. It is obvious that some of the powers which resided in the White House earlier, even quite recently, were no longer evident there. We know that the president cannot send troops to fight overseas without a positive assent by Congress. We know that his capacity to "deliver" on foreign aid promises made to other countries is questionable. We know that his powers to persuade Congress have been severely diminished. President Carter's few legislative victories were obtained at the cost of vital concessions. His most widely heralded foreign policy triumph, the negotiation of the Israeli-Egyptian agreements, came with a large price tag attached, according to various official and unofficial estimates, but Mr. Carter had not submitted to the House and Senate that particular bill for payment as of mid-1979. Generally speaking, we know what a president *cannot* do, but we are very hazy on what he *can* do.

If this situation were peculiar to President Carter alone, it could have been chalked up as an aberration, rather than as a turning point. But there was no reason to believe that another president would have found himself in a better situation. The members of the Congress were not mad at Mr. Carter. They just saw no reason to coalesce behind a president who so very obviously lacked command over broad stretches of public opinion.

The 1980s may reveal a series of one-term presidents, a trend continuing into the indefinite future, when presidents are placed in office without any real passion or commitment on the part of the voters. There is a singular absence of both qualities in our present politics. The polls and personal observation both came to the same conclusion—no one is passionately in favor of our set of leaders as of the end of the 1970s, but no one is passionately against them either. Relatively small groups feel strongly about a variety of relatively narrow issues, but people no longer discuss politics in terms of what happens to the nation as a whole. It is as if no one cares what happens to the nation as long as some one or another narrowly defined issue is resolved to a person's satisfaction.

Some parallels with the decade that preceded the Civil War were striking. No one seemed to care then either. The United States elected a series of presidents who are recalled today only by academic experts or devotees of trivia games. One political party went out of existence altogether, and the other suffered from a split—with the public at large apparently paying little attention. That, of course, was a period of tremendous economic change as the nation shifted to increasing factory production. We too are going through tremendous economic changes, including a shift to a highly managed economy which could feature various forms of rationing in the 1980s as resource scarcities multiply.

Whatever the specifics of the economic situation as of the end of the 1970s, we were clearly marking time in the political situation. It is more than unfortunate that this was also a period of disillusionment. One wants to predict that, eventually, a sense of national cohesion and purpose would be recaptured, but without confidence in the White House that time could be long delayed. In one sense, it might have been better if Mr. Carter had triggered sharp and widespread public antagonism rather than indifference. Antagonism could foster a diligent search for alternatives; indifference merely fosters apathy.

It was obvious enough that something had to happen somewhere along the line. In the modern world, we are facing too many problems to permit a continuation of drift. Inflation, the energy crisis, the clashes in the Middle East and Southeast Asia and Africa were issues that would not go away of their own accord. The United States needed to act, and under our governmental system that meant that the president had to act. There is no substitute for our chief executive.

The question became: How far will the nation follow if the president leads? To say that the president can act is only a partial truth. It is more accurate to assert that only the president can lead. He does not exist as a self-contained unit, however. He is effective only when the people are willing to follow. As of the end of the 1970s, nobody could predict with confidence how far the public might go if the president called them in a certain clear voice, but on that question was hanging the probable future of the presidency. One could doubt whether the office would, could or should recover the strength that it had exhibited for most of the forty-plus years prior to 1980. But it was possible for it to recover enough strength to give the nation adequate leadership. This issue was larger than the future of the presidency. It was also a matter of the future of the nation.

A Call for a Politics of Institutions, Not Men

*Martin A. Levin**

In the past few decades, Americans have developed an inordinate interest in learning what our presidents are "really like." Barbara Walters merely gave voice to this national obsession when she earnestly asked Gerald and Betty Ford whether they slept in twin beds. Journalists have always focused on personalities and explanations emphasizing the importance of individual actors and their personality and character traits. But recently this has received scholarly legitimization with the popular and academic attention given to James David Barber's *Presidential Character*. The editor of a leading national newspaper recently told me that both journalists and political scientists had been greatly influenced by Barber's analysis and by Richard Nixon who made Barber's analysis appear to be correct. I agree with his assessment. For instance, in *Marathon: The Pursuit of the Presidency*, Jules Witcover of the *Washington Post* defends media focus on the 1976 candidates' personality and character on the grounds that the Johnson and Nixon experiences taught the media how important these factors were.

In the spring of 1976, journalists, many political scientists, and most of Washington started asking: "What is Jimmy Carter like?" . . . "What is he likely to do in office?" But to answer the question of what any president is likely to do in office by analyzing what he is like misdirects our understanding of policy-making. In this essay I want to make two broad points. First, a descriptive one: presidential policy-making is primarily a function of the interaction between the president and the elements and institutions of our political system. Presidential personality, background, and attitudes on particular issues are less influential; moreover, their impact on presidential behavior is mediated through their interaction with institutional and situational factors. In the language of political strategy, what a president will do in office is less a function of what he is like than it is of what we do to him—the kind of demands we make of him and how we make them. By "we" I mean the rest of the political system; not so much "the people," as political organizations—labor organizations, state and local party organizations, religious, ethnic, business, professional, and "public interest" organizations, the bureaucracy, Congress, and state legislatures. In politics, knowledge may not be power, but organization surely is the key to power. Mass participation in politics—even in elections—is not as significant as the participation of organizations. And in organizations, it is the actions of their executives and permanent staffs that are most significant.

My second point is prescriptive: we need a politics of institutions, not men; a presidency that is shaped and influenced by the rest of the political system; a Madisonian conception of the presidency, especially among those writing about it, which sees it as part of the web of government. This is in opposition to the dominant postwar view of those in and out of politics that the presidency is the government. We also need a different conception of the role of other political institutions, particularly Congress, emphasizing their ability to contribute to policymaking and to speak for the national interest. We should focus on increasing the power and stature of these other institutions rather than diminishing that of the presidency.

Policy-making would thus reflect more of a Madisonian competitive balance among institutions, interests, and organizations—more sharing of power among them. Such policy-making, especially with a presidency open to these influences, seems likely to produce better policies because they are more responsive and have been subject to more error detection and correction.

I am not, of course, proposing a narrow and naive view of our political system in which the president is merely a political cash register upon which groups bang out their demands. To the contrary, in a mass democracy like ours there has to be more reliance on leaders than on the led, even when the latter are organizations. Indeed, the attitudes and behavior of the led are to a considerable degree shaped by their leaders' cues. Thus, the need for outstanding leaders is increased rather than diminished in a democracy. I am proposing, however, reliance on the institutions and organizations which these persons lead and that policy should be the product of the interaction between a competitive plurality of these institutions and organizations. In the following pages I will sketch the view opposing my two points. Then I will provide some historical and contemporary material from six presidencies which I think supports these points. Finally, I will suggest a critical look at this "politics of institutions." These sections were written in the summer of 1977. For this volume, I have added an epilogue written in April 1979.

The Presidency Is the Government

Among both practitioners and academics the dominant postwar view of the presidency and of national policy-making in general has been that the presidency is the government. William Andrews summarized this view as it was expressed in the early 1960s: "[They] allowed for no other national political or governmental leadership than the president's. He was called upon to be absolute Number One in each area of activity of the national government . . . . So far as Congress entered the picture at all, it followed the president. The president was alone in the driver's seat. At best, Congress was a loyal helpmate . . . at worst, it was an aggressive backseat driver, grabbing at the steering wheel, fighting to put on the brakes, threatening to overturn and destroy the whole vehicle. 'One of the few political truths about the American system of government,' wrote Walter Johnson, 'is that the president alone can give the nation an effective lead.'" In this view, for the presidency, checks and balances, the separation of powers, are either an anachronism or a Republican "cover" (or a Democratic, when there was a Republican White House) to oppose the president's policies. (I do not refer to this view by its usual label of the strong or activist presidency school of thought. Activism or strength is not the essence of this view; rather it is the almost complete predominance of the presidency over other institutions and interests in national policy-making. Furthermore, a strong and activist presidency is not excluded from the model of policy-making by competing institutions and organizations which I am advocating.)

After Vietnam and Watergate, for the first time in the postwar era there was significant dissent from the presidency-is-the-government view, even among some of its leading advocates such as Arthur Schlesinger, Jr. and James MacGregor Burns. However, most of this switch in institutional preference seemed to be due to their reaction against these and other specific policies. Thus, if and when the "good guys" got back in the White House, it seemed likely that these writers would switch back again. Indeed, as soon as Carter entered the White House that began to happen.

A major reason for the widespread and long-lasting acceptance of this view seems to be the popularity of a major corollary of it—the presidency is best able to stand for the public or national interest. This view holds that a president ought to represent something more than the sum and resolution of interest group conflict. He ought to be something different than a broker of interests. If there can be such a thing as a public interest on a given issue, according to this view, there is not likely to be a voice for it from any institution other than the presidency.

Later I will discuss the merits of this traditional view of the public interest and the presidency. My point here is to analyze why it is so widely held. One important element seems to be that as Louis Hartz argued persuasively, America has always had a liberal tradition. And the strong, activist presidency has always been advocated as the single voice that could achieve what have come to be thought of as liberal goals. Thus, even erstwhile opponents of an "imperial presidency" and associated policies such as the Vietnam War keep gravitating back to the presidency-is-the-government view. For instance, in

1977 the Senate moved toward deregulating the price of natural gas with liberal opponents of regulation of a wide variety of areas such as airline fares and broadcasting joining for the first time with conservatives and oil state senators. President Carter opposed it and criticized the Senate for yielding to "special interests." He was joined by recent critics of the presidency such as an old socialist and Vietnam dove like Murray Kempton who said that Congress was showing itself to be only responsive to narrow and parochial interests and thus forfeited all right and ability to speak for the nation as a whole. On the other hand, Kempton went on, in Carter's opposition to deregulation, we again see that only the president can speak for an serve the single national interest against these narrower interests.

Support for this view is even more strongly held at the White House, as Thomas Cronin's interviews of the presidential staffs of Kennedy, Johnson, and Nixon indicate. The first two consisted of liberal activists, the third of conservative activists. But all voiced impatience and frustration with all other elements of the government, especially with the cabinet departments and the bureaucracy. It was best summarized by one White House aide who said: "Everybody believes in democracy until he gets to the White House and then you begin to believe in dictatorship, because it's so hard to get things done. Every time you turn around, people just resist you, and even resist their own job."

There is another view of the presidency which tends to run counter to my prescriptive argument, as well as reinforce the presidency-is-the-government view: the character and personality view of interpreting presidential behavior. These two views usually are not thought of as being closely associated, but I will suggest some of their common assumptions and values. The character and personality view is most elegantly voiced by James David Barber, who focuses on presidential personality—personal style and political world view, as well as the climate of expectations and power situation with which the president's personality interacts. For Barber, the core of personality is *character*: "The way the President orients himself toward life—not for the moment, but enduringly . . . . [It] grows out of the child's experiments in relating to parents, brothers and sisters, and peers at play and in school, as well as to his own body and the objects around it." In character he focuses on two dimensions— *"activity-passivity"* and *"positive-negative" affect toward one's activity*, which refer to how much energy an individual invests in his activity and how he feels about what he does. From this Barber has four character types for analysis: *"active-positive," "active-negative," "passive-positive,"* and *"passive-negative."*

This is not the place to deal with the significant problems in Barber's methodology, and his theory constructions and testing. Instead, I wish to discuss the potential political and policy effects of this interpretation of presidential behavior and the values underlying it. Barber's scholarly and provocative analysis and other excellent examples of psychobiography such as Alexander and Juliette George's *Woodrow Wilson and Colonel House: A Personality Study* seem to me to have reinforced and legitimated the predilection in both journalism and the popular mind to explain policymaking in terms of personalities and individual character traits. Together, this scholarly work and journalistic predilection seem to have the following sort of negative effects on how we view and react to the presidency. This interest in what our presidents are really like leads to a political fatalism which seems to assume that once we elect someone president, he is beyond our control. In this view, to understand and anticipate a president's behavior, we ought to know his character traits. This contributes to a false ideology of personalism that in turn tends to legitimize quiescence and political passivity on the part of citizens, organizations, and institutions in the face of presidential power. It tends to develop a political voyeurism which seeks to identify and personalize the traits and tastes of public leaders so as to have a personal figure with whom to identify. It reflects and reinforces our tendency to look for a father figure in the presidency. (It does, however, help the media because it is easier to talk about personality than about structures, institutions, and complex issues; it is also easier to convey to an audience.) Thus, this view does not contribute to a politics of institutions. Most importantly, it is refuted by recent history which indicates that we can influence a president's policy and that this satisfies democratic values and indeed often improves policies through error detection and correction.

The character and personality view of interpreting presidential behavior tends to flow from the same activist values and assumptions that underlie the presidency-is-the-government view. Barber, for example, emphasizes the virtues of the active-positive type of president: Active-positives (Franklin D. Roosevelt, Harry Truman, John F. Kennedy) "display personal strengths which enable them to make of that office an *engine of progress*." As Alexander George has argued, Barber does not give sufficient consideration to the risks associated with active-positive presidents: "The historical example [of these risks, which Barber] cites [is] FDR's effort to pack the Supreme Court [and it] is hardly reassuring in this respect." By contrast, Barber is critical of passive-negatives (Calvin Coolidge, Dwight Eisenhower) because they leave "vacant the *energizing*, initiating, stimulating possibilities of the role." He notes, but does not elaborate upon in a more general model, that in certain historical circumstances, passive-negatives can provide a "breathing spell" for recovery after a period of frantic politics.

From a policy perspective the most serious flaw is Barber's failure to make qualitative distinctions among actual levels of activity and positivity. The presidency-is-the-government writers, such as Richard Neustadt, also fail to do this with regard to activism. Perhaps the most important of these distinctions is the question of the values which an active and positive president will pursue. Like Neustadt, Barber tends to be more concerned with creating an efficient machine—one that moves briskly and feels positive about itself, so it won't be self-destructive. Indeed, he wants the office to be an "engine of progress." But neither he nor Neustadt are very explicit about where they think this engine should be going, toward what goals and to achieve what values. Neustadt's *Presidential Power* is about how a president should obtain and keep power. There is almost no discussion of the ends for which the power should be used. Neustadt tends to treat power as if it were an end in itself and as if it could be exercised in a neutral fashion; Barber treats activism and positive affect in a similar manner. Of course, their New Dealish, liberal Democratic sympathies do show through. But they tend to avoid explicit discussions of values as if there were societal consensus on where we want the presidency to take us and on how to get there; as if the goal of "more progress" meant the same thing to different people. This is part of the corollary noted earlier—the presidency is best able to stand for the public or national interest. The dubious assumption behind it and reflected in these writers is that if the president wants it, it must be good; after all, he is elected by all the people. So he must be more representative of a national interest than others who are elected as parochial representatives.

A Politics of Institutions, Not Men

A presidency open to both a variety of interests and views and to the task of brokering among them results in a policy-making process that is bumpy, indirect, unsightly, wearing on the president, and sometimes even inefficient. But tidiness has never been the source of our political system's virtues. Nor is efficiency our highest political goal. Indeed, by the mid-twentieth century, politics seems to have replaced economics as the "dismal science" in most democracies that try to cope with social problems through policy intervention. They have found it difficult to move men and organizations to obtain agreements and social action. The more open political institutions are to a variety of interests and pressures and the more leaders see their role as brokering among them, the harder will it be to move people and organizations and secure agreements. However, for a democracy such difficulties are probably appropriate and have positive value. In this age of omnipresent government, before it acts everyone ought to have a chance to slow government down and search for alternatives, including no government action at all. This may cause some inefficiencies but it maintains democratic values through a more representative politics and policy-making. Compromises inherent in an open politics with dispersed power may alter a policy's objectives and effects and reduce its effectiveness, but they seem to be the essence of representative policy-making in a large, heterogeneous society.

But the most significant point here is that policy-making characterized by competing institutions, each of which—including the presidency—is open to a variety of interests and pressures, is more efficient and wiser in the long-run. We cannot expect the president or any policy-maker to be completely free of error or even to come close to that. Thus these competing institutions and interests can make a major contribution as sources of error detection and correction.

The failures of Vietnam and Watergate, for instance, can be read as instances in which the presidency was resistant to error correction. By contrast, Eisenhower was able to avoid an inappropriate and untimely U.S. intervention in Indo-China because of his openness to error detection and the vigorous efforts of competing institutions. The ultimate success in the Watergate case was the work of competing institutions—the courts and the Congress, operating independently of each other, with no central guidance.

Nevertheless, I do not think that presidents voluntarily will be open to this type of policy-making. First, the view that the presidency is best able to stand for the national interest is accepted at the White House and reinforced by its popular support. Second, as George Reedy has persuasively argued in *The Twilight of the Presidency*, structural characteristics of the office run in the opposite direction: "The environment of deference [in which the president operates], approach[es] sycophancy . . . . [It] helps to foster another insidious factor . . . a belief that the President and a few of his most trusted advisers are possessed of a special knowledge which must be closely held within a small group lest the plans and the designs of the United States be anticipated and frustrated by enemies." Third, and related to all this, presidents seem to have adopted the view that since they ultimately are going to take the responsibility for most national policy-making, why should they share the decision-making with others who do not share that responsibility and its costs.

These factors are manifested in a plebiscitary conception of the presidency which is held by others than Richard Nixon. In the fashionable rhetoric of today, President Carter has deplored the growth of an imperial presidency. Yet his emphasis on direct access to the people, without any intermediate bodies, is central to a plebiscitary presidency. He often talks of "special interests" as the obstacle to desired policy. If he does not get his way, Carter has promised to go directly to the people, as he did in his legislative battles in Georgia. Mayor Lindsay of New York City also did not like "deals" and bargaining with special interests, power brokers, party bossess, and union bosses, which were all morally tainted. Nor did French President Charles deGaulle, who spoke so contemptuously of political parties and had an explicitly plebiscitary presidency, with direct access to the people. Similarly, in his first administration and in the 1972 election, Nixon even set himself apart from the rest of his own executive branch. President Carter seems so different from Nixon that maybe this potential similarity tells us something about our current political system and how the institution of the presidency is evolving. Perhaps with the decline of political parties, all presidents will take this plebiscitary, no-intermediate-groups approach.

If presidents will not be open voluntarily to a more competitive Madisonian policy-making, then to improve error detection and correction, these other institutions and organizations must take the initiative and press their views on the White House. This will be difficult because of the presidency's predominance for over forty years. But a place to start is Aaron Wildavsky's suggestion that ''the institutional lesson . . . is not that the Presidency should be diminished but that other institutions should grow in stature . . . . The wisdom of a democracy must be in its 'separate institutions sharing power' . . . . The first order of priority should go to rebuilding our political parties because they are most in need of help and could do most to bring presidents in line with strong sentiments in the country . . . . [A] party provides essential connective tissue between people and government . . . . So does Congress; strengthening its appropriation process through internal reform would bring it more power than any external threat could take away. The people need the vigor of all their institutions.''

Of course, one person's error correction is another's obstructionism; one person's error is another's statesmanship and principled behavior. Underlying part of this analysis of alternative policy-making processes is value conflict: the simple preference for a particular policy which is associated with one institution at that time. For instance, the presidency plays an important error-correcting role for the rest of the system. But there is much more than value conflict here. First, there is the question of balance: The presidency as an error-correcting device is widely advocated and accepted, but we seem to have lost the perspective that the presidency also needs to be subject to some error detection and correction.

Second, both the White House and these other institutions and organizations commit errors. Thus the crucial question is which one can more readily admit error and thus contribute to correction. Because of the dominance of the presidency-is-the-government view and the office's structural features discussed by Reedy, the presidency seems to be less able to publicly admit error than have Congress and some interest groups. Congress seems more likely to admit error because it is a plural body with more individuals potentially available to make such admissions and to depersonalize the blame.

This is probably the strongest argument for more competitive, plural policy-making. Reedy in effect suggests that the nature of the modern presidency has largely vitiated its own error detection abilities. It has thrown up around itself a fog of dissonance reduction: "If I am the president and I do this; given all that I alone know, all my unique responsibility . . . . then it *must* be right." Vietnam and Watergate are striking examples of this, but much recent presidential policy-making has fit this pattern.

Pressure, Error Correction, and Responsive Policy-making

An examination of some issues in the Truman and Kennedy presidencies and brief discussions of the other postwar presidencies will illustrate the two themes of this essay. In the instances of successful error detection and correction, the president's personality and openness to different views may have been contributing factors, but the pressure on him from other institutions and organizations seems to have been at least as influential. In the cases in which presidential error correction failed to occur, it seems to have been a product of inadequate pressure from others (especially congressional abdication of responsibility) as well as of the president's personality and views on the issue.

Truman and Kennedy

The policies toward Israel and on civil rights in the Truman and Kennedy administrations are best understood by analyzing the demands made on these presidents once in office rather than by looking at their prepresidential careers, attitudes, or behavior. Most organizations and coalitions interested in these issues were and are shrewd enough to ignore the question of what a president is "really like." Instead, they concentrate on how they can pressure him and the other organizations and institutions in our political system. Jewish organizations did this with Truman and have continued to do so successfully since then. Since the 1940s blacks and their allies have followed the same strategy with general success, as the Truman and Kennedy administrations indicate. In both instances blacks were faced with administrations that at the outset were at the most moderate on civil rights, but they eschewed any fatalistic acceptance of the prepresidential record and used pressure to turn both into administrations that were quite progressive on civil rights for their day. Both presidents were at almost every step reluctant to pursue the policies pressed on them. Thus while these cases hardly constitute proof, they are suggestive of this essay's arguments, especially concerning the relative influence of personality and background compared to pressures from other institutions and organizations.

Before becoming president, Truman had not personal or policy predispositions toward Zionism. Indeed, whether it was his own personal predilection or merely political expediency in his area of Missouri, Truman's and his wife's behavior was publicly cool to Jews. Yet on balance Truman's policies as president greatly benefited Zionism. They were strikingly the product of demands made on him and on congressional and party leaders by the Jewish community, which was a significant element of his party's coalition and strategically concentrated in states with large electoral votes. This in turn produced political pressure on Truman from his own White House staff. All this occurred despite Truman's own ambivalence and despite strong counter-pressures within the executive branch. As Snetsinger has shown, it is only a "popular myth" that Truman was an unswerving supporter of Israel. His support was a function of political pressure and thus oscillated quite a bit.

Truman's very significant pro-civil rights policies were developed through a similar pattern of political pressure. In this policy area, Truman's pre-presidential views and actions were ambiguous. More importantly, they were the product of the same type of coalition expediency in Missouri that he was to face as president, rather than of his own background or personal preference. Truman's symbolic and substantive presidential civil rights policies were quite progressive for the 1940s and were important building blocks for later aspirations and more advanced policies. The relative influence of various factors is capsulated in an off-the-record comment to a young political scientist in the late 1950s, which as far as I know has never been printed before. After completing an interview with the former president on another topic, the researcher said that he wanted Truman to know that he has always admired him for his strong stands on civil rights. Truman replied matter-of-factly, "Well yes that's true . . . . But you know I never really cared much for the Negra [sic]. Most of them are lazy . . . . They aren't clean . . . . But when you are President, you have got to be for the Negra [sic]." Truman of course did not "have to be for the Negro" just as he did not have to be reelected; indeed, few thought he would be. Hoover wasn't reelected, nor was Johnson or Ford. But Negroes and their allies were strategically positioned elements of the national Democratic coalition. In the face of significant pressure, he moved for them and helped his administration survive politically, as well as producing responsive public policy.

The state of Israel and the blacks benefited from Truman's policies, but it is also significant that Truman prospered as well. His 1948 election victory was a stunning upset. Truman had many political disadvantages and made several political errors, but after the 1946 election defeat, he was able to make significant corrections. An important aid in this was his staff, which was quite responsive to intermediate groups and their pressures. It is difficult to attribute the presidential votes of even one ethnic group to particular policies, but most observers feel that the adoption of policies favored by blacks and Jews greatly helped Truman keep these groups in the New Deal coalition. Both blacks and Jews were concentrated in states that had both a large number of electoral votes and very narrow victory margins for Truman. He carried Ohio, California, and Illinois by less than 4,000, 9,000, and 17,000 votes, respectively.

The development of President Kennedy's civil rights policies indicates a similar pattern. There was little in Kennedy's prepresidential background or actions that would predict his presidential civil rights policies which eventually were rather progressive. Politically and personally he probably had less exposure to the race issue than the average northern Democratic politician of his time. Kennedy's court historian, Arthur Schlesinger, could only describe this pre-presidential attitudes and behavior on civil rights as "sympathetic but detached."

Pressures on Kennedy with regard to race and poverty began in his presidential campaign. He reacted with some progressive promises on combatting Appalachian poverty, his "stroke of the pen speech," and his effort to get Martin Luther King released from jail, though race was barely mentioned in the Kennedy-Nixon debates. As president these pressures grew much greater: sit-ins, freedom rides, and voting rights demonstrations by the standards of the times involved quite a bit of civll disorder. In turn, within his party coalition liberal congressmen and their allies pressured for legislation. In a different approach, lawyers for the National Association for the Advancement of Colored People brought desegregation lawsuits. Yet Kennedy clung as mucy as he could to a modest approach to civil rights because through 1962 he perceived the counterpressures as being even greater: civil rights still lacked widespread support among whites, and southern counterpressure was especially influential in Congress. Most objective observers would agree with that estimate of the relative political influence then. Through early 1963 Kennedy seems to have concluded that civil rights legislation was politically unnecessary, unlikely to pass, and likely to harm other legislative goals if he tried to get it passed.

Nevertheless, by the end of 1962 Kennedy had moved a long way in the direction of greater civil rights: the Justice Department brought many southern voting suits, sent 600 deputy federal marshalls to protect freedom riders in Alabama in 1961, brought the National Guard to the University of Mississippi to protect James Meredith; at the University of Alabama, Kennedy federalized the Alabama National Guard and sent Deputy Attorney General Katzenbach to present Governor Wallace with a federal court desegregation order as he stood in the "school-house door." Kennedy followed the latter two with eloquent national television speeches criticizing resistance to civil rights. However, these actions were all *reactive* to some specific crisis or court order; they were not initiated by the president nor were they institutionalized civil rights policies. Indeed, Kennedy resisted pressure to introduce civil rights legislation until 1963.

His strategy was to maintain "consensus" with both southern congressional support as well as black and white liberal support. But pressure by civil rights action and by anti-civil rights counterattacks finally shifted him. The pressure reached a highpoint with the huge (by pre-Vietnam standards) and peaceful Civil Rights March on Washington in August 1963. Even before the March, the pressure led Kennedy to propose comprehensive civil rights legislation to Congress. In light of the counterpressure in Congress and elsewhere, all this was quite progressive for those times, and it was almost exclusively the product of pressure from the civil rights movement and its Democratic party and congressional allies. As Fairlie, who otherwise is critical of Kennedy for creating excessive expectations, accurately concludes, Kennedy "waited until violence had actually erupted, or was immediately threatened, before he intervened."

Kennedy did not live to face reelection, and it is difficult to attribute votes to particular policies. Also, in addition to the Democratic civil rights policies affecting blacks, the 1964 Republican candidate was especially antithetical to blacks. Yet it is striking that in the 1964 election his Democratic successor, Lyndon Johnson, increased the Democratic proportion of the black vote from about sixty-five percent in 1960 to ninety-five percent in 1964.

Some Other Postwar Cases

A brief examination of some cases in the other postwar presidencies will also illustrate the themes of this essay. In several cases we find significant and successful error detection and correction of presidential policies through the interaction between the White House and other institutions, interests, and organizations. In other cases these institutions and organizations made inadequate efforts to press their views, or the president was not open to such pressures.

Perhaps the most striking and successful presidential error correction comes in a too-often forgotten but very important case: President Eisenhower and Indochina. Briefly, in 1954 as the French were being defeated in Indochina, they privately asked for U.S. intervention; later they specifically requested air strikes to relieve the besieged garrison of Dienbienphu. Eisenhower and his influential secretary of state, John Foster Dulles, seemed inclined to give such aid, though the former would do so only with congressional approval. (Ike spoke of a "row of dominoes" falling if Indochina were lost.) There was consultation with eight bipartisan congressional leaders, including the Senate minority leader, Lyndon Johnson. Most of the Democrats (including Johnson) opposed intervention, and all eight pressured Dulles first to seek the support of allies such as Britain. He did and failed to get any; the possibility of intervention ended. The significance and irony of this case need hardly be remarked on today.

Eisenhower followed a similar pattern of interaction with Congress in two other major foreign crises. However, in a striking illustration of the presidency-is-the-government view, its proponents were critical of Eisenhower's actions. They felt it represented an abdication of presidential responsibility and authority in an area that should be dominated by the executive.

By contrast, as Reedy and others indicate, while he was evolving his Vietnam policy Lyndon Johnson was not open to the variety of congressional and other pressures which might have led to error detection and correction. Vietnam was an unsuccessful policy for the nation and for Johnson, who was in effect forced to resign; earlier the war had weakened his ability to carry out his ambitious Great Society programs.

Ironically, Johnson had been superbly successful in the Senate as an open broker of a variety of interests. Reedy thinks it was the structure and nature of the presidency that led to a different approach in Vietnam, and the Nixon White House's similar approach gave credence to his argument. However, in both cases it is hard to distinguish the effects of the office and the effects of waging an unpopular war. Gerald Ford's White House seems to have been different, but he did not have the war. Barber explains Johnson's approach to Vietnam in terms of personality. Both elements probably were influential, but I suggest that another factor may have been significant. My reading of 1965 to 1968 suggests inadequate pressure by Congress, party leaders, and other members of the Democratic coalition such as labor and civil rights leaders. They waited quite a while before they began to think independently about U.S. policy in Vietnam, and most were not aggressive in making their doubts known to the administration until as late as 1967 or 1968. More importantly, many potential critics, such as some civil rights and congressional leaders, allowed themselves to be bought off by administration support of their goals in other areas. To be sure, the White House is powerful. But party and congressional leaders should have viewed their self-interest in a long-term perspective and understood that the White House was not only bringing itself down but also splitting the entire Democratic coalition.

The Reedy and Barber views—one emphasizing the nature of the office, the other the personality of its occupants—help explain why Nixon isolated himself so much on Watergate. But this is too simple a picture of Nixon's policy-making. In other areas, he showed himself open to a range of views, in his first term, such as sponsoring a national income-maintenance program and new policies toward China and Russia. Most of the ideas and pressures in these areas came from within the White House, but even on Vietnam (especially with regard to Cambodia in 1970) Nixon responded, though slowly, to outside pressures. Thus there is some possibility that Nixon might have been open to warnings from his party and congressional leaders on the dangers of Watergate to his popular support. However, as with Johnson and Vietnam, such warnings were not forthcoming, and the near absence of national leaders in the weak Republican party contributed to this. Of course, Nixon did nothing to reverse the decay of his party.

Gerald Ford's presidency does not fit Reedy's model. It seemed open to error-correcting pressures. The most significant instance seems to have been his struggle for the nomination. From his dumping of Vice-President Rockefeller to his trimming on a whole variety of issues on which he had been criticized by the party's conservative wing, Ford was open to such error correction from his party's coalition. He and his advisers correctly read the distribution of influence within their party's coalition and acted boldly, as in the Rockefeller decision. Although he also had the powers of incumbency going for him, his responsiveness to these influences does seem to have been crucial in saving the nomination for him (and perhaps beneficial for his party, because he was probably its most effective candidate for the general election).

What about President Jimmy Carter? I have discussed his emphasis on direct access to the people, without any intermediate bodies; his attacks on "special interests"; and his representation of himself as standing above them in a direct relationship with the people. However, there is reason to believe that Jimmy Carter will make policy, at least in part, in response to pressures from leading elements of his coalition. Near the end of his presidential campaign, Carter changed his views on a number of substantive policies such as tax reform, the Humphrey-Hawkins bill, abortion, and busing. After six months in office (at the time of this writing), his responsiveness to changing circumstances had been significant. Some would even say that after firing off strong rhetoric, he had fallen back too often and too quickly: the Sorensen CIA nomination, removing several water projects from his initial "hit list," the international human rights controversy, the fifty dollar tax rebate, and even some elements of his "moral equivalent of war" against the energy crisis. After some aloofness, he has worked with some groups such as civil rights organizations, who had strongly criticized his alleged neglect of blacks, and the maritime unions on the issue of U.S. crews.

Yet there also are signs of an absence of openness to error correction with regard to the *procedures* for making policy rather than with its substance. Jack Knott and Aaron Wildavsky persuasively argue, "If there is a danger for President Carter, it is not that he will support unpopular policies, but that he will persevere with *inappropriate procedures* . . . He is not an ideologue of policy." He seems more concerned with the procedures for policy-making. He advocates, and in fact followed as governor of Georgia, the procedures of the old "scientific management" approach: simplicity, uniformity, predictability, hierarchy, and comprehensiveness. Some of his pronouncements on policy may have been campaign rhetoric or legislative bargaining chips, but his beliefs about procedures seem sincere, even passionate, and as governor he practiced what he preached.

Congress is a good source of error correction. Thus another disturbing sign has been the Carter White House's unrealistic attitude toward Congress and the distribution of power between the two. In some ways it is as if thus far nothing had been learned from the Johnson and Nixon experiences. For instance, a Carter aide told a reporter after the congressional investigation which lead to the resignation of Office of Management and Budget Director, Bert Lance, that Carter's entourage's greatest surprise in Washington was the recognition of Congress' political power and ths real sense of challenge and opposition to the White House when opinion there runs against the president. In the Lance case the White House damaged itself by acting as if it were still dealing with the Georgia legislature.

My reading of the other postwar presidencies suggests this for Carter in the long-run: His personality and character have been pretty completely formed now that he is fifty-four years old. We cannot now give him a different mother or different pre-presidential career experiences. But his presidential behavior, to a great extent can be shaped by how citizens, organizations, and institutions interact with him. In the face of complex policy issues, they should not shirk this task. After this essay was drafted its themes were echoed by the National Urban League's Vernon Jordan when he spoke about the Carter administration's policies toward blacks: "I do not believe Jimmy Carter is an insensitive man. He cares, and he has our interests in his heart, but it is our job to get them out of his heart and head and into public policy."

A Critical Look at this "Politics of Institutions"

I have suggested that rebuilding our political parties would contribute much to creating more plural and competitive national policy-making. Nostalgia is powerful but often misleading. Strengthened parties would greatly aid our politics in many ways, in addition to improved presidential error correction. But this does not seem to be a realistic expectation. As Edmund Burke observed, "Circumstances . . . give in reality to every political principle its distinguishing colour and discriminating effect. The circumstances are what render every civil and political scheme beneficial or noxious . . . ." The circumstances for American parties have not been favorable for the past 30 years and they do not seem likely to change. The social bases for strong parties is eroding. As income and educational levels increase, the proportion of people who identify with the major parties has been declining. On a policy and ideological level, the picture is even darker. Almost all considerations of parties in the postwar period and all party "reform" have either been explicitly directed at weakening them or have had that effect. Even their manifest functions as a channel of communication between candidates and voters and as an instrument for winning elections have been taken over to a significant degree by the media and by professional campaign consultants.

The circumstances do not seem much more favorable for other organizations and institutions that might contribute to error correction for national policy-making. There has been a great proliferation in the number and activity of so-called public interests lobbying organizations (Common Cause, Nader affiliates, Energy Action) in Washington in the past decade, and they seem to have given a "greater balance" to the inputs of national policy-making. But even without considering the policy biases of these organizations it is too early to know what their long-run significance will be. Moreover, it seems likely that they will not be an adequate substitute for either strong parties or a strong Congress.

Perhaps we can look for a bit more aid from Congress than from the parties, but the situation is still problematic because of the nature of Congress. As Nelson Polsby once said, "Congress has a hard time standing on its 1,070 feet." For the most part this has been more of a problem during the past decade than earlier this century. One source of strength, direction, and focus for Congress would be aggressive, strong leadership. Today many have high expectations in this regard for Speaker Thomas O'Neill and Majority Leader Robert Byrd. My advocacy of strengthened congressional leadership is in terms of mechanisms of increased *institutional centralization* rather than a search for strong men. But my feeling is that the weakness of recent congressional leadership has been more a function of the members' unwillingness to have strong leaders rather than the weakness of the particular leaders involved. Even if O'Neill and Byrd were able to assert strong leadership temporarily, I do not think that congressmen will allow strong leadership for the long-run. The reform, democratic, participatory ethos that has been prevalent in our society increasingly for the past quarter century is getting stronger. It has come into Congress in the past decade and it strongly militates against the centralization of power within Congress. With a few exceptions recent congressional "reform" has largely meant weakening the leadership and other centralizing forces in this large, structurally fragmented body. (The somewhat increased strength of party and regional caucuses probably will add some centralization and discipline to Congress, but at the same time many committee chairmen have been weakened. More importantly, the power of these caucuses relies on the sufferance of their members who have had limited willingness to sacrifice some of their individual influence to some central unit or person.)

Congress' tendency to abdicate policy-making responsibility and therefore power may even be a greater factor militating against a pattern of national policy-making by competitive institutions. This tendency has promoted the growth of presidential power in the field of foreign affairs. But the congressional flight from responsibility also has been occurring in the less excusable area of domestic policy. The most serious instance of this has been with respect to spending. Congress could have more power here but until very recently it seems to have been content with taking credit for individual pieces of spending and letting presidents take the heat for cutting appropriations. In part this was a major issue in the Nixon impoundment controversy, though it was hidden behind liberal and conservative labels. The first few years of the new and strengthened congressional budget process do not indicate a major reversal in Congress' behavior on this. For one thing, thus far there has been no central direction within the congressional budget committees and the process itself. Congress' lack of interest or ability to make real inputs into the policy *implementation* process is another instance in which it has failed to take an opportunity for seizing some responsibility. After the Great Society there has been much loose talk around Washington about the need for better implementation of what Congress passes. But as far as I can tell Congress has done almost nothing in this area. Its interest in oversight still seems to be merely seeing to it that money is spent honestly. Because of the absence of political incentives for Congress to become genuinely interested in implementation, this is not likely to change.

The absence—in the nation and among congressmen themselves—of a conception of Congress as being competent and legitimate in voicing the national interest is perhaps the most formidable obstacle to the development of national policy-making by competitive institutions. Since the presidency and Congress are both fallible, a crucial question is which one is more likely to be able to publicly admit its errors. There seems to be reason to believe that Congress and some interest groups are more able to do this than is the presidency, or at least they are less disabled from doing this. This presidential disability means that when the occasion arises congressmen must stand up and say that an error has been made (or is about to be made), that the public interest is not being served, and that they have as much ability to accurately see the public interest as does the presidency. For instance, congressmen advocating the de-regulation of natural gas should be willing, if they so believe (as many do), to say that this policy is in the national interest and its continued regulation, as was advocated by President Carter, is not in the national interest.

Congressmen will only be willing to do this and can only do it effectively, if both the nation and the congressmen themselves view the institution as being competent and legitimate. However, it now seems that neither of them do because of the impact on their thinking of behavior—presidential and congressional—and the impact of ideas. Since Franklin D. Roosevelt almost every president has acted in such a way as to preempt Congress' position of making such statements and acting in this way. At the same time Congress reinforced this preemption by its abdication of policy-making responsibility and its particular disinclination to make these statements. During the Eisenhower and Nixon-Ford administrations there were frequent exceptions to this congressional abdication and often this resulted in significant competitive policy-making and error correction.

Nevertheless, these exceptions seem to have done little to change anyone's conception of Congress as failing as a spokesman for the public interest. Perhaps this is because throughout this period the presidency-is-the-government view was eloquently advocated by many academic and popular writers, with almost no writers expressing a contrary view. This reached a high point in the early 1960s with the wide popularity of books like Neustadt's and Rossiter's. Thus through both the effect of behavior and these writings a process of "labeling" of Congress occurred. Congress has been described and thought of as lacking in this public interest competency so much that congressmen seem to have come to believe it and act as if they cannot fulfill this role. (Such internalization is probably even more likely among the brightest congressmen who are more likely to be exposed to such ideas.) It has been said that early in the Carter administration Congress has been continuing to reassert some of its power as it did during Nixon's time. Even if this continues, it involves power relationships. But nothing seems to be happening in word or deed about altering the conception of a Congress that fails as a spokesman for the public interest.

There is one other critical point to consider in this call for a politics of institutions. There seem to be significant limits to the possibility of it developing. But if it did develop, what would be some of its consequences? One possibility is that there would be too much of a good thing. This plural, competitive policy-making produces error correction and tends to satisfy the goal of representativeness. Yet there is a dilemma here. In one person's view there may be responsiveness and error correction of presidential policy, but to the next one this may be unprincipled opportunism. Although the evidence is indirect and sketchy, it seems that a major element in the peoples' feeling of trust and legitimacy for a leader is the leader's consistency. Thus the tradeoff here seems to be between presidential policy-making which tends to be responsive and subject to error correction and a loss in presidential popularity. My own preference is for the former, since modern presidents seem so likely to suffer decline in popularity anyway. Yet this tradeoff should be kept in mind when evaluating the suggestions made here.

In the past few decades popular and academic interest in personality have deflected a proper appreciation of the importance of institutions and organizations. During the eighteenth and nineteenth centuries the most important persons and institutions shaping national policies often were someone other than the president. In the twentieth century, this has changed less than we might think if we exclude periods of war and the Great Depression. For instance, ten years from now will Presidents Nixon and Ford be seen as the dominant forces behind the foreign and domestic policies of their eight years in office? Perhaps not. Was President Eisenhower, or the Supreme Court, or Congress more influential in shaping domestic policies of the 1950s? Nevertheless, we will and should continue to look to the executive branch for the execution of policies, especially foreign policy. Yet there is much writing on the presidency, with comparatively little attention to the other thousands of top officials in the executive branch. The initiation and development of policies—and later their day-to-day implementation—also will be done by persons *and* by institutions other than the presidency.

Of course, persons do shape institutions; analyzing the interaction between the two is essential to understanding policy-making. However, since the 1930s, first because of domestic and then foreign crises, we have overemphasized the importance of presidential leadership.

Yet process isn't everything; not even when the process is competitive and involves multiple institutions sharing power. We ought to be even more concerned with the values and ends that these institutions will pursue. As we consider what we want from our institutions, including the presidency, we must first know who we are and what we want.

An Epilogue

The preceding sections of this essay were written in the summer of 1977. This epilogue, written in April 1979, tries to assess the current state of our political institutions. President Carter has tended to behave as I suggested he might, with one major exception. Many observers have been critical of his performance and have argued that this is evidence of our need for a stronger presidency. My own conclusion is very different. Between 1977 and 1979 almost all of the factors which I initially discussed have tended to endure for the most part. Therefore, I would emphasize my initial prescriptive point: a call for a politics of institutions; a presidency that is shaped and influenced by the rest of the political system. However, I was also concerned then that these institutions were not up to the task. In 1979 I must continue to acknowledge that to assert this Madisonian model as a value preference is different than being able to claim that it exists at present.

The Presidency

Carter's first two years seem to have been characterized, as I suggested they might, by a tendency to resist error correction with regard to the procedures for making policy, an emphasis on direct access to the people—without any intermediate bodies, and an unrealistic attitude toward Congress and the distribution of power between it and the White House.

Carter has tended to persevere with inappropriate procedures like his emphasis on the old "scientific management" approach. For instance, almost every major policy initiative has emphasized comprehensiveness (comprehensive welfare reform, a comprehensive Mideast settlement, a comprehensive energy package, a comprehensive health policy) even when it seems inappropriate. Many felt that his welfare proposals were inappropriate. So many incremental improvements have been made in the welfare system in the past ten years that a comprehensive proposal now might be too radical and risky. It might lose some of these improvements and bring in potentially negative changes, as well as being very costly. His opposition to a step-by-step Mideast settlement and his October 1977 call with the Soviet Union for a comprehensive approach at Geneva focusing foremost on the Palestinian problem seems to have been so inimical to the two most important principals, Egypt and Israel, that they undertook their own incremental process starting with Sadat's visit to Israel. Even after the initial September 1978 agreement by these principals to the Camp David accord, Carter kept pushing a more comprehensive approach (even more than desired by Egypt) which almost destroyed the agreement.

Carter has adopted the style of a plebisectary presidency: direct contact with masses of people (phone call-ins and town meetings), constant public criticism of "special interests," and the perhaps unnecessary alienation of major elements of his electoral coalition such as organized labor, blacks and Jews. Similarly, he has made little effort to build ties with local Democratic party groups and leaders, which, like his alienation to these other elements, may cause serious renomination problems.

It is one thing to prefer to deal with "the people" over the heads of intermediate groups. It is quite another, leading to self-inflicted political wounds, to fail to consider the existence and responses of such groups in one's political and policy calculus. But Carter has often done the latter. For example, he was "surprised by the intensity of the outcry among Jewish leaders in the United States" in response to his October 1977 call for a comprehensive Mideast settlement and expected "that it would pass" (New York *Times* Magazine, Jan. 21, 1979, p. 22). But rather than passing it seems to have been the beginning of the Jewish leaders' alienation from the president. The benefits to the president of contact with leaders of "special interests" is illustrated by the important communications—with forewarnings about his declining support among this group which was important in his 1976 victory—that the president has received from the Congressional Black Caucus.

But his unrealistic attitude toward the power and nature of Congress may create the most immediate threat to his own power. The Carter entourage's belated recognition of Congress's power and willingness to challenge the president, which I wrote of in 1977, seems to have taken a long time to take hold. Moreover, they have tended to adopt the curiously apolitical perspective of Congress as an undifferentiated mass of actors, with insufficient sense of its internal hierarchy and distribution of power. During the summer of 1976, one of Carter's top aides told the late Jeffrey Pressman that one of their major legislative goals would be the passage of broad tax reform. When Pressman asked how this would be accomplished in light of the likely opposition of the influential Senate Finance Committee and its powerful chairman, Russell Long, the aide replied: "You don't understand. All the political rules have changed. The media is so important today, that we will go over Congress's head and go directly to the people with this issue. We proved this in Georgia." After the election this apolitical view of Congress seems to have persisted. At a private White House meeting on welfare reform, Russell Long began his remarks there with the sardonic introduction "Hello, I'm Russell Long and I'm chairman of the Finance Committee." When an interviewer asked a White House aide how part of their energy package would go over with the influential Senator Henry Jackson, chairman of the Energy Subcommittee, the aide retorted: "We don't need Scoop Jackson; we beat him for the nomination." And from the time of the inaugural festivities to the Griffin-GSA affair, the White House dealt with House Speaker O'Neill in a clumsy manner.

It might be argued that presidents need to be feared and respected by Congress rather than loved. But Carter seems to be coming up short on all counts. In early 1979 a group of senators responded to the question of "who is President Carter's man in the Senate" by saying that it was "no one." One of these senators, Bennet Johnston, Jr., a Louisiana Democrat added: "each president has always had a large number of Senators and Congressmen he could identify as his own, but not Carter. When you get in trouble, that's when you need friends, and he just doesn't have that."[1] During the same period, "in dozens of interviews with a wide range of Democratic legislators," a New York *Times* reporter found that "few expressed any deeply held loyalty to the president." The Democratic Majority leader of the House, Jim Wright, explained how twelve of his fourteen recommendations of people for federal appointments had been turned down because "the president thought there was something tawdry about the idea of political appointments." Wright meets regularly with the president, but he feels that the president seldom listens to him or any other politician: "he may suffer from the delusion that elected officials are all a bit corrupt, and that their advice is not any good."[2] Because of Carter's approach toward Congress and the further decay of the party system, Congress may operate as if it were the "opposition" even when it is controlled by the president's own party.

But perhaps such splits in the predominant majority party are to be expected no matter what individual is in the White House. In fact they correspond to Samuel Lubell's sun and moon theory of parties:

> We find relatively few periods [in American history] when the major parties were closely competitive, with elections alternating between one and the other. The usual pattern has been that of a dominant majority party, which stayed in office as long as its elements held together, and a minority party which gained power only when the majority coalition split. Our political solar system, in short, has been characterized not by two equally competing suns, but by a sun and a moon. It is within the majority party that the issues of any particular period are fought out; while the minority party shines in reflected radiance of the heat thus generated . . . . For the minority party the immediate problem of political strategy always revolves around one question: Which element in the majority coalition can be split off most readily? . . . The key to the political warfare of any particular period will be found in the conflict among the clashing elements in the majority party. This conflict controls the movements of the minority party as well as of the third parties which may appear. The Moon and the lesser planets revolve around the majority Sun.[3]

Indeed, many party patterns of the post-war period correspond to Lubell's model: Nixon's early successes in splitting off elements of the Democratic party coalition including southerners and blue collar ethnics; the major third parties occurred as spin-offs of the Democrats: the Wallaces, Henry and George, and the 1948 Dixiecrats.

More Leadership but Where Is it Going to Come From?

I do seem to have been incorrect in arguing "that Jimmy Carter will make policy, at least in part, in response to pressures from leading elements of his coalition." I failed to fully appreciate another point that I made in 1977: while "the pressures on the post-war presidents seem to have been at least as influential as any other factor," the one element of their personality which may be a crucial contributing factor is their "openness to different views." Carter's own career background, primarily as an engineer and businessman rather than as a politician, may have reinforced this lack of openness to error correction by legislative and party leaders. But the inadequate constraints and resources provided by these other institutions seem to have been equally significant.

Carter's tendency, noted in 1977, to fire off strong salvos of rhetoric and then later fall back, seems to continue. But I consider this less a pattern of plural decision-making open to error correction than merely a process of splitting the difference with the opposition. For instance, congressional leaders frequently complain that they are only consulted after the fact.[4]

My own reaction to these past two years is that they largely reinforce the need for a politics of institutions rather than near total reliance on the presidency. But the consensus among the large majority of academic and journalistic observers is very different: First, they suggest that Carter has been politically inept; second, that this is explained best by his personality and character; third, that the nation once again needs a strong president. (That the president-is-the-government model has remained foremost in the minds of most despite the memories of Vietnam and Watergate indicates how strong the sources of this model are, especially when there is a Democratic incumbent. More generally it indicates how much our political preferences and thus our institutions are shaped by the force of ideas. An especially influential one today seems to be our lack of trust and respect for Congress and parties as institutions.)

I agree that on the whole Carter has been politically inept. I am afraid that my anticipation that Carter's emphasis on the "scientific management" approach would come at the cost of political sensitivity has been borne out in his inability to set political strategies and build coalitions behind them.[5] But the consensus explanation of this political inability and their solution seem misguided.[6] My guess is that his career background has been at least as important in this as his personality or character. The insufficient responses, contributions, and pressures from these other institutions seem to have been even more of a factor in allowing his presidency to develop as it has in all the ways noted here. But whatever the cause, the remedy of greater reliance on these other institutions probably is a wiser strategy than the calls for a more powerful president which we hear now. By focusing on all these institutions, this would help develop a Madisonian conception of the presidency, which sees it as part of the web of government. Leadership is required. But for better error detection and correction, it ought to come from several institutions rather than solely from the White House. But as the next section will indicate there seem to be serious limits to the contributions which these institutions are able to make as they stand now.

Are These Other Institutions Up to the Task

What more do we know in 1979 about these other institutions and their limitations? The importance of a broad range of institutions contributing to policy-making remains strong as my value preference, but it is less persuasive today as a description of reality. My conclusions here are more sobering than those about Carter. Even if Carter's shortcomings are greater than I suggested, the consequences tend to be limited by his tenure in office. But these institutions' limitations will be with us for a much longer time. It seems that, as I predicted, these institutions generally have not provided sufficient resources or constraints for the president. This is the pattern of the previous postwar presidencies noted above: presidential error correction failed to occur because of inadequate pressure from others as well as the president's lack of openness to such pressures.

The circumstances for American political parties still are not favorable. Moreover, the ideological pressures against parties seem to have accelerated rapidly. Parties and party involvement in government, whether it be in Congress or in the nomination of the president, continue to be considered the antithesis of "good government" both by the mass of voters and by opinion leaders.

Though this view has been held by many of the latter group since the Progressive Era, in recent years it increasingly seems to be an idea whose time has come in the most widespread manner. Its ascendency seems closely related to the rise of an educated, idea-oriented public. From 1966 to 1976 voter self-identification with the parties decreased for the Democrats from fifty-three to forty-five percent and from thirty to twenty-two percent for the Republicans. Since the mid 1950s, the number of self-identified independents approximately doubled. In recent years, even those with a party identification are not so as likely to follow it when voting as did voters in the 1950s. Interviewers report that voters with a higher educational background "are not content merely to vote the party ticket. They consider themselves capable of making sophisticated judgments on the individual worth of the candidates they have seen on their living-room screens. They tell you proudly, 'I don't vote for the party; I vote for the man.'"[7]

In observing a prevailing hostility to capitalism in capitalist countries, Schumpeter said that "to condemn it and declare one's aversion to it has become almost a requirement of the etiquette of discussion." Today in America there seems to be an analogous "required" aversion to political parties and some of the same inability to understand their latent functions seems to lie behind these views. For instance, even amóng those who write about politics, there is almost no appreciation of the valuable latent functions performed by parties which I discussed earlier. One would be shocked if John Gardner of Common Cause spoke positively about the favorable functions which parties perform. Moreover, such influential opinion leaders continue to advocate various "reforms" without any consideration of their serious negative effects on parties. For instance, the 1974 campaign financing reform which provides for matching public financing of presidential campaigns probably will further weaken the parties. The public money is given directly to the candidates ($67 million in 1976) rather than using the parties as conduits; the parties received only a few million dollars for convention expenses. If public financing of congressional campaigns is enacted by Congress, it probably will be designed to serve the advantage of incumbents and thus further weaken the grip of parties.

The continued frailties of our parties also adversely affects Congress's power. Without the bond of strong party ties and strong party leadership, building coalitions in Congress has become quite difficult. President Carter has not been adept at political bargaining and coalition building, especially with Congress. But the necessity of constructing new and separate coalitions for most major questions before Congress begins to defy the abilities of any president or any skillful political leader. For instance, the very able Speaker, "Tip" O'Neill, has been constrained in this area and in other leadership tasks by the House members' assertion of their individual power especially in the context of increased activity and influence of subcommittees.

Caucuses, especially party caucuses like the House's Democratic Study Group, in principle could be centralizing forces which in turn would strengthen Congress as an institution. But in practice they have not. Since the regional caucuses do not exert any discipline over their members, they provide individual congressmen with significant services and regions with an organizational base, but they are not a centralizing force. On the whole the same is true of the House's Democratic Study Group. It helped depose some committee chairman and weakened the role of all committee chairman, especially through its pioneering efforts at developing mastery of information so that individual congressmen no longer had to rely on their committee chairman or party leaders for it. However, the dimunition of their power has not been transferred to the party or the leadership but to the decentralizing mechanism of subcommittees.[8] By the mid-1970s, on average one of every two Democrats in the House was chairman of a subcommittee, while every Senate Democrat chaired an average of two subcommittees. This has added to individual Congressmen's power and independence from House as well as committee leadership, and it has tended to move the House away from centralization and more in the direction of individualization in the pattern of the Senate.[9] Thus, like the "reform" of public financing of campaigns, these committee "reforms" have contributed to the atomization of important political institutions.

Finally, for a variety of reasons congressmen have increasingly emphasized their casework, ombudsman, and district oriented activities rather than policy-making activities and a national orientation. At first blush this change appears likely to diminish Congress's contribution to Madisonian policymaking, but perhaps not. Several political scientists have argued that this increased emphasis on casework is one of the major reasons for a marked increase in the number of safe districts in Congress. For our purposes the precise causes are less important than its policy implications. One possibility is that with more Congressmen coming from safe districts, they may feel less constituency or interest group pressure to vote in a particular way. They then—as individuals, and the institution as a whole—may feel freer to make policy and suggest error correction in a "statesmanlike" manner.[10]

However, coming from safe seats will give congressmen independence from congressional and party leadership as well. For Congress to be effective as an institution, it needs greater centralizing forces to compensate for the opposite forces created by the nature of its size, diversity, and the postwar patterns discussed here. Thus, on balance, it is possible that increased safety of congressional seats will make the institution a less effective contributor to plural policy-making and error correction.

There are, however, two recent significant positive developments in Congress. First, my 1977 pessimism about the new congressional budget process may have been accurate then. But there is now some rough preliminary evidence that Congress is in fact slowly gaining institutional strength in this area. For the most part it seems that the work done now will not produce visible gains for another decade because of the incremental nature of the budget process and the longstanding nature of the relationships between the bureaucracy, congressional committees, and interest groups with which this new process must compete. (For example, the House budget committee is not as strong as the Senate's in part because the former was created only as a temporary committee with rotating members. This was a result of the pressure of the House's existing powerful budget-oriented committees—Appropriations, and Ways and Means.) But these current efforts seem to have the potential of paying the future dividend of the development of the congressional budget process as a significant information system.

Second, perhaps some of the changes in the committee structure will lead to opportunities for some inventive party leaders to rebuild the parties within Congress. There is some preliminary evidence that Speaker O'Neill is trying to do this. Because of the weakened committee structure, O'Neill finds it necessary to form special task forces to guide important bills through the House such as the crucial budget resolution and *ad hoc* committees to supplement the standing committees in the preparation of especially complex legislation such as the 1977 energy bill and welfare reform. His appointments to these chairmanships are either very junior House members or more senior ones who are not standing committee chairmen.[11] These appointments seem to contribute to an increased centralization of the Speaker's power, though it is still too early to make any final judgment. Nevertheless, it may indicate a very significant potential for building a type of party politics within Congress which would not have to rely on the voters' direct interest and which would co-exist with the members' increasing district orientation. Interestingly this would be similar to how the Jeffersonians developed the parties in the first place.

Some Dilemmas Of Madisonian Policy-making

My 1977 essay was intended to state briefly a general argument that tried to restore some balance: The presidency is widely advocated and accepted as an error-correcting device, but we seem to have lost the perspective that the presidency needs to be subject to some error detection and correction. In such an essay I was unable to go into all the specifications and qualifications of my argument that would apply to particular issues and circumstances. Of course, I am even less able to do so in this epilogue, but I want to briefly suggest my response to some of the specific dilemmas involved in Madisonian policy-making.

Policy-making by multiple, competing institutions seems particularly appropriate when the optimal policy is to stop or slow down an action. Some of my cases above of effective error correction indicate this pattern in the foreign policy area. On the other hand, in some circumstances bold initiatives are required. Indeed, in a small but very significant number of instances, policies are required that are based on a future orientation, an orientation to the national interest, sometimes even to a world interest. Often there is understandably no organized constituency demanding or even supporting these actions. Those who emphasize the significance of these circumstances stress that they often exist for foreign policy and that the presidency is the only institution that will perceive the need for these policies in such circumstances and the only one able to act on it. (According to this perspective, the cases of black and Jewish organizations shaping Truman and Kennedy administration policies through their influence with Congress and the parties are not relevant for the situations described here, especially since they involve two of the better organized interests in the U.S.).

It is argued that the dilemma in these circumstances is that in the name of plural and error correcting policy-making, these other institutions interfere with the bold and future-oriented initiatives of the presidency. They either totally block them, irreparably delay them, or cannibalize then in an amending process which reflects narrow, parochial interests. The latter is said to be especially damaging to intricately developed presidential foreign policies which must remain intact and unamended if they are to be effective. For example, it is said that this type of congressional amending process was barely tolerable in the 1978 Panama Canal treaty ratification process, and that the more complex SALT treaty cannot be subjected to such a process if it is to remain a viable foreign policy instrument. Therefore, it is argued, that in an even smaller but even more significant number of instances, almost exclusively dealing with national security, these other institutions should be totally excluded (except for some *post facto* consultation with a few of their leaders) from the policy formulation process which should be wholly presidential.

These arguments raise the right questions, but I want to suggest, first, some different distinctions concerning particular circumstances, and, second, some different answers to these dilemmas. The latter take cognizance of the constant, endemic pressures for an overextension of presidential freedom from Madison constraints.

First, these dilemmas do not exclusively exist for foreign policy. For domestic policy the optimal policy often is to stop or slow down an action, especially with regard to spending levels. For example, both Congress and the presidency need to rely on each other to help themselves control expenditures. Similarly, when New York City's mayor shared power with the separate and competing Board of Estimates (a semilegislative institution composed of the independently elected city council president, controller, and five borough presidents) it aided him in the difficult tasks of saying no to certain expenditures and maintaining reasonable general expenditure levels. A charter "reform" under Lindsay reduced the Board's power, and the mayor was less able to control expenditures. This seems to have been one of the several factors contributing to the city's fiscal crisis.

Other dilemmas seen in foreign policy also are present in the domestic area. There is often a need for bold departures based on a future orientation and without the benefit of an organized constituency's pressure or support (e.g., the early proposals for a negative income tax). For domestic policy the suggestions and interventions of institutions other than the presidency often weaken rather than correct policy (e.g., the mayoral and congressional expansion and thus dilution of the initial Model Cities legislation from a concentrated demonstration program for a few cities to a thinly funded one for over 150 cities). In domestic policy there are also intricately developed policies which must remain intact and unamended if they are to be effective (e.g., a negative income tax requires uniformity for administrative effectiveness rather than a host of regional and occupational exceptions; many tax bills can be vitiated by excessive amendments or failure of Congress to inact the legislation at the optimal time in the business cycle).

Thus, to suspend generally these Madisonian constraints for foreign policy is fickle. It is based on the policy preferences of the moment rather than on an orientation to general institutional arrangements regardless of the exigencies at hand. One indication of this is that among liberals and conservatives arguing for a distinction between foreign and domestic policy in applying Madisonian constraints each opts for a different area to be exempt: Conservatives want to constrain the presidency domestically but not in foreign policy; liberals want to do the reverse. Furthermore, even "bold departures" in both domestic and foreign policy ought to be subject to a process of error detection and correction. Indeed, one could argue that such policies require the collective wisdom of multiple decision-makers precisely because they are innovative and did not initially percolate through other institutions and organizations. Even if one argues that the presidency needs more discretion to maneuver in foreign policy, this should not be extended to the unwise extreme of shedding all or almost all Madisonian constraints on the presidency in this area. Nor is such an extreme justified by the fallacious view that the foreign policy contributions of institutions other than the presidency are inherently negative. More power is required for the presidency under certain circumstances, but there is also a need for the maintenance of a balance of power among institutions. The framers of the constitution wisely saw these dual needs. They created separate institutions sharing powers even in foreign policy. The president is somewhat predominant as the commander-in-chief, but Congress must declare war and raise the resources for the armed forces.

To suggest that the presidency is better suited than other institutions to take the initiative to develop innovative and intricate foreign policies does not indicate the the presidency is infallible. Thus, even those policies ostensibly so complex and intricately crafted that they must move through the policy adoption process almost intact, at some stage probably would benefit from the consultative wisdom of other institutions. If these policies in fact should not be subject to the intense public amendment, bargaining, and logrolling of the legislative process, they still can and probably ought to be shaped by Congress's leaders and foreign policy specialists *before* the proposals leave the White House and are sent to the full Congress.

Finally, there is a need for bold innovations despite the absence or even the opposition of organized constituencies, but in principle these need not come only from the presidency. In domestic policy this certainly has not been the case. Some of the innovative policies that have come from institutions other than the presidency include the civil rights initiatives in the 1950s from the Supreme Court and the Congress (the 1957 and 1960 civil rights bills)—while the presidency was inactive and the spate of environmental and safety legislation during the past ten years. There are, of course, well-known reasons why in the past the presidency in practice has been more likely than the Congress to develop foreign policy initiatives. Most of the factors contributing to this disparity are likely to continue. But perhaps we should not be too quick to give almost all the foreign policy discretion to the presidency. For instance, in the past few years we have seen Congress's ability to begin to reassert some of its power and expertise in the highly complex budget-making process. A decade ago most observers assumed that they had almost totally abdicated it to the presidency, just as they now assume is true of foreign policy.

Second, as I suggested in 1977, the central dilemma is that one person's error is another's statesmanship and principled behavior. What to one person may be the addition of collective wisdom may to the next be unprincipled opportunism. An answer, not *the* answer, to these dilemmas probably can only be made in the concrete rather than in the abstract. In large part answers depend on one's values and the particular context in question. (Was it error detection to avoid aiding the French at Dienbienphu? I think it was, but who knows? Maybe we will know in fifty years. Maybe not. As Henry Fairlie suggests, "the most important fact about what politicians do is that they do not know what they are doing . . . A politician must deal from day to day with what Bismarck called imponderabilia.") Yet, I would suggest some general guides: First, I would advocate certain general tendencies in institutional arrangements—multiple, competing ones, with adjustments for particular circumstances. Second, it should be recognized that consultative, collective decision-making is a matter of degree rather than an absolute. These institutions should share most but not all decision-making and at some but not all stages nor in all contexts. Therefore, perhaps for certain complex foreign policy issues the contributions of institutions other than the presidency should be minimized. Third, while I have no definite answer to these dilemmas, I feel confident in suggesting that *there are numerous, strong pressures within the presidency and from outside it to over-extend the policy area that is relatively free of these Madisonian constraints.* This is at least as significant as the dangers from other institutions weakening and obstructing presidential initiatives. *It is in the face of these pressures that I urge so strongly a maintenance of balance in the sharing of power by our national institutions.*

These pressures ars so significant because they seem to be endemic to the presidency and to the nature of our political system today with its fragmentation and dispersion of power. There are the frustrations of the office of the president in the context of the type of political system: "everybody believes in democracy," said one presidential aide, "until he gets to the White House and then you begin to believe in dictatorship, because it is so hard to get things done." There are the structural characteristics of the office that Reedy describes which leads to the White House view "that the president and a few of his most trusted advisors are possessed of a special knowledge which must be closely held within a small group." There are the expectations from outside the office which put such broad responsibility on the presidency (especially for foreign policy and the management of the economy) that presidents seem to adopt the view that since they ultimately are going to take the responsibility for most national policy-making, why should they share the decision-making with others who do not share that responsibility and its costs. These seemingly self-serving views are given an aura of legitimacy by the widely held view that the presidency is best able to stand for the national interest.

The combination of these pressures and the typical difficulties that the president faces creates incentives for the presidency to seek to evade Madisonian constraints. But in our system it is difficult to legitimately evade them unless there are unusual circumstances. Faced with these pressures and expectations, what is the White House to do then? It probably will feel impelled to move toward an operating style of creating crises to justify an evasion of these constraints. It seems easiest to justify such evasions in foreign policy and the examples of it are clearest there—the Gulf of Tonkin incident and the Mayaguez incident. But it also happens with domestic policy—the swine flu case and President Carter's 1977 (and subsequent) characterization of energy problems as the "moral equivalent of war."

Thus, strong efforts are needed to sail against these prevailing winds and maintain a balance among our national institutions. Perhaps the most significant justification for maintaining this balance except in the most unusual circumstances like urgent national security questions is precisely the importance of just such situations. If the president has not constantly sought to evade the Madisonian constraints, he will have developed a reserve of goodwill with institutions like Congress. Then when he needs broad and unfettered discretion in a policy-making area like national security, he is likely to get it. But if he has not created this reserve, as seems to be true of Carter today, then the Congress is likely to intrude in these sensitive areas to an excessive extent. This seems to be the scenario to which we can look forward during the SALT treaty ratification process.

What Can Be Done?

The over-emphasis on the importance of the presidency that I criticized in 1977 still exists today even with the constant criticism of the incumbent's abilities. (And most of those who continue to look so much to the presidency were for the most part also critical of the performance of the previous three incumbents. But they seem to persist in idiosyncratic rather than systemic explanations for these incumbents' shortcomings.) But equally disconcerting is the increased atomization of the institutions that I suggested should share more policymaking with the presidency. The force of ideas continues to help shape these patterns. The views that the presidency is the government, that political parties contribute little to democracy and should be "reformed," and that Congress is much less competent to legitimately voice the national interest, seem to continue to dominate the nation's political thinking. In part they seem to be interrelated: Perhaps we are content to see the deinstitutionalization of our parties and Congress because we feel that the presidency is more important and that it remains intact.[12]

Can anything be done about these patterns? Probably not. These ideas are strongly held, rarely challenged by influential writers, and their social bases of increased education and income are here to stay. We can try to make clearer, however, the costs of ''reforms'' in contributing to the atomization of Congress and the parties. From previous reform experiences we should have learned that there is no free lunch. Though it may be worth it, there is a price to pay for reform. Since important societal values rarely can be simultaneously maximized, trade-offs ought to be anticipated. Thus it should not be surprising that these reforms may have moved us from an imperfect situation to a worse one; or at least to one that is no better, and that we may have sacrificed important values in the course of achieving others. We must weigh whether the benefits of these reforms are commensurate with their costs. If we do not carry out such a calculus, in the name of democracy we may render our parties and Congress so weak that the presidency in fact will become the government. Indeed, if these trends continue the only possible governmental elements that are likely to stand as a peer to the presidency are the bureaucracy and the courts. But neither of these are elected or responsive.

The call for a politics of institutions and for strengthening and centralizing these institutions rather than atomizing them seems to go against the grain of most current popular thought, the practice of most of our institutions, and the social bases of these ideas and these institutions. But today the force of ideas in politics is so influential that perhaps the ideas advocated here could gain rapid acceptance if some opinion leaders would take a second look at them, although the past two years do not lead me to be sanguine.

As it was in 1977, it is important in conclusion to stress that our ultimate concern ought to be with the values and ends that these institutions will pursue. Yet a policymaking process that is competitive and involves multiple institutions sharing power inherently contributes to democratic and representative policy-making because it is so plural and tends to aggregate interests.

Notes

*My thanks to Gene Bardach, Seyom Brown, Vincent Davis, Chris Leman, and Frank Levy for their perceptive comments on an earlier draft.

1. The New York *Times*, March 3, 1979, p. 18.
2. *Ibid*.
3. Samuel Lubell, *The Future of American Politics*, pp. 212-217.
4. After this was written, President Carter sent to Congress a large new energy

proposal including decontrol of domestic petroleum and a "windfall profits" tax on oil companies. Unlike his 1977 comprehensive energy proposal, this 1979 one was the result of extensive consultation between the White House and congressional leaders and included some of the congressional proposals. A senior White House aide explained, "we learned something in two years. An energy plan didn't have to come down as tablets from Mt. Sinai." But we do not yet know whether something lasting was learned or whether this consultation is merely the exception that proves the rule. Incidentally there is no evidence that his 1977 energy proposal was a more optimal one because it avoided prior congressional consultation.

5. I would note, however, that he has been unfairly criticized for many areas—like inflation and Mideast conflict—in which even a politically capable president would have serious short-run difficulties. Presidents receive such intense scrutiny that it may be that neither I nor most critics would be satisfied by any incumbent's political ability. For my own part I do not think this is true. Carter's shortcomings are rather great. Indeed, without resorting to a comparison with the now mythic FDR, some significant contemporary contrasts in political ability are provided by Walter Mondale and Daniel P. Moynihan. For instance, recently Mondale has been criticized as a professional protege and Moynihan for engaging in excessive flattery. But both (despite their modest backgrounds) have thereby successfully furthered their own influence and careers and along with that some useful programs and issues along a broad range of political opinion. Gary Wills, "Moynihan's Flattery," *New York Magazine*, December, 1977; Martin Tolchin, "The Mondales," *New York Times Magazine*, February 1978, pp. 15-16.)

6. Former presidential speech-writer James Fallows' fascinating critique of Carter ("The Passionless Presidency," *The Atlantic*, May 1979) is a good example of the continuing emphasis on personality explanations.

7. Broder, "Of Presidents and Parties," *Wilson Quarterly*, Winter 1978, p. 105.

8. The DSG developed a subcommittee bill of rights which freed subcommittees and their staffs from the chairman's control.

9. A key step in this individualization process in the Senate was Lyndon Johnson's practice as majority leader in the 1950s of giving each freshman senator at least one major committee assignment and the subsequent growth of subcommittees and select committees headed by relatively junior senators.

10. This hypothesis is consistent with Richard Fenno's conclusion that Congressmen actually have a good deal of independence because they are elected on the basis of their "homestyle." He found that they are not dependent on party for reelection but rather than on their own personal relationship with their district and thus have a good deal of stored credit with voters. Richard Fenno, "Congressmen in Their Constituencies," *American Political Science Review*, 1979.

11. Richard Cohen, "Tip O'Neill—He Gets By With a Little Help From His Friends," *The National Journal*, Sept. 2, 1978, p. 1384.

12. Henry Fairlie's persuasive argument to the contrary notwithstanding, we tend to believe that in recent years there has been an institutionalization of the presidency. By contrast, Fairlie argues that "a myth has been created since the Second World War that [does] not add up to saying much more than that the president does many things which the president did not do before, and needs a larger staff to help him . . . . There is no high political office which is less institutionalized . . . The Presidency, as organized in the White House, seems to me a form of unencumbered, arbitrary, personal rule." "Thoughts on the Presidency," *The Public Interest*, Fall 1967.

Congress, the President, and the Cycles of Power

Lawrence C. Dodd

Almost a century ago a young political science graduate student at Johns Hopkins wrote a provocative little book entitled *Congressional Government*. The author's name was Woodrow Wilson. He argued that a twofold power shift was occurring in American politics: (a) a shift of power from the state to the federal level; and (b) a shift of power at the national level from the Supreme Court and the presidency to Congress. Wilson saw these shifts as historical necessities.

In the intervening century, *Congressional Government* has become one of the most influential studies of American politics. It was the first systematic and widely read book to argue that institutional politics in America is characterized by a shifting balance of power. In addition, Wilson's analysis was sufficiently cogent and provocative to provide a classic interpretation of American politics, an interpretation that political analysts continually restudy for its insight and method. For those of us who would attempt to assess the current shifting balance of power between Congress and the presidency, Wilson's book provides three lessons.

The first lesson—one unique for Wilson's time though widely acknowledged today—is that power and power relations are not constant. They are not indelibly imprinted on institutions by a constitution. In Wilson's time political analysts assumed that the Constitution guaranteed power to institutions. They assumed that a separation of powers, check and balance system of government would endure as written in the Constitution. They assumed that the chief threats to government were invasion from abroad or civil war at home. Political analysts in Wilson's day did not perceive that a slow transformation of power relations among American national institutions might substantially alter the government from within.

Wilson argued, in a dramatic departure from the legalistic mentality of his day, though consistent with the arguments of Madison a century earlier, that the power of institutions rests not only on their constitutional mandate but also on the ability of institutions to organize themselves so as to utilize their power prerogatives. In order to use their constitutional power authoritatively, institutions must be organized in a cohesive manner that maintains their decision-making integrity. If an institution cannot organize effectively, its power will ebb away and other institutions will fill the void. In his own day Wilson saw the presidency and the Supreme Court as less able to organize effectively, while Congress, through the expanded use of the committee system together with a strong speaker, was organizing in a cohesive fashion. Thus the shift of power to Congress.

The second lesson of *Congressional Government* is that political analysts must be cautious and hardheaded in their interpretation of the shifting balance of institutional power. We must take care not to extrapolate current patterns indefinitely. Short-term events and power shifts may well disguise the real nature of long-term power dynamics; long-term shifts of power in one direction may be reversed by critical crises or changes in societal context and governmental role that send power dynamics off into wholly new directions. Because we are all products of our time, we may be blinded by immediate preoccupations from seeing the real historical dynamics. We thus must seek historical interpretations of power relations that are as rigorously logical, empirically accurate, and broadly inclusive as possible.

The lesson at hand, thus, is that political/institutional change is complex and interactive. At the time Wilson wrote he was basically correct in perceiving the existence of the two patterns he identified. But, because he relied too extensively on immediate patterns as enduring guides, his long-term prognosis was incorrect. Thus he saw Congress as becoming the supreme branch of American government because it seemed to be moving toward predominance during the Reconstruction era. Less than thirty years later he was to play a major role in creating the modern presidency and setting it on its course toward predominance. Ironically, Wilson's misinterpretation of the shifting balance between Congress and the presidency occurred partly because of the accuracy of his forecast that power was shifting from the states to the national level. As will become evident later in this discussion, the rise of the national government played a major role in the decline of Congress, a decline that simply was not evident in Wilson's time. In addition, Wilson largely missed the important influence that changes in the social, economic and international order can have on the role of government and on particular institutions, their organization, and their power potential.

Finally, the third lesson that Wilson taught us was that each generation must attempt to assess anew the shifting balance of institutional power. Every historical era has its own crises and its own potential. The actors of each era can be so buffeted by change and so unaware of the character of change that crises overwhelm them and potential goes unfulfilled. Few generations will ever completely resolve their own problems or exploit their own opportunities. Nevertheless, the performance of a generation will improve significantly as it comes to understand the historical forces that are operating.

Wilson was trying to make sense out of a world that had suffered a devastating Civil War, a debilitating Reconstruction, and a string of weak presidents and strong-headed Congresses. By dropping the constitutional blinders that other analysts had worn, Wilson accurately perceived the shift of power from the states to the national government; this perception proved a major building block of the legislative programs of his presidency. In addition, Wilson perceived that power relations do vary and that the way institutional actors behave within an institution influences the power of that institution. This insight led him to emphasize the speakership of the House and the potential importance of the congressional committee system, an organizational device that political analysts had not come to appreciate fully. In addition, Wilson's understanding of the importance for external power of an institution's internal behavior was critical to his own reinterpretation of the presidency in later years and to his recognition that the behavior of the particular president could be critical for the power of the presidency.

While the immediate forecast of the young Woodrow Wilson concerning presidential-congressional relations was wrong, the intellectual style reflected in his early analysis later proved immeasurably useful to him and to other political analysts. Wilson's example teaches us that to understand the nature of our time, to take short-term events and derive from them their underlying significance, to forecast the kinds of problems we are likely to face and thus to envision the kinds of responses likely to be required of us, we must actively and honestly seek to understand the broad historical dynamics that shape the power relations among our political institutions. While our efforts will be necessarily incomplete and in some instances misguided, the end result will be greater self-awareness and a better opportunity to respond intelligently to the forces at work in our generation.

I

In our own time we have witnessed a series of events at least as dramatic as those of Wilson's time. In the sixty years since Wilson's presidency, power has shifted from the Congress to the presidency, with the late 1940s serving as an era of short congressional resurgence. With the long-term power shift toward the presidency, the president has increasingly become the nation's chief legislator, chief budgetary officer, the primary overseer of the bureaucracy, the leader in foreign policy, the nation's chief tribune. For a generation, at least, the rise of the presidency was often glorified as necessary to govern the country. During the 1950s and 1960s political analysts wrote that the presidency was the nation's one truly democratic institution, the president the only officer elected by all of the people. The Congress was seen as an outdated, obsolete institution elected to serve parochial rather than national interests. The interests of the presidency were seen as essentially parallel to those of the nation at large, which meant that it was a safe, responsive, humane institution, whose actions would necessarily be good for the whole country.

In the late 1960s and early 1970s a series of events led analysts to challenge both the benevolence of the presidency and the historical necessity of its rise. The Vietnam War, Nixon's impoundment of duly appropriated funds, the credibility gap of the Johnson administration, the Watergate crisis, the rise of a secrecy system which saw the executive branch suppressing a wide range of information, presidential politicization of the FBI and CIA—all of these have led to a serious and widespread challenge to the desirability of presidential government. We have come, rather, to see a strong presidency not necessarily as a benevolent guardian of democracy but rather as a potential imperial threat to political liberty.

In response to growing apprehensions about an imperial presidency, the 1970s witnessed a new congressional resurgence, a new shift of power momentum from the president to Congress. In this shift, Congress tried to regain its legislative power by strengthening the power of its party leaders. Congress sought to regain control of the budget by creating a new congressional budget process. It sought to regain control of the bureaucracy by reforming its oversight procedures. It attempted to reassert its war-making prerogatives by passing a war-powers act. And it hoped to improve its role as popular tribune by broadcasting its legislative sessions. These and other reforms, the most widespread congressional changes in sixty years, present a picture of a newly invigorated and assertive legislature that has retaken its place in the constitutional order.

Political analysts today often worry less about presidential power and more about a return of congressional government. The short-term reforms and the congressional resurgence, extrapolated into long-term power shifts, fill many an observer with dread. It is not uncommon, in fact, to hear the assertion that the presidency has been crippled and that the nation is moving pell mell into an era of congressional dominance. With the imperial presidency still a warm memory, we are cautioned that the real problem we should fear is an imperial Congress.

Thus, the dilemmas that we face in trying to understand the movement of events in our time: Do we extrapolate the long-term power shift, i.e., the rise of the presidency, as the fundamental reality shaping our politics and our future? Do we highlight the short-term shift, i.e., the resurgence of Congress, as the new reality likely to persist? Do we suspect a totally new development in institutional power dynamics? Do we envision a balanced equilibrium now emerging between these institutions? Do we simply throw up our hands and conclude that no sense can be made of these events? Or, do we conclude that it simply does not matter what the balance of power really is or how it is shifting?

To take the last question first, it should be clear to us that the balance of power does matter, and that understanding it matters. The balance matters because the alternative may be to leave decision-making power in the hands of one person, an imperial president—and that scheme is rejected by the full force of Western political thought. The difficulty is not merely that philosopher-kings are difficult to select; it is also, as Bruce Buchanan so clearly demonstrates in *Presidential Experience*, that the immense burdens and stress of the presidency itself may distort personality and make judgment unreliable. Thus government by separate institutions sharing power, including a legislature composed of numerous elected representatives, commends itself to us today as it did to the framers of the Constitution. Because we are committed to government by separate institutions sharing power, understanding the shift of power among those institutions is critical.

So what sense do we make of the events of our day? What is the nature of the shifting balance of institutional power? What institutional problems are we likely to face in the coming decades for which we should now be preparing? A key to these questions lies, much as with Woodrow Wilson, in developing and discussing a broad historical interpretation within which to view and interpret the short-term events.

II

In the late eighteenth century and early nineteenth century, the national government was not immensely powerful. Congress was a debating society, a forum for the great ethical struggles of the day. The leaders and careerists of Congress were individuals gifted in debate, in identifying and articulating broad principles, and in compromise, the Websters, Clays, and Calhouns. During this era Congress was in relatively clear command of its role as legislative decision-maker for the nation. The decisions it made, however, were, with a few notable exceptions, of mild import to the daily lives of the nation's citizens.

Events of the late nineteenth century altered this situation dramatically. The Civil War ended ambiguities about supremacy by clearly establishing the hegemony of the national government in political affairs. The industrial revolution helped create an interdependent economy based on interstate commerce, thus expanding the power potential of the national government by confronting it with social and economic decisions of considerable magnitude that lay within its constitutional mandate. The industrial revolution also provided America (as well as other nations) with the technical means to span the oceans, conquer far-off lands, and gain international markets for American goods. America thus discovered the world, the world rediscovered America, and the national government discovered anew its constitutional responsibility for foreign policy and the regulation of American involvement in foreign commerce. Congress became the center of this expanded national power, because the constitution gave to it the delegated powers to regulate interstate and foreign commerce, to give advice and consent (on the part of the Senate) to treaties and ambassadorial nominations, to control defense authorizations and appropriations, and to declare war.

During the Civil War Reconstruction period and its aftermath, consequently, ambitious politicians focused more intently on Congress. Voluntary turnover of members began to decline. Committee work was taken more seriously and significant committee reforms and changes, such as the separation of the Ways and Means and Appropriations Committees, were instituted. Party leadership began to assert itself more strongly, with the leaders gaining considerable authority because they offered services—such as selection of committee members and chairmen, policy development and guidance, mediation of parliamentary conflicts, scheduling of legislation—that were necessary to avoid the chaos implicit in the changing Congress.

The late nineteenth century thus constituted an era of party government in Congress, with increasingly strong party leaders dominating an increasingly active committee system and an increasingly powerful Congress. This was the era documented by Woodrow Wilson, one in which it did appear that Congress was emerging as the supreme branch of government. Congress during this period seemed to justify Madison's fears that a cohesive Congress led by strong central leaders and in control of the power of the purse, taxation, and the tariff could dominate the Court and the president. This dominance was not to last indefinitely, however.

At precisely the time that party leaders were consolidating their power within Congress, changes were occurring that laid the foundation for yet a new era of American politics and congressional power. The Progressive era, particularly the years from 1905 to 1920, should therefore be regarded as the second major societal transformation, one as significant in many ways as the transformation of the Civil War and Reconstruction era, in American governmental history. First, the nation became increasingly concerned with "democracy," with popular participation in politics, and in equalizing power among elected representatives. This growing popular viewpoint undercut support for political machines, including party machines in Congress. Secondly, the Progressive era witnessed a rise in the involvement of interest groups. While this rise emanated from concern with participatory politics, it served to legitimate strong ties among corporations, bureaucratic agencies and congressional committees—ties that bypassed party organizations. Third, during this period the nation became convinced of its unlimited power—power internationally to remake the world order, power nationally to secure a good life for its citizens. The business corporations, government agencies, and congressional committees that developed in the late nineteenth century were seen in the early twentieth century as needing not so much coordination by a national machine or party leadership but rather more freedom to act and to cooperate so as to nurture the well-being of the interests they effected. The best government, in other words, was decentralized, with power exercised close to relevant interests. The Progressive era, therefore, provided popular pressure and ideological justification of the overthrow of party government in Congress. This societal pressure meshed well with the emerging interests of the individual members of Congress.

By the Progressive era, congressional careerists no longer found that a centralized system of power within Congress served their personal interests. Rather than seeing strong party leaders as an aid to the effectiveness of their legislative service by reducing organizational chaos and providing needed policy guidance, careerist legislators of the new Congress saw party leaders as arbitrary tyrants interfering with personal careers and policy specializations. Thus, in a quest for personal autonomy and power, and nurtured by the political forces activated in the Progressive period, early twentieth century members of Congress moved dramatically against strong party leadership in Congress, stripping the speakership in the House of most of its power and eventually discarding the role of a powerful majority party leader in the Senate. In place of party government, members turned to committee government.

The emerging system of committee government was held together by institutional norms and rules that had been developing over the preceding decades as turnover had declined, the most important of which was seniority. The system of committee government served the interest of the individual members of Congress by spreading far more widely the access to significant power positions. It meshed with Progressive ideology by seeming to democratize Congress. And it found considerable support from the business community and executive agencies because it allowed the sweetheart relations to flourish unfettered by party leaders who, if nationally oriented, might question the wisdom of particular committee policies seeming to serve only the interests of particularized sectors of the society or economy. The move to committee government, however, failed to serve the interests of Congress as an institution concerned with protecting its power position in the constitutional order.

The move away from strong congressional party leadership and toward committee government knocked out a major underpinning of the Madisonian system of government, namely the assumption that Congress would maintain its institutional will because it would be composed largely of nonprofessional politicians who would centralize congressional power. This major move thus was a qualitative change in Congress and a watershed occurrence for the relationship between Congress and the presidency.

III

As a form of organization, committee government distributes policy-making responsibilities among a series of relatively autonomous groups each having significant control over policy decisions in a specified jurisdictional area. Although this system denies every member the opportunity to control all policy decisions, it ensures that most members can hope to satisfy a portion of their power drive if they remain in Congress long enough to acquire a chairmanship.

Despite several advantages, committee government possesses severe flaws that undermine the ability of Congress to fulfill its constitutional responsibilities to make public policy and oversee its implementation. Among these flaws, three stand out: first, committee government is without strong, centralized leadership, and thus lacks the ability to develop comprehensive programs that cut across committee jurisdictions; moreover, it leaves Congress without an authoritative spokesman to justify its policies to the nation. Second, committee government is without a mechanism to ensure that decisions of the authorization, appropriations, and revenue committees bear some reasonable relation to one another; lacking fiscal coordination, Congress finds it difficult to develop a rational national budget. Finally, committee government provides no safeguards against self-interested policy-making; the committees that create and fund programs also oversee program implementation; and because the creators and funders are normally the most visible supporters and are backed by lobbyists and interested bureaucrats, they are loathe to undertake critical investigations of a pet agency or program. In this manner, committee government leads to a failure of vigorous, coordinated, objective congressional oversight of the executive.

Committee government thus produces a cruel paradox: the wide dispersal of power within Congress creates such immobilism that Congress is unable to play a strong role in national decision-making. Or, put differently, the desire for power by individual members in combination with the support and pressures from lobbyists and bureaucrats, creates an organizational dispersion of power that undermines the ability of Congress to maintain its institutional cohesion and its constitutional power, and thus diminishes the long-term value of power positions within the institution.

This inherent tension between personal power and institutional power in the twentieth century Congress generates an explosive dynamic within Congress, and between Congress and the presidency. This dynamic is cyclical in nature, and follows a relatively clear long-term pattern. At the outset, the natural tendency within a large institution like Congress is to develop a fairly centralized power structure so that a few strong leaders, even within committee government, can organize decision-making processes in a way that avoids chaos and allows coherent decision-making. It is also natural, of course, for such leaders to use their positions to favor their personal policies and influence, and to remain in office as long as possible to exercise their hard-won power. These career interests of the central leaders are at odds, however, with the career interests of other members of Congress who do not possess power positions and who seek to move up in their career progression. As time passes, these members will shore up their constituency ties enough to seek policy influence and power positions, only to face the fact that a few congressmen control the limited number of organizational positions that carry with them parliamentary prerogatives and organizational resources. In an effort to gain power positions, these members will support the decentralization of power, spreading control over parliamentary procedure and organizational resources among a wider number of power positions.

The coming of congressional decentralization produces two divergent patterns. First, it does bring more innovation into the policy process, and it does bring more members into the possession of some element of organizational power. But decentralization carries with it real costs, particularly a decline in the ability of the institution to provide internal and external leadership, to provide policy and budgetary coordination, to oversee executive implementation of policy, and to respond decisively to broad national policy sentiments. The end result is policy immobilism particularly with respect to broadly focused, nationally oriented concerns. Decentralization thus undermines the ability of Congress to make decisions in a coherent manner.

In the wake of this kind of congressional immobilism, the country elects a strong president in a dramatic electoral realignment and the strong president moves to exert national policy leadership, supported by a large number of new members elected on his coattails. The immobilism within Congress is broken, and innovative policies flow forth in an avalanche. The end to immobilism is temporary, however. With the strong presidency comes executive disregard for Congress, the members of Congress and their prerogatives. Congressional willingness to follow presidential leadership declines. Congress once again attempts to rely on its own internal devices, experiencing renewed immobilism. The immediate response within Congress is to see the problem as the result of a few obstreperous leaders who possess too much power to thwart the will of Congress in particular policy areas. Based on this perspective, reformers move to undermine the power of these individuals, increasing congressional decentralization. Such efforts fit well with the immediate career interests of the many members of Congress who lack significant power positions, and thus succeed. The end result, however, is more policy immobilism and renewed executive aggrandizement of congressional prerogatives.

The reassertiveness of the presidency mobilizes the members of Congress into action. They see that their individual positions of power within Congress are meaningless unless the institution can impose its legislative will on the nation. Searching for ways in which to regain legislative preeminence and constrain the executive, they identify part of the problem as an internal organizational one, and seek to reform Congress in a way that will reduce congressional susceptibility to presidential usurpation of power. Such reform efforts come during or immediately following crises in which presidents clearly and visibly threaten fundamental power prerogatives of Congress. The reforms are marked by attempts to strengthen centralized party leadership, improve budgetary and policy coordination, and strengthen congressional oversight of the executive, all of which make this a centralizing reform era.

Because the quest for personal power continues as the underlying motivation of individual members, the centralizing reforms are basically attempts to strengthen the value of internal congressional power by increasing the power of Congress vis-a-vis the executive. The reform efforts are constrained by consideration of personal power prerogatives and by pressure from lobby groups and bureaucratic officials that benefit from the pre-existing system of decentralized congressional power. The attempt to protect personal prerogatives while centralizing power builds structural flaws into the centralization mechanism, flaws that would not be present were the significance of congressional structure for the national power of Congress itself the primary, overarching consideration. These flaws provide the openings through which centralization procedures are destroyed when institutional crises pass and members again feel free to emphasize personal powers and careers. Because policy inaction within Congress often will be identified as the immediate cause of presidential power aggrandizement, and because policy immobilism may become identified with key individuals or committees that have obstructed particular legislation, reform efforts also may be directed toward breaking up the authority of these individuals or committees and dispersing it among individuals and committees who seem more amenable to activist policies. Even centralizing reform eras, therefore, may include significant decentralizing reforms as part of the overall reform package.

During the recentralizing stage, Congress experiences considerable membership change. Involuntary turnover rises because the public punishes the party of the president whose actions have created the appearance of executive aggrandizement of congressional power; the presidential party thus will receive significant electoral losses in Congress. In addition, as the centralizing era proceeds the senior members of Congress who benefited from the old power structure will perceive that the reforms undermine their power positions and that Congress is not as much fun as it was. For these reasons, together with the fact that they are reaching the late years of life and do find congressional service more demanding, they voluntarily retire in large numbers, with Congress thus experiencing a large influx of new members.

As Congress moves to resolve internal structural problems and circumscribe presidential power, presidents begin to cooperate with Congress. This cooperation stems from a desire to defuse the congressional counterattack and protect the power prerogatives of the presidency. To do otherwise would open a president to serious personal attack as anticongressional and thus antidemocratic, tarnishing the legitimizing myth of the presidency as a democratic institution representing all the people, and identifying presidential motivations as power aggrandizement rather than protection of the Republic.

The presidential effort to cooperate with Congress moves the nation into a quiescent era in which political conflict over constitutional prerogatives fades and conflict over policy takes center stage. In the quiescent period, Congress is resurgent. Yet, because Congress still lacks truly strong leadership and sound structural mechanisms suitable to a more assertive role, it uses its resurgent authority primarily in a negative fashion, to stop presidents from acting or to alter and trim presidential proposals. Because the reform era failed to create a truly strong and durable system of congressional leadership, and because individual members continue in a quest for personal power, Congress is largely unable to engineer a coherent, aggressive set of programs.

The large new generation elected in the reform and quiescent eras becomes frustrated both with congressional inability to act in an aggressive manner and with the impotence and harassment of the centralized elements of the new Congress. As this new generation ages and learns the electoral ropes, its members turn attention to personal policy influence, power positions and personal legislative autonomy within Congress. Untempered by the lessons of the past, and enticed by the electoral, policy, and power rewards to be gained by a closer and deeper personal connection with lobbyists and bureaucrats that comes in a decentralized Congress, these members provide a major block of supporters for weakening or bypassing central policy organs and renewing and expanding power decentralization within Congress.

And so the authority of the centralized power organs ebbs away. Congress relies on and expands its decentralized authority structure—the committees and subcommittees. Congress becomes increasingly immobile and enfeebled, lacking confidence even in its negating powers. At first the calls for presidential government are faint and muted. But as time passes and the government lacks clear direction, the clamor for presidential government grows, leading again to presidential dominance of policy processes and to yet another era of presidential imperialism and constitutional confrontation.

Inherent within the organizational dynamics of a professional Congress based on committee government, then, is a cyclical rhythm of organizational change. The organizational power cycle has roughly five stages:

Stage I   (Decentralization and Immobilism)

Stage II   (Electoral Realignment and Presidential Government)

Stage III   (Renewed Immobilism and Decentralization)

Stage IV   (Renewed Presidential Government, Constitutional Crisis, and Congressional Recentralization)

Stage V   (An Era of Quiescence)

During the era of committee government, the cycles have occurred at approximately thirty-year intervals. Their existence, and the evidence of these stages, is clearer in the House of Representatives than in the Senate, owing to the fact that the greater impact of organizational structure on the power potential of House members makes them struggle more overtly over organizational structure. Yet, in both, the general patterns associated with the cycles and stages exist.

IV

During the twentieth century experiment with committee government, Congress has experienced two power cycles. The first occurred during the period from around 1920, after Congress had thrown off the shackles of party government and developed the basic outlines of committee government, through the mid-1940s. The process of decentralization that started in the 1910-20 period proceeded throughout the era from 1920 to 1946, with Congress attempting to break legislative logjams by ever greater reliance on a proliferation of committees, subcommittees, special committees and joint committees. With decentralization came immobilism, the 1920s and early 1930s being the great era of congressional impotence on national policy issues. In the 1930s, facing policy immobilism, the country turned to strong presidential government, experiencing a realigning presidential election, initial policy breakthroughs, and then a return to congressional intransigence. The era of constitutional confrontation began roughly with Roosevelt's court-packing plan of 1937 and continued into the 1940s, marked by his decisions to serve a third and fourth term, his forceful use of power as commander-in-chief, and executive preeminence in legislative policy-making. The era of centralizing reform came in the 1940s, highlighted by the 1946 Legislative Reorganization Act. That reform effort was essentially a reinforcing reform movement, one that solidified and recommitted Congress to committee government.

The transition to the second power cycle came in the late 1940s and early 1950s as the nation moved to an era of quiescence in which conflict centered over policy rather than constitutional power. In this quiescent era, the presidency was less aggressive than in the Roosevelt era, and a new decentralization stage began to emerge. Congress ignored the centralized budget procedure established in the 1946 Act and in the 1950s and 1960s came to rely increasingly on subcommittees for legislative activity. The move toward decentralization was fueled by a high turnover in the late 1940s, particularly among Rooseveltian Democrats, a high turnover that brought to Congress in 1946, 1948, and 1950 new members less sensitive to the dilemmas of decentralization. As these members pressed decentralization, Congress became increasingly immobile. Facing this immobilism, the country turned away from the somnolent presidency of Eisenhower, just as it had turned away from the passivity of Hoover, toward the activism of Kennedy, Johnson and Nixon. In the midst of this move toward presidential government the country experienced the realigning election of 1964, bringing a short-term rise in congressional turnover and breaking the policy deadlock within Congress. The second cycle came to a head with the renewed congressional decentralization of the late 1960s and early 1970s and, particularly an institutionalization of subcommittee dominance within committees, and the constitutional confrontations over such issues as impoundment, war powers, and secrecy of information. In response came the centralizing congressional reforms of the 1974-76 period, including strengthened party leadership, a new budget process, ethics legislation, and reform of congressional oversight. Significantly, this centralizing reform era left largely untouched the decentralization from committee to subcommittee power that preceded it, and in some respects expanded the reliance on subcommittees.

Today the nation is in a quiescent period. Constitutional confrontation between the president and Congress is behind us. The era of centralizing reform in Congress is over. Congress is somewhat resurgent, but its resurgence seems expressed more in its willingness to stall the president's programs than in an ability to offer clear alternatives to them. The president is uncertain, and ineffective in dealing with Congress. Presidents in such eras, after all, face the double standard of being expected to emulate the positive leadership of their immediate predecessors (without the resources of an imperial president) while facing a resurgent Congress that their predecessors were spared. Thus we hear calls for an activist presidency while Congress stands ready in principle to cripple most presidential initiatives and the press stands ready to denounce any presidential activism that seems to portend a power aggrandizement.

The future today looks all too clear. With the continuance of the quiescent era we can expect renewed congressional decentralization—including efforts to bypass or limit the power of party leaders and the authority of the new budget process. As the breakdown of the central policy organs proceeds, Congress should become increasingly immobile. With immobilism will come calls for presidential government. And with presidential government will come constitutional crisis.

Unfortunately, there is reason to expect that the next crisis era will be more devastating than the preceding ones. There are two reasons for this. First of all, there is the nature of the drift in institutional power that characterizes the power cycles. The power cycles of the twentieth century do not appear to be mild fluctuations around a constant balance point, as envisioned by Madison. Rather, the executive branch gains more authority and power with each cycle than it is forced to give up during congressional reform and resurgence. In each cycle, presidential roles and responsibilities are legitimized that previously were nonexistent or ambivalent, and the presidency's power base is thus expanded. Moreover, with each cycle presidential transgressions of constitutional comity are more severe beacuse the executive's power base is stronger, the Congress is increasingly weaker as it is more decentralized, expectations of modern government and its capacity to solve social and economic crises are greater and more politically salient, and popular acceptance of the legitimacy of presidential activism increases with each cycle. In the next generation, therefore, we can expect that a president or presidents, in building on the expanded power base of the office, will provide a much greater assertion of presidential power during a national crisis and act with still greater disdain for the constitutional division of power between Congress and the presidency. This expectation is reinforced by a second consideration, the observation that the nation today is undergoing another dramatic environmental transformation, one that is meshing with the congressional changes of recent decades to transform Congress as fundamentally as at any time in the past, a transformation that will produce a qualitatively weaker Congress.

V

During the past two decades, the environment of Congress has changed as dramatically as it did during the Civil War and Recontruction era or during the Progressive/Wilsonian era. First of all, there has been a significant change in the nature of group politics. Segments of society have been brought into the political arena that have largely been excluded heretofore—the blacks and poor whites of the South, the chicanos of the Southwest. Other groups largely silent heretofore, such as women, consumers, welfare recipients, and environmentalists have become increasingly conscious and organized, as have general "public interest" groups. This expansion of the groups involved in politics has been fueled by the increasing balkanization of our economy into ever more specialized technicians, social service workers, professional white collar workers, agribusiness concerns, blue collar craftsmen and tradesmen, government workers, and so forth, all of whom view themselves as having special needs, problems and interests that require government attention. All of these groups, together with a widening range of single-interest groups concerned with specific issues such as abortion, have descended on Congress in the last several decades, expanding considerably the issues and pressures to which the members must respond. In addition, these groups increasingly bypass or give limited loyalty to the traditional political parties because they eschew the compromise and coalition politics such parties necessarily must undertake. Rather, the groups demand relatively immediate action on their specific concerns, the concerns falling into two broad categories: redistributive politics in which social and economic goods and services previously denied them are given to them, or corrective politics in which major symbolic and substantive policies of the government that they find abhorrent are reversed. The politics of the twentieth century, in which government has sought to respond to needs and social priorities dominant social and economic sectors of the nation, has led these particularized groups to expect similar attention to their interests, an expectation that government in the last several decades, as in the Great Society, has fueled.

This expectation of government action, particularly redistributive action, is increasingly unrealistic because of a second major change in the national environment: resource scarcities. For most of its existence, the United States proceeded on the assumption that its resources were limitless. The primary political struggle during this century, therefore, has been devoted to tapping the fruits of the nation's resources. Groups were excluded from this political struggle and its rewards not because of an assumption of resource scarcity but because of the avarice of the dominant social and economic groups, longstanding prejudices and legal barriers, a lack of technical economic knowledge about how to adequately and effectively "spread the wealth," and the low political consciousness, efficacy and political expertise of the disadvantaged groups. Unfortunately, just as these latter groups have reached a point in political awareness and development where they can seriously challenge the hegemony of dominant social and economic groups and force greater sensitivity to their social priorities and a redistribution of economic resources, the nation is entering an era of genuine scarcity in resources.

The problems associated with limited national power in foreign areas and domestic resource scarcity are augmented by a third change. Many of the basic corporations that have helped provide the stable economic national base have become international corporations capable of actually benefiting from, or at least being largely untouched by, the economic misfortunes of the nation. These multinational corporations owe their loyalty less to the United States than to an international economic order in which profits and corporate success may not be commensurate with the economic affluence and social well being of this country. Having built their international economic power largely with the support of this country and their use of its resources and governmental aid, these corporations may well be prepared to invest their money, build their factories and spread their wealth in more profitable environs abroad, creating a "resource drain" for the United States.

The existence of resource scarcity, which limits the ability of the government to fulfill the needs and demands of emerging groups, nurtures a fourth major change in national politics, a widespread disaffection from government, a crisis in the legitimacy of the state. The major institutions geared to deliberative action, such as political parties and the Congress, are seen as particularly ineffectual. The disaffection leads to lower voter participation in elections and, simultaneously, a more intense nontraditional political involvement by frustrated social groups. Because the groups seeking economic redress of grievances often overlap somewhat with groups seeking corrective action on symbolic policies of the government, individuals with membership in both types of groups become particularly bitter and disaffected, and supportive of social protest movements, particularly single-issue movements in which concentrated activity seems to provide some possibility of political success. Thus major political characteristics of this new era of American politics include a decline in the identification with and support for political parties, growing disaffection from government, a questioning of its legitimacy, and a rise in the number, intensity, size and political involvement of special or single interest protest groups that focus attention on symbolic corrective change in public policy.

The foregoing changes in the congressional environment have rather serious implications for Congress, its organizational life, and its position vis-a-vis the president. First, the balkanization of the electorate into a wide range of special interest groups concerned not with broad issues within broad policy domains but with particularized issues in narrow domains creates strong external support for the institutionalized subcommittee government that has arisen in the last decade. Because the subcommittees concern themselves with narrow policy issues and thus provide formal access points and pressure points for single or narrow interest groups, such groups can be expected to devote considerable attention both to "playing subcommittee policies" and to opposing efforts to weaken subcommittees or to move toward a more centralized organizational system. This balkanization of the citizenry into numerous factions also provides support for the creation within Congress of numerous subcaucuses devoted to particularized interests. It fuels the rise of single-interest and narrow-interests lobbying within Congress. It provides support within the bureaucracy for decentralization of bureaucratic power from agencies down to bureaus that correspond more closely to the narrow clienteles of modern politics, a decentralization also nurtured by the dispersion of congressional power from committees to subcommittees, with bureaus in the executive branch roughly paralleling subcommittees in Congress. In many ways, then, the interests of individual power-seeking members of Congress in sustaining subcommittee government are served and reinforced by the rise of particularized interest groups capable of providing external pressure and support for subcommittee government, and by the concomitant rise of "bureau government" within the executive branch, with bureaus strongly attached to and supportive of their sister subcommittee in Congress.

The pressure of the particularized groups for attention to their needs and interests, however, conflicts directly with the interests of dominant groups and corporations in American society. This conflict arises because the age of scarcity does not allow a "widening of the pie," simply creating a more inclusive system of distribution of government services and economic supports. If the government is to respond affirmatively to the new political forces, it must do so through a redistribution of existing resources and services. In an age of scarcity and contracting resources, responding to new political forces would entail not only redistributing existing services, but, given the contracting nature of the economy, greater tax burdens on the affluent class and on corporations. Thus tax politics and national budgetary politics emerge as a dominant focus of political concern, with significant portions of the electorate, particularly the more affluent and economically powerful factions, pressing Congress and the president to concern themselves with constraining budgetary growth and holding down taxes. These forces create support for centralized budgets and policy coordination by centralized leadership. These forces pushing for constraints on taxes and the national budget simultaneously demand maintenance of pre-existing services and programs that benefit them. Ironically, they may gain support from a number of the disadvantaged segments of society who, seeing the failure of redistributive politics and questioning the legitimacy of government itself, see constraints on taxes as a corrective policy that can at least provide them some degree of personal financial relief. In their frustration with government, then, members of the disadvantaged groups may well appear irrational by supporting tax and budget protest movements that help ensure the inability of government to provide them the social and economic services and resources that they desire, and continued government support of programs that support the affluent class.

In this new world, then, there are two main dimensions of congressional conflict. First, the push for and conflict over redistributive and corrective social and economic policies that surface in the subcommittee system and reach national visibility in floor fights in the House and Senate. Secondly, conflict over comprehensive budget-making and revenue policy, where ultimate priorities are established and money for policies is raised. Within Congress today this conflict emerges in the Congressional Budget Office, the two budget committees, and the two revenue committees; this conflict rises to a boiling point in the spring and fall budget resolutions. Amidst these two dimensions of conflict, the cross-cutting pressures on members obviously will be immense, as they seek to respond to demands of newly politicized special interest groups in their constituency and to the pressure of economic groups that carry considerable financial and political clout. The world of the members will be complicated additionally by a range of corrollary factors: particularized groups may often be in conflict with one another; the salience of particularized issues may vary in unpredictable ways; individual citizens will, in a seemingly unpredictable and irrational way, move back and forth across the policy spectrum, alternatively and perhaps simultaneously demanding redistributive policies, supporting protests over symbolic corrective policies, and urging constraints on taxes and the national budget.

Political parties at a national level will be of little value to the member in his struggle to make sense out of, and mend her or his way among, the conflicting pressures, since parties will be torn by the same particularized and generalized interests that the member is. Within Congress party leaders will be pressured to create viable policy and budgetary coalitions that respond to immediate political pressures. Because of the lack of clear guidance and support from the national party, the unpredictability of single issue politics, and the long-term difficulty of balancing the demands of particularized interests among themselves and with broader and more traditional social and economic interests, viable coalitions will be difficult to create, membership in the majority coalitions will shift overtime considerably, and party leaders will find their positions precarious if they lack the skill to remold their supporting coalitions from month to month, session to session, Congress to Congress. And while there will be greater demand for skillful party leadership in the emerging era, even the most expert leaders may face conditional situations so complex and conflictual that viable policy-making majorities are impossible to produce, given the limited resources of congressional party leaders.

A key characteristic of the new era, then, will be volatility. Coalition politics will lack the order and clarity it had during the era of committee government, where the conservative coalition and northern liberals were the dominant political realities. These coalitional terms may well cease to have the same meaning as in the previous era, with new conceptualization of the coalitional processes needed that focuses on the shifting roles of particularized interest groups and the constraining influence of the affluent class (regardless of whether its members be social liberals or social conservatives) and large corporations. In the midst of the shifting and volatile internal politics of Congress, members of Congress will find their own electoral security more precarious than in the past and their long-term commitment to congressional service somewhat diminished.

In the era of committee government, low turnover of members of Congress resulted from a variety of factors. Involuntary turnover was low because the strong role of party and partisan identification conditioned voter response in elections, helping secure the election of incumbent members of dominant state and regional parties; incumbents were able to build powerful supporting coalitions through attachments to broad lobby groups such as the AFL-CIO or the business community; porkbarrel and casework activity by members developed attachment from a core attentive constituency in their district which, given the low voter turnout in off-year congressional elections, could dominate congressional elections; and the low saliency of congressional elections allowed party and incumbency factors to mold the voting decisions of the public. As we move into the new congressional age, all of the factors should be less influential in congressional elections. Political parties are disintegrating as objects of attachment and mechanisms of organizational support, and the broad lobby groups are no longer the primary and most visible pressure groups and financial support groups in the electoral arena. Rather, congressional elections should become increasingly salient areas of protest for those groups that believe themselves left out of the mainstream of governmental life and unrepresented in policy making, the salience of congressional elections deriving from the fact that they are one of the most immediate and accessible electoral arenas in which protest groups can strike.

Congressional primaries and general elections should increasingly be characterized by protest efforts against incumbents, with incumbents caught in a peculiar bind. No matter how homogeneous a constituency, politics is fragmenting to the point that any constituency is sufficiently diverse for there to exist groups that believe themselves unrepresented by the actions of their member in Congress. The more heterogeneous the constituency, the more likely the rise and success of countervailing radical and reactionary protest movements that hold members accountable for their moderate actions, with the Senate being the arena most likely to experience severely the defeat of incumbents. In these protest movements, the member's power within the Washington Establishment may not prove as great an asset as in the past, since it allows the member to assist only a subset of his constituency, while exclusion from that establishment and its services constitute the problems alienating other constituents and making congressional politics a salient dimension of life to them. Thus, over the long-term we should move into an era in which the cyclical pattern of turnover occurs at a higher level than in the era from 1920 to 1970, this higher turnover a product of defeat as well as retirement. Changes in electoral environment and turnover will be reflected in significant increases in the number of marginal districts, decreasing statistical advantage of party and incumbency, and increasing electoral volatility (i.e., upset defeats of powerful and "safe" incumbents). The changing electoral environment, together with changes in the authority structure within Congress, should alter the nature of congressional careerism.

Throughout the era of committee government, members sought long-term congressional careers because they sought political power that congressional service could provide. The length and precise characteristics of normal careerism in this era, however, was a product of the conditions in which members sought a congressional career. Because committee government created a hierarchy of power, with only a relatively small number of real power positions (i.e., committee chairs), it took a considerable length of time to attain power. However, since the committee chair positions afforded considerable personal influence on policy, the wait seemed worth it. Additionally, because the nature of partisan and national politics allowed incumbents to nurture electoral security, and because members could use their time in Congress to nurture their financial security through extracurricular activity such as consulting, real estate investments, and ventures into the stock market (all of which could benefit immeasurably from knowledge and contacts developed in Congress), members could envision relatively stable and rewarding long-term careers.

All of the supporting conditions of long-term congressional careerism are changing today. Increasingly incumbents will find that they do not have secure electoral margins, or that the large margins they have afford little security because of a volatile electorate. The power positions they gain in subcommittee government carry with them less policy influence than did power positions in committee government. The power positions also take less time to attain, with long-term service not bringing significantly greater increments of formal power. Additionally, the ethics reforms of the seventies place greater financial burdens on congressional service, burdens that make lifetime congressional careers inordinately costly from a private perspective (with Congress becoming one of the few professional "careers" wherein members are essentially prohibited from significantly advancing the size of their personal estate).

For these reasons, the nature of careerism should be transformed. It will not be the case, as in the early nineteenth century, that politicians largely will avoid attempting significant long-term service in Congress. Congress as an institution will still be seen as an arena in which significant power can be attained, and as an avenue to even greater power. However, with less real power and more uncertainty characterizing congressional service than in the past, members will be willing to leave earlier than in the past in search of higher elective or appointive office, or to move into supportive professions in the Washington Establishment, such as lobbying or legal consulting. Careerism will also drop because members will be defeated more often. Thus, instead of twenty to forty years constituting a realistic career expectation, probably fourteen years or so and upward will constitute the real goal of "careerists," with members more readily envisioning a "life after Congress" than in the last sixty years.

The rise in turnover and the transformation of careerism will not mean a flight from subcommittee government and toward elite or party government, as during the eras of high turnover in the nineteenth century. First of all, the level of turnover should not rise to the norm of fifty percent that existed in much of the nineteenth century, but simply range more often above the five to ten percent level of the postwar years. Secondly, subcommittee government should persist because of the peculiar interaction we can expect between the power motive of politicians and the requisites of interest group politics in this new era. In this new age, the effort to adjust to scarcity and retrenchment will necessarily involve the federal government more in the daily lives of its citizens as it seeks regulations that keep the economy afloat. Thus the national government will remain the arena in which most political/governmental power resides in this country. And, as in the past, Congress will be the national political institution most accessible to power seekers. Thus, politicians will continue their quest for power within Congress, with the quest simply occurring in a shorter time, in less predictable conditions, and perhaps leading to postcongressional careers in the executive branch or Washington Establishment for more members than in the past.

Through all of these changes, subcommittee government should persist as the most immediate mechanism through which members can gain and exercise an element of personal power over policy. It thus is a form of organization not given up lightly. In addition, while turnover may rise and careerism decline, these electoral changes will not signal less concern of most members with their immediate congressional careers. Rather, most members will seek re-election and will seek to draw on whatever advantages they can derive from congressional incumbency. As subcommittee government provides them an avenue to develop some supporters, they will concentrate extensive energy on utilizing subcommittee service to benefit them electorally, including attempts to expand subcommittee activity to increase its representativeness of disadvantaged groups. In addition, the persistence of subcommittee government will be reinforced by the existence of a professional staff system that has arisen in Congress as it has decentralized and institutionalized subcommittee government. The professional staff members of subcommittees, who increasingly are becoming careerists with considerable expertise in congressional politics and policy-making, will provide continuity in the congressional subsystem arena somewhat analogous to the continuity provided by civil service bureaucrats in the executive. These staffers, who themselves will have considerable vested interest in maintaining autonomous subcommittees, will provide not only policy guidance to revolving members of subcommittees, but also political guidance and contacts with supportive bureaucratic agencies and interest groups, contacts that can help sustain the existence and authority of subcommittees from reformist onslaughts.

In sum, then, the changing environment of Congress should serve to institutionalize and protect the decentralization of Congress that occurred during the second organizational power cycle of the committee government era. In the process, Congress is moving into a totally new era unlike any in the past. In this era, the dominant organizational force will be subcommittee government. The dominant struggle for power will occur among subcommittees and subcommittee members, and between subcommittees on the one hand and the centralized leaders of the revenue and budgetary process and the party leadership apparatus on the other. This new age will be characterized by volatile coalitional politics in Congress, with Congress hard put to produce viable legislative programs amidst the pull of the different particularized interests and the conflict between forces of redistribution and the forces of fiscal retrenchment. The members of Congress will also face a more volatile electoral world. Torn between the demands of single interest groups and pressure from middle and upper classes for protection of past services together with tax relief, the electoral benefit of incumbency will decline. In the new era, in attempts to improve their electoral chances, widen their resources, and reduce internal congressional pressure on them, members will move to decentralize Congress in much the cyclical fashion of the past. Objects of decentralized reform will include moves against party leaders and the revenue and budgetary process, hoping that to kill the messenger will suppress the message. The decentralizing efforts also will include further attempts to institutionalize and rigidify subcommittee government, providing greater protection for members within it, increases in professional staff available to members and subcommittees, and increases in congressional computerization, thereby increasing the members capacity to make sense of and deal with the volatile world they face.

Within Congress, members will climb the congressional power ladder faster than in the past, moving up to subcommittee chairs and, in many cases, out to significant positions in the federal government or the Washington Establishment. Congress itself will increasingly become a professionalized institution whose professionalization rests on the size, expertise and career longevity of its staff as much as its elected members. In this sense, we are moving into a totally new era of legislative professionalism at the national level, with the staff being the core of the professional Congress. Unfortunately, while a professional staff can sustain Congress as a functioning organization, it will not be able to replace the members as political actors, or nurture the institutional power of Congress.

VI

Ultimately, the power of Congress rests on the ability of its elected members to legislate, to respond effectively to political demands, to act. To be an effective representative institution, Congress must generate leadership that can unite a majority of its members and speak for them authoritatively. It must possess effective mechanisms to coordinate its policy process, and it must be able to ensure that the executive executes its policy. The coming of committee government undermined all of these requisites of congressional power. Subcommittee government, based on a far greater dispersion of power and a more volatile and unpredictable politics, should increase the problems of congressional leadership, coordination and oversight manyfold. At the same time, subcommittee government will not possess the large number of elected careerists and the long-term, powerful elected congressional experts that existed in committee government and that served somewhat to counterbalance the executive branch. Its professionalism will rest in a staff that lacks the capacity to act formally, and whose personal interests may conflict ultimately with the interest of individual members and the institution itself. Thus, subcommittee government should create far greater policy immobilism than committee government, and it should prove far less effective in counterbalancing executive power than did committee government.

In the face of a weakened Congress, the pressures on the president to act, to break policy immobilism, will be immense. These pressures will be greater than in the era of committee government because of the very nature of the president's new environment—the perception of a loss of national power abroad producing a greater sense of insecurity, the budgetary pressures at home, his own difficulty in building a viable supporting coalition given the balkanized nature of interest group politics and the conflict over redistribution versus retrenchment. Such conditions tempt presidents to establish their popularity and power by bold strokes of leadership, and by forceful efforts to "save the Republic." In short, the power vacuum created by Congress, together with presidents' own sense of the inability of "traditional" leadership to nurture national and international security and to ameliorate social problems, will lead them to dramatic efforts that should show little regard for constitutional constraints. Thus we can expect far more severe incursions of presidents into the constitutional powers of Congress, with the incursions coming at a faster pace than in the era of committee government, the faster pace occurring for three reasons: Congress is more decentralized than in the past, so its potential immobilism is greater; given the greater electoral pressures on members and the greater personal stake members have in power decentralization, Congress should move more rapidly to a new era of decentralization; the pressure on the president to act—external pressure deriving from the greater problems of the country in the era of retrenchment at home and abroad, and internal psychological pressure deriving from the greater stress of his job should be greater than in the past. Within the next generation, then, assuming that there are no countervailing changes in the systemic setting of national or international politics that I have ignored, much as Woodrow Wilson ignored key changes in his era, we shall surely witness the further decline of Congress, the rebirth of the imperial presidency, and a severe constitutional crisis surpassing any previous one.

What we are witnessing, in effect, is the self-destruction of the Madisonian system of government. Increasingly, Congress lacks the organizational capacity to know and assert its institutional will. As Congress decentralizes further, it exacerbates its inability to play its legislative roles and it necessarily invites power aggrandizement by the executive. Short-term reform attempts at recentralization of organizational power within Congress do not redress the long-term drift toward congressional decentralization and the long-term weakening of the institutional power of Congress. Rather, the increasing balkanization of American society and the rise of the age of retrenchment domestically and internationally, together with the natural power drive of politicians, fuels long-term congressional impotence and the consequent rise of an imperial presidency.

Ironically, the self-destruction of our constitutional order is not necessarily the result of malevolence, evil motives, or evil people. The quest for power by members of Congress may derive from the most noble and genuine desire to serve humanity. The effort of members of society to seek a redress of personal grievances and protect personal interests is merely a reflection of their constitutional rights and a major reason for representative government. Finally, presidential assertiveness and "imperialism" may derive from a very real presidential concern for economic stability or national security, and from a very accurate perception that Congress cannot act.

Nevertheless, the self-destruction of the system is real. Because of the cyclical nature of the changes, and occasional recentralization and resurgent eras within Congress, the long-term weakening of Congress and the long-term rise of presidential government are not crystal clear. Congressional reassertiveness suggests that Congress is still a viable institution. Short-term congressional resurgence, however, simply diverts attention from the long-term momentum toward congressional impotence and greater presidential power. In fact, when we examine the likely long-term characteristics that will emerge from the recent "reformed" Congress, in light of concomitant changes in our national environment, what we foresee is far greater likelihood of congressional impotence and far greater executive usurpation of congressional power. In the sweep of history, this congressional reform period may well be a major transforming era as significant as that of the Civil War/Reconstruction era and the Progressive era within Congress, a reform era that moves us into a qualitatively new world characterized by extreme congressional decentralization, organizational and electoral volatility, policy immobilism, and political impotence.

Against this dark horizon we are necessarily forced to wonder whether this black future can be averted. The answer to this query necessarily is complex. Part of the resolution of our dilemma, however, lies with recognizing that a major portion of our problem lies not in Congress or the presidency per se but in the Constitution, in its failure to provide constitutional provisions that nurture congressional cohesion and centralization in ways comparable to those provisions that nurture the institutional cohesion of the court and the presidency. In retrospect it is understandable why the founding fathers failed to provide specific functions and organizational structures for Congress that would help ensure its institutional integrity. They were structuring a constitution for a very different world in which it could be realistically assumed that Congress would naturally maintain its organizational cohesion, in which, indeed, a strong Congress would be the chief threat to other separate organs of government. Unfortunately for the operation of our constitutional system, there have been and continue to be significant changes in the world since the age of the founding fathers, changes that clearly alter significantly the way in which the provisions of the Constitution operate. In particular, the rise of industrial America, and now the coming of a postindustrial era of scarcity, both serve to create conditions conducive to congressional decentralization and the inability of Congress to maintain sufficient institutional integrity or will to balance the other branches, particularly the presidency.

So, what is to be done? Clearly, it is time to reconsider the appropriateness of our constitutional structure to the problems and realities of our age. In this reconsideration, two paths suggest themselves as viable options. First, it may be that the necessary changes can occur within the confines of the current Constitution. Perhaps we can alter and create constitutional provisions in such a manner as to create an incentive system within the Constitution which, while permitting enough congressional decentralization to encourage innovation and expertise, will lead members of Congress naturally to support centralizing mechanisms and majoritarian politics, thereby sustaining the institutional will of Congress.

A variety of constitutional changes are possible. For example, the Constitution could give greater authority to the Speaker of the House, president pro tem of the Senate, or similar organizational leaders; such authority might include significant responsibility to appoint committee members and/or leaders, greater procedural powers, and greater control over congressional prerequisites. Such action would help redress problems of congressional leadership caused by committee government and give the congressional leaders "bargaining chips" they could use in coalition building analogous to the "chips" the president possesses (nomination and/or appointment of political appointees in the executive branch and White House Office, nomination of federal judges, veto power, and so forth). Similarly the Constitution could create a Congressional Security Council that could exercise congressional war-making authority under specified emergency conditions, helping Congress regain constitutional control of warmaking. The constitutional creation of a Congressional Budget Committee and a Congressional Budget Office, together with specification of certain powers, could legitimize and protect those central policy organs, improving the capacity of Congress for serious control of and coordination of the budget. Constitutional specification of congressional responsibility for oversight of the executive, perhaps with the creation of an Oversight Committee and recognition of legislative veto power, could strengthen the capacity for oversight. In all of the cases, the committees could be made joint congressional committees, giving constitutional encouragement to a joint committee system that could bridge the two houses and reduce the problems caused by bicameralism. Finally, a revision of the presidential veto authority (making overrides easier or vetoes harder) could enhance congressional control of policy-making; this revision seems particularly in order since the founding fathers did not intend presidents to use the veto as a policy weapon, but rather in cases of constitutional conflict with Congress.

All of these constitutional changes would be designed to mesh with the preexisting system of separation of powers and checks and balances. Their intent would be to strengthen the ability of Congress to know and express its will authoritatively by creating a constitutionally-supported environment conducive to the creation of majority coalitions in Congress nurtured by strong congressional leadership and institutionalized mechanisms of policy coordination and oversight. In other words, we would simply accept the basic constitutional design of Madison, and recognize that environmental changes have undercut certain expectations he had about the operation of the system, particularly expectations about the operation of Congress. We would develop constitutional remedies that adjust the separation of powers/check and balances system to the realities of our day, focusing on the creation of constitutional provisions designed to nurture congressional cohesiveness. Constitutional enactment of these provisions, rather than legislative enactment, would be critical to avoid successful attempts by ambitious members within Congress to unravel the provisions after the attention of the nation moved elsewhere. Properly undertaken, and with due regard for some additional provisions that might be necessary with respect to other branches of government (such as Bruce Buchanan's call for a plural presidency), such "corrective surgery" might be able to create a political order in which Congress would be more capable of fulfilling its proper functions and constraining the rise of presidential imperialism.

Such "tinkering" with the current constitution, though politically quite difficult, would seem by far the surest, easiest and most direct way to redress the constitutional dilemmas of our day, at least in so far as they flow from congressional organization. These changes do not alter in any fundamental way the constitutional structure of government or the specified powers of specific branches. They are merely designed to make the system work as it was intended to work, by recognizing that a changing environment alters the logic underlying the justification of the system and necessitates remedial action. A basic problem with this approach, however, is that it is designed to reassert a separation of powers, checks and balances system, and political analysts often lament that such a system may necessarily produce deliberative decisions in which majoritarian politics is slowed by the force of institutional pluralism. This argument is a strong one, and suggests that a second path should be considered—a complete revamping of our constitutional system. One model often suggested for such a revamping, a suggestion that goes back at least to Woodrow Wilson, is to move toward parliamentary government. Other alternate models can also be envisioned. The problem with any such fundamental revamping, of course, is that it is extremely difficult to undertake politically, and the effects of large-scale constitutional change in a particular national environment are difficult to forecast with any degree of accuracy, as the experience of the Weimar Constitution in Germany illustrates.

Despite the problems of constitutional change, however, the country clearly should not shy away from facing up to its current institutional dilemma and considering significant constitutional tinkering or restructuring. The alternative, I fear, is a painful transformation of our political order into strong presidential government in which Congress increasingly lacks the will and capacity to balance presidential assertiveness and constrain presidential imperialism. Such a transformation seems an inevitable result of the forces at work in Congress and in society unless constitutional action is taken. Yet in envisioning constitutional action, we must recognize the difficulties it poses and beware a major pitfall.

Constitutional revision is serious and difficult business. It requires a realistic and hardheaded assessment of human nature, of the implications of different institutional arrangements, of the social conditions within which politics is to be conducted, and of the consequences that will derive from the interaction of these elements of political life. In many ways Madison in the *Federalist Papers* is still the best guide to this type of undertaking. And a major rule followed by Madison and the founding fathers was that a constitution establishes structure and procedure, it does not legislate specific policies. In constitution-making, the great temptation is to address not the organizational and legal problems of an era, but its policy problems, writing into a constitution policy solutions that destroy the ability of the government to flexibly adjust to new policy realities from year to year. In many ways the greatest problem, or pitfall, with introducing constitutional revision as an approach to resolving our institutional dilemmas is that self-interested political forces will seize the opportunity to seek constitutional enactment of particularized policy proposals and, simultaneously, to nurture personal ambitions.

What the nation needs today is serious attention to constitutional provisions touching on institutional structure and procedure, particularly that of Congress. What the country does not need is a series of specialized constitutional amendments such as provisions requiring a balanced budget or provisions authorizing or prohibiting abortions. Unfortunately, the very immobilism of Congress, combined with the growth in single interest groups and the preoccupation of affluent classes with budgets and taxes, suggests that such movements for specialized constitutional policy provisions are likely to proliferate over the coming decades, and possibly even become the basis on which an ambitious politician gains the presidency and attacks fundamental policy-making powers of Congress. In other words, a major way in which presidential imperialism may emerge is through presidential leadership to constitutionally enact specific politics that considerably limit the policy-making prerogatives of Congress. Such amendments would be particularly onerous, and supportive of presidential imperialism, if their operation were keyed to presidential decisions (as, for example, an amendment calling for balanced budgets except in conditions where presidents verified a particular type of emergency).

In conclusion then, the nation today faces a very serious set of dilemmas. It possesses a constitutional structure ill-designed to mesh with the realities of the twentieth century, especially the emerging era of retrenchment and scarcity. In particular, the Constitution fails to provide provisions that help Congress maintain its institutional cohesion and integrity, given the conditions of the contemporary world. As a result, Congress faces serious difficulties in attempts to organize itself and play a strong policy role. Overtime, while Congress experiences cyclical attempts at serious reorganization, the fundamental institutional drift is toward decentralization and immobilism, a drift that encourages the rise of presidential imperialism. If this drift is to be reversed, the nation must attempt to seriously strengthen the organizational cohesion of Congress through specific changes in the Constitution. Any movement toward constitutional change, however, probably will fuel the desire of special interest groups for constitutional amendments that enact their particularized policy concerns and activate a propensity among presidents or aspiring candidates to support such policy-making through constitutional revision. Any such constitutional policy-making, however, will weaken rather than strengthen Congress by removing its ability to legislate in key policy areas and thus restrict its legislative role. In addition, constitutional policy-making might well provide a means through which a specific president or series of presidents effects constitutional changes that expand presidential discretion and tilt the constitutional balance further toward presidential government.

Today, as much as ever before, the well being of the nation requires a sensitive recognition on the part of the citizenry and political leadership alike of the seriousness of the dilemmas facing the nation. If representative government is to be secured and presidential imperialism constrained, Congress must be seriously strengthened. The reforms of the past decade do not ensure congressional resurgence; given the realities of contemporary politics, internal congressional reform cannot work. Rather, the nation must have constitutional reform designed to improve the position of Congress within our contemporary constitutional system. Unfortunately, constitutional revision itself may lead not to strengthening Congress but rather, in the hands of a politicized electorate and imperially-minded presidents, to a crippling of Congress and our separation of powers system. The nation thus faces a difficult road, one in which wise leadership, tempered ambition and judgment, and widespread recognition of our national institutional problems all are necessary to enact the constitutional changes critical to our survival as a free and democratic society.

The Evolving Relationship Between the White House and the Department of Defense in the Post-Imperial Presidency

Lawrence J. Korb

Introduction

The Department of Defense (DOD) came into existence in 1947. For the greater part of its first three decades DOD confronted a strong imperial presidency. During that same period of time, the defense establishment dealt with a relatively stable and uncomplicated force planning environment. The interplay between these two factors structured the relationships that existed between the White House and DOD from 1947 through the early 1970s. However, as DOD enters its fourth decade both the nature of the presidency and the force planning environment have changed dramatically. The presidency has entered into a post-imperial phase while the force planning environment has become both complex and unstable.

DOD and the Imperial Presidency

The parameters which govern the formal relationship between the president and the defense hierarchy, that is, the secretary of defense and the five-member Joint Chiefs of Staff, are found in the National Security Act (NSA) of 1947 and its subsequent amendments. These laws establish a single cabinet level department, the Department of Defense, under the control of an appointed civilian, the secretary of defense. In addition to controlling or managing DOD, the secretary also functions as the deputy commander-in-chief of the operational forces, and the chief spokesman for the department within the National Security Council (NSC) system and before the Congress.

The NSA also sets up a five-member Joint Chiefs of Staff (JCS) to serve as the principal military advisers and military staff to the president, the secretary of defense, and the Congress. Membership in the JCS is gained through appointment to a four-year term as chief of one of the nation's four armed services or to a two-year term as chairman of the JCS, that is, as the presiding officer of the structure with no service responsibilities. JCS advice to the secretary of defense is provided primarily through the Joint Strategic Planning System, that is, through a series of seven long, medium, and short range plans which assess the military threat facing the nation and recommend a military strategy to meet the perceived threat and execute the current policy. Military advice to the president is given through the NSC system and in annual meetings with the chief executive on the defense budget. The chairman is an advisor to the council itself and either he, or his representative, sits as a member of the major NSC committees and subcommittees. Congress normally receives JCS inputs at the annual hearings on the defense budget. Both the chairman and service chiefs prepare written reports (known as posture statements) on the overall military balance and the condition of each of the services.

During its first quarter of a century of existence, DOD was almost completely dominated by the White House. The White House-DOD relationship was one of the clearest manifestations of the existence of an imperial presidency.

In the pre-Korean War period, President Truman demanded that the defense hierarchy acquiesce in his post-World War II demobilization policy or quit. The majority of the JCS not only acquiesced but enthusiastically supported the policy. General Omar Bradley, the first chairman of the JCS, went so far as to tell the Congress that he would be doing a disservice to the nation if he asked for a larger military force, while General J. Lawton Collins, the Army Chief of Staff, stated to a somewhat astounded Congressional (House) Appropriations Committee that Truman's reductions in the size of the Army actually made it more effective. After the outbreak of the Korean War, Truman insisted that defense officials support his containment strategy and his rearmament policy against its critics. Again the military responded enthusiastically. During the last two years of the Truman administration, General Bradley made fifty-seven appearances before Congress, civilian groups and over radio and television in support of administration policy. Bradley's most outspoken defense of Truman's policies was delivered in a March 20, 1952 speech to the Pasadena Chamber of Commerce. In it he characterized the president's Republican critics, like Hoover and Taft, as selfish and defensive.

Those defense officials who could not or would not enthusiastically support Truman's national security policies did not remain in their posts very long. James Forrestal was relieved as secretary of defense after only eighteen months because he wanted to implement containment prior to the Korean War and Admiral Louis Denfeld was dismissed as chief of naval operations after less than two years in office for opposing the draconian economic measures of Forrestal's successor, Louis Johnson.

During his eight years in office, President Eisenhower functioned as his own secretary of defense. The civilians he appointed to head DOD acted essentially as business managers trying to get "more bang for the buck." Like Truman, Eisenhower sought support for his policies from the uniformed military on the JCS. Indeed the former general made it clear before appointing an individual to the JCS that he expected loyal support for his military policy of massive retaliation with its emphasis on strategic forces as opposed to conventional, as well as his economic philosophy of refusing to allocate more than ten percent of the GNP to defense. Eisenhower publicly accused those military leaders, like General Matthew Ridgway and Admiral Arleigh Burke, who could not give strong backing to his policies of legalized insubordination. The president forced some of his recalcitrant chiefs into early retirement, the others he simply ignored.

The relationship between DOD and the White House during the Kennedy-Johnson years was dominated by Robert McNamara, who served as secretary of defense from 1961 through the early part of 1968. McNamara was the first secretary of defense to serve through two administrations and the first individual to serve an extended period of time in that office. Prior to 1961, the average tenure of a secretary of defense was less than two years.

McNamara, who was picked by Kennedy to take control of the Pentagon, did exactly that. He demanded unequivocal support not only for the policies of the administration but for his decision-making style as well. The military leaders who made public their dissatisfaction with McNamara's style of management, which virtually excluded them from any meaningful participation in the policy-making process, were quickly dismissed. Within his first two years in office McNamara replaced every member of the JCS.

For the greater part of the Kennedy-Johnson years, McNamara's methods plus his strong support within the White House so overwhelmed the JCS that they gave their endorsement to such critical policies as: the Test Ban Treaty with the Soviet Union, the strategy of gradualism in Southeast Asia, and the intervention into the Dominican Republic. This approval was given in spite of the fact that the chiefs played no meaningful role in the formulation of these policies and that the chiefs disagreed with these decisions. In the last year of the Johnson administration McNamara was victimized by his own methods. When President Johnson discovered that McNamara's enthusiasm for the administration's policies in Vietnam was waning, the secretary was sent packing to the World Bank. Lyndon Johnson had no reservations about, and paid no political price, for relieving the most powerful secretary of defense in history when he became a dissenter on Vietnam.

Although the exact date is difficult to pinpoint, it is clear that, sometime during the first Nixon administration, the powers of the presidency began to decline, and the impact of this new phenomena was clearly felt in White House-DOD relationships. Moreover, it has continued into subsequent administrations. In 1972, the Nixon administration was forced to "bribe" the JCS into supporting the SALT I agreement by promising to build at an accelerated pace a new array of strategic weapon systems, including Trident, Minuteman III, and the B-I. The Nixon White House also felt compelled to put up with "legalized insubordination" not only from the professional military but also from its own appointed civilian head of the Defense Department. Secretary of Defense Melvin Laird openly opposed many of the major national security decisions of the president, including the invasions of Cambodia and Laos and the B-52 bombing of Hanoi. Not only was he not fired, like Forrestal or McNamara before him, Laird was not even rebuked. The weakened state of the presidency vis-a-vis DOD was vividly demonstrated when President Ford fired Secretary of Defense James Schlesinger for his overly hawkish views on detente and his arrogance toward the White House on the size of the defense budget. Schlesinger was hailed as a hero and a martyr and Ford judged incompetent for not tolerating dissent. Similarly, during the Nixon and Ford years, the White House was forced to allow outspoken and openly critical military officers like Admiral Elmo Zumwalt and General George Brown to remain in office until their terms were completed.

The Force Planning Environment

The fact that the White House was able to dominate its relationship with DOD through the late 1960s was attributable not only to the power of the presidency but also to the force planning environment which existed during that period. If that environment was not so relatively stable and uncomplicated, the power of the military to resist White House pressure may have been much greater. Therefore, before speculating on future White House-DOD relations, seven essential features of that environment will be summarized.

First, the United States enjoyed overwhelming superiority in nuclear weaponry, with an initial postwar monopoly on the technology, and, later, general superiority as the Soviet Union entered the field. As a result, the U.S. could reasonably assume that the threat of countervalue strikes against an enemy's population and industrial targets was sufficient to deter attacks against the U.S. itself, and military actions against its principal allies. The strategic nuclear umbrella also provided insurance against conventional force deficiencies, allowing reduced emphasis upon this category of forces.

Second, views of conventional warfare were shaped by the experiences of World Wars I and II, both of which involved drawn out campaigns whose outcomes were largely determined by national abilities to replenish attrited forces. The U.S. entered the post-World War II period supreme among the world's nations in terms of the industrial and reserve mobilization base upon which the military could draw should war ensue. As had been demonstrated during the two world wars, this imposing capability permitted U.S. officials to size conventional forces for the purpose of delaying an enemy's success only long enough to allow our industrial supremacy to assert itself.

Third, the United States enjoyed a dramatic absolute advantage in naval forces relative to those of any potential adversary. This advantage allowed the U.S. freedom of maritime operations and the ability to deny the same to any hostile state. Additionally, because of the lack of any credible threat to U.S. naval forces, planners were able to allocate naval capabilities away from the traditional sea control mission and to the mission of power projection. Because naval projection forces (both carrier air and marine amphibious forces) had evolved to levels of technical capability relatively commensurate with those of corresponding land-based forces, the ability to exploit secure sea-based forces led to several advantages, including flexibility and mobility, rapid responsiveness, independence from foreign influence, and ease of insertion and disengagement of forces. Naval projection forces became a substitute for land-based forces in many theaters, and an important complement to it in others, including Central Europe.

Fourth, the potential adversaries of the United States, including the Soviet Union and the Peoples' Republic of China, were generally restricted in their use of military force to geographic areas contiguous to their own boundaries. Only the United States emerged from World War II with the overseas bases and logistics support facilities necessary to sustain operations distant from its homeland. As a result, potential conflict scenarios could be limited in terms of geography. Moreover, within most of the developing world, no major power threat to U.S. interests could be identified.

Fifth, the United States emerged from World War II as the world's only strong and independent state in terms of economic capabilities. The previously industrialized nations of Europe and Asia came out of the war with dramatically reduced industrial bases and labor forces, and the Communist nations generally suffered from the war and previously fragmented processes of industrialization. The United States, on the other hand, sustained notable levels of nonmilitary production during the war and suffered no industrial attrition from the war itself. In addition, U.S. resource wealth was itself sufficient to leave the nation in a largely self-sufficient position in terms of strategic materials, at least for moderate periods of time. The U.S. economic advantage was so strong that it was able to embark on programs to rebuild the economies of Europe and Japan through support of the international trade and monetary system and direct grants.

Sixth, the United States emerged from the war with general national consensus regarding the nature of the military threat facing the nation. The Communist movement, led by the Soviet Union, was generally perceived to be hostile, expansionist, and the antithesis of fundamental U.S. values and objectives. As a result, barriers were erected thwarting essentially all economic, cultural, and political intercourse between the world's superpowers.

Seventh, the U.S. could afford to spend whatever was necessary for defense without adversely affecting its economy or denying its social needs. During the war in Korea, defense spending increased fivefold and during the war in Vietnam it doubled. Between 1950 and 1970, DOD consumed 10.5 percent of the GNP and 46.7 percent of the federal budget. Yet all throughout this period the U.S. economy remained strong, inflation was low, and social programs did not suffer from a lack of funding. This nation was certain it could have whatever was necessary for defense, that is, both "guns and butter."

Clearly this environment has changed. Moreover, this change has occurred almost simultaneously with the decline in the powers of the presidency. U.S. national interests, while remaining worldwide, have evolved considerably. Western Europe, having recovered from World War II and developed into a set of modern industrial economies, remains a key U.S. ally, economically as well as militarily. Warsaw Pact forces, now clearly superior to those of the NATO countries, remain poised on the boundaries of Western Europe, representing the one continuous threat since the end of World War II. The rest of the world has not remained so stable. Asia and the Pacific may be generally viewed as in a state of flux, with the recent normalization of relations with the Peoples' Republic of China, the end of the U.S. involvement in Southeast Asia, and the planned withdrawal of forces from Korea dramatically changing the picture there. Similarly, the developing world, including the Middle East, the Persian Gulf, Africa, and Latin America, has emerged as a growing economic force as the result of U.S. (and allied) requirements for energy supplies and raw material resources. Along economic dimensions, the United States has evolved from a position of dominance and independence to the present state of extensive linkages. Certainly as a result, the global nature of U.S. interests has been magnified.

The Soviet Union, which has itself enjoyed considerable growth along economic dimensions, has evolved into a military threat with capabilities not dissimilar to those of the United States. Three dimensions of the Soviet military buildup are particularly critical: their strategic force capabilities, their naval capabilities, and their projection capabilities.

By most assessments, Soviet strategic nuclear forces have reached a position of at least parity with those of the United States, a parity which has in fact been formalized through the SALT treaties. As a result, the strategic umbrella over conventional forces that existed during the first several decades of the post-

World War II period no longer exists, requiring new concern about the conventional force balance in Europe. More importantly, Soviet nuclear capabilities have evolved to the point where counterforce applications of their forces are within reasonable grasp.

Soviet force evolution has been significant in the naval and projection arenas as well. The Soviet navy has progressed from a coastal defense force to one with open ocean capabilities through growth in their submarine forces, surface forces, and maritime air forces (although the latter remains mostly land based). Coupled with the numerical decline of U.S. naval forces, the Soviets have reached a position where, at minimum, they can significantly impede and delay U.S. naval operations. Their overseas projection capabilities have advanced rapidly in recent years, with the development of allied and proxy forces operating in distant nations. While the Soviets have had difficulty in sustaining any system of overseas bases, their capabilities are at least sufficient to extend the number of regions within which military options are feasible. In addition, their ground and air forces in Europe and Asia have progressively grown and been modernized throughout the postwar period.

Coupled with the overall rapid growth of Soviet military capabilities has been a technologically induced evolution in the nature of conflict itself. Through technological improvements in weaponry (principally missile systems which require only modest platform support), the nature of war has changed dramatically in terms of the levels of violence and destruction which can be unleashed over short time periods. This newly emerging feature of high intensity conflict has among its implications the rapid attrition of forces on the modern battlefield and the potential for one side to gain rapidly a decisive advantage, thus negating any mobilization potential.

Finally, the United States simply can no longer afford to spend what is necessary for defense without neglecting its social needs or upsetting its economy. In spite of the fact that its major adversary, the U.S.S.R., spends at least twelve percent of its GNP on defense and increases its defense budget by at least five percent per year in real terms, this nation has great difficulty in allocating five percent of the GNP to defense without neglecting its social programs or weakening its economy. Moreover, the president is forced to resort to slick bookkeeping devices and rubber yardsticks to show even a three percent real increase in a defense budget which has been falling for a decade.

Finally, as a result of these changes the national consensus regarding the nature of the military threat facing us and our national strategy has been undermined and bipartisan foreign policy destroyed. Neither the American public nor its elected representatives can agree on how and why our military forces should be deployed, who our enemies are, and where our real interests lie.

Future White House-DOD Relationships

The weakened state of the post-imperial presidency and the changed international environment have and will continue to bring about significant changes in the nature of the interactions between DOD and the White House. The dominant factor in this new relationship is an increase in the potential power of the uniformed military leaders, particularly the JCS.

The increase in the potential power of the JCS is attributable to three interrelated factors. First, the Congress will play an increasingly influential role in the national security decision-making process. In order to increase their impact on policy, legislators they will seek more advice and opinions from the JCS. They will no longer be content with pro forma JCS endorsements of administration policies and will demand access to unconstrained military advice.

The new congressional-JCS relationship has been very much in evidence in the first two years of the Carter administration. In 1977, Congress used inputs from some members of the military to delay the B-1 decision for eight months and then only failed by three votes of overturning it. The following year, Congress at the urging of Navy officials transferred funds from the Carter administration's NATO programs to the Navy for the construction of a large nuclear powered aircraft carrier (CVN) in FY 1979. The legislature did this in spite of the fact that the president wanted a medium size conventional carrier (CVV) built in FY 1980. Although the Camp David meetings on the defense budget prevented Congress from overriding the president's veto of the bill and authorizing the CVN, the legislature showed its resentment by refusing to restore the NATO funds.

The second reason for the enhanced power of the JCS lies in the increased complexity of the force planning environment and of modern warfare. These phenomena make technical military expertise more important. Very few civilians will be able to compete successfully with the military in dealing with such complex areas as verification, single-shot kill probability, vulnerability of carrier battle groups, and close air support doctrine. Moreover, given the smaller margin for error, it is not likely that decision-makers will want to take the risk of ignoring military advice.

The final source of the increased power of the JCS is that it is now much more difficult to get rid of an individual chief than in the past. An amendment to the 1967 defense authorization bill provides that service chiefs are appointed to a fixed four year term instead of a two-year renewable term. Since the passage of that law, no chief has left office unwillingly before the end of his term.

As a consequence of these three factors, the administration now must deal with the JCS in formulating and implementing its national security policy. The chiefs can no longer be ignored or dismissed as Eisenhower could safely ignore

JCS complaints about his strategy of massive retaliation, and retire those who complained too much; as Kennedy could exclude the JCS from the test ban negotiations and fire those who were unhappy with its contents; and as Johnson could bypass the chiefs on both the major and minor details of the conduct of the war in Southeast Asia. President Carter needed JCS support for the Panama Canal Treaty so desperately that he acceded to their demands about reserving the right to retake the canal by force. Similarly, he has had to involve the JCS in every step of the SALT II process and has already made many concessions to their views, including a commitment to raise defense spending substantially in the 1980s.

This administration and its successors are likely to attempt to counter the increased potential of the JCS in several ways. First, they are likely to appoint only "team players" to the JCS and other high military posts. Demonstrated loyalty to administration policies and a willingness to support publicly even those policies to which one is opposed may become the key criteria for selecting the service chiefs and the chairman.

It is widely acknowledged that Air Force General David Jones was appointed to the chairmanship in 1978, instead of Army General Bernard Rogers, because of his willingness to "change his mind publicly" on the B-1 and other issues. Similarly, General Lew Allen who had not flown a plane in twenty years was chosen to be the Air Force Chief of Staff because of his eight years of faithful service to Secretary of Defense Harold Brown during the 1960s.

Second, individuals selected to be secretary of defense will be those who possess recognized expertise in national security affairs and who lack a political base. The future secretaries are more likely to resemble Harold Brown and James Schlesinger instead of Charles Wilson, Melvin Laird or Donald Rumsfeld. The White House will use this expertise to offset and counter that of the military, if the uniformed officers should oppose administration policy. Lack of a political base will make it much easier for the White House to persuade the secretary to support its policies and to use his expertise to oppose that of the JCS, and will make it easier to threaten to fire the secretary if that should become necessary. The Carter administration has successfully employed Harold Brown, an acknowledged expert in the defense area, to counter the arguments of the JCS on the B-1 and large carriers even though Brown supports the JCS position on these issues. Brown has had to do this or risk being fired because he lacks any constituency within the Carter camp or the Democratic party. The administration chose Brown, not the secretary of state, to plead the case for SALT II.

Third, future administrations are liable to structure the way in which the JCS participate in the decision-making process to make it appear that the JCS support a policy when in fact they do not. For example, the JCS were never asked by President Carter if they favored U.S. withdrawal from Korea. Rather, they were asked how best to undertake a withdrawal from the peninsula. Their withdrawal plans were brandished publicly by the White House as JCS consultation on and support of the withdrawal. Similarly, in the formulation of the FY 1980 defense budget, the Chiefs were directed to draw up a program that implemented the Consolidated Guidance (CG) which was formulated by Harold Brown and his staff without JCS input. The Chiefs' program was then displayed as an indication of their support for the CG.

Conclusion

While the relationship between DOD and the Pentagon during the imperial presidency was far from perfect, it may well have been better than that which is likely to exist in the post-imperial period. This new relationship is likely to cause serious problems for this nation. Choosing only team players for the JCS will probably prevent the most competent military officers from rising to the top and could undermine the military professionalism of those who do. The most capable officers are the ones most likely to refuse to support policies which are contrary to their professional judgments, while the pressure to be team players will make it difficult for the officer to live up to the code of his profession which demands that expert advice be presented openly and without reservation. Moreover, if the Congress and the public come to perceive that only team players are selected for the JCS, they may not pay attention to the advice of the chiefs even when it is not given under duress. General Jones is already confronting this credibility problem.

Similarly, expert secretaries of defense without their own political constituencies will be more likely to support ill-conceived White House policies, thus prostituting their expertise to legitimize poor policy. Finally, structuring the process to make it appear that the JCS support a policy could have the same result.

Whether these problems will surface cannot be stated with certainty. But, in the new international environment and in the era of the post-imperial presidency, they are certainly plausible outcomes and there are already indications that they are occurring.

The Advantages of a Presidential Executive Cabinet (EXCAB)

*Graham Allison**

Richard Nixon

Promise: "Mr. Nixon has fallen in line with the popular conception that the cabinet is a collectivized body on which the president can lean heavily in matters of policy."

—Richard L. Strout, *Christian Science Monitor*, (December 9, 1968).

Performance: "Despite his campaign talk, Mr. Nixon continues the traditional neglect of the Cabinet as any sort of broad policy making or advisory group. Cabinet meetings not only are infrequent but also when they do occur they are usually briefing sessions or pep rallies rather than decision shaping sessions."

—Allen Otten, "The Scorecard: the President's Cabinet Officers get mixed reviews for efforts to date," *Wall Street Journal*, (September 8, 1971).

Jimmy Carter

Promise: "We've initiated and maintained a weekly Cabinet meeting that further strengthens the Cabinet-level authority and responsibility."

—Jimmy Carter, announcing Executive Office Reorganization Plan, (July 15, 1977).

Performance: " . . . The changes suggest that the president is pulling back from the notion of 'Cabinet government' . . . Recently, (he) decided to cut back on the Cabinet meetings to once every two weeks. What is not generally known is that some Cabinet members had suggested the same thing as long ago as spring of 1977."

—Dom Bonafede, "Carter Sounds Retreat from 'Cabinet Government,'" *National Journal*, (November 11, 1978).

I. The Cabinet Idea: The Historic Context[1]

In British terms, the definition of cabinet function is simple: it *is* the govern-ment. A decision-making body in which binding votes are taken, the British cabinet collectively embodies the political will of Britain's parliamentary system. It acts, subject to parliamentary votes of confidence, as the final repository of executive authority.

The U.S. cabinet possesses no such authority. Executive responsibility in the American system rests exclusively with the president. The cabinet has no formal authority: it does not collectively make decisions, nor does it normally advise on questions of importance. While there exists language establishing "Executive Departments and Heads of Departments" whose "opinion in writing" would be an important source of advice to the president, the cabinet as such has no constitutional mandate. Its institutional legitimacy derives solely from custom and function.

It was George Washington who, acting upon what he saw as "the impossi-bility that one man should be able to perform all the great business of state,"[2] began calling his executive secretaries and the attorney general into collective collaboration on a regular basis. To him it was clear that the chief executive alone could neither dig deeply enough into the vast range of presidential problems to be assured that all the dimensions of any given issue were covered, nor see to it that his decisions and overall priorities were faithfully carried out at all levels of government. Only by giving responsibility to specialists whose expertise and administrative authority spread over the entire range of issues and having them meet regularly could he begin to overcome this institutional predicament. In order for the administration of government to reflect coherent goals and strategies, therefore, a number of serious people had to be involved in the policy formation process. For Washington, it was the heads of the executive departments who collectively best met these requirements.

Copied by his successors, Washington's organizational initiative (dubbed "the Cabinet" by James Madison) was quickly accepted as a permanent feature of the executive office. This institutionalization was a clear signal that the cabinet was indeed serving an important function in the presidential decision-making and coordination process, giving the president both a relatively com-plete display of the issues before him *and* an opportunity to extend his control throughout the Executive bureaucracy. Its exact status, however, continued to change as presidents sought to establish clearer lines of authority within their administrations.

By the mid-nineteenth century a new, more permanent relationship between the president and his cabinet had emerged—a relationship epitomized by President Lincoln's often-repeated quip: "Seven noes, one aye; The ayes have it."[3] According to Richard Fenno, the cabinet had come to live "in a state of institutional dependency to promote the effective exercise of the president's authority and to help implement his ultimate responsibilities.''[4]

Today the cabinet's mandate seems more compelling than ever. The extraordinary complexity and range of issues on the presidential agenda has compounded the chief rxecutive's inherent organizational difficulties, limiting still further his ability to carry out his central decision-making and coordination responsibilities. Much more than in Washington's day, the contemporary president is forced to rely upon others to both advise him and carry out his policies. Who should these ''others'' be? With close ties to interest groups, Congress, and their own bureaucracies, the men and women who head the departments of the executive branch still collectively appear the best suited to fulfill these functions.

It is therefore not surprising that each newly elected president is attracted to the traditional cabinet idea. When faced with the necessity of organizing his office for central decision-making and coordination, it seems an entirely logical approach; the cabinet *should* make a major contribution to the effectiveness of any administration.

But *can* it? Is the cabinet in its present form well suited to these tasks? Can it, as a collegial body, be a successful part of the president's organization for effective policy-making and implementation? To answer these questions intelligently requires that we first define the tasks of the contemporary president more precisely.

II. The Presidential Task: Central Decision and Coordination

President Nixon and the New Economic Policy

On August 15, 1971, President Nixon announced his ''New Economic Policy'' (NEP), a sweeping set of measures designed to strengthen the U.S. economy at home and abroad. That package included a suspension of the convertibility of the dollar into gold, a ten percent surcharge on all imported goods, and a thinly veiled demand that the United States' major trading partners permit a unilateral devaluation of the dollar against their currencies. The new policy ended the era in international economics that the United States itself had begun at Bretton Woods in 1944.

The Bretton Woods system had established the dollar as the foundation of the international monetary order. The United States had pledged itself to maintain the dollar's value at thirty-five dollars per ounce of gold while other countries pegged their currencies to the dollar at fixed exchange rates. The dollar thus became a form of international money, an unofficial legal tender for the world economy, since the strength of the U.S. economy made other countries willing to accumulate dollars and to treat them ''as good as gold.'' Thus, during the first two decades of the Bretton Woods regime, the American balance of payments deficit was not only tolerated but welcomed: it was an important source of the liquidity needed to finance the economic recovery of Europe and Japan. By the late 1960s, however, that recovery was largely complete. Continuing deficits were no longer useful; instead, they were producing a massive "overhang" of dollars held abroad. During the Vietnam years U.S. demand for imports increased, while overvaluation of the dollar made American goods less competitive abroad. The result was a rapidly worsening U.S. trade and payments position, culminating in a massive hemorrhage of capital from the United States in early 1971—the United States' official reserves transactions balance was headed for a record deficit of 30 billion dollars for the year.

Something had to be done, and correcting the overvaluation of the dollar relative to other currencies—a chronic problem since the mid-1960s—clearly had to be part of it. Yet the action taken—President Nixon's abrupt and unilateral suspension of the dollar's convertibility into gold and imposition of a ten percent surcharge on all imports—rocked the international economic system. It violated the principles of cooperative action and of free trade, two pillars of the West's unprecedented postwar prosperity. Even more than the substance of the decisions, U.S. shock tactics in taking them raised questions about the U.S. commitment to orderly international processes and unnecessarily threatened cooperative practices in which the United States had a very large stake.

The short-sighted character of that decision clearly reflected the unbalanced process that produced it. The group that President Nixon relied upon to make the decision was dominated by a newly appointed Secretary of the Treasury, John Connally. It included the Chairman of the Federal Reserve, Arthur Burns, and of the Council of Economic Advisers, Paul McCracken, together with the director of the OMB (Office of Management and Budget), George Shultz. Domestic perspectives were therefore weighted heavily. But the group contained neither the secretary of state nor the president's assistant for National Security Affairs, nor any senior subordinate of either. No one was engaged whose job required him to think hard about the consequences of the decisions for larger foreign policy objectives. Yet the purpose of those decisions was exactly to affect the relation of our economy to those of our closest allies and trading partners.

Thus, the decision process precluded any serious effort to assess how the NEP (New Economic Policy) would affect other important foreign policy issues: SALT and European fears of a U.S.–Soviet deal at their expense, the China summit and Japan's uneasiness over the sudden American policy reversal, or U.S. relations with the expanded European Economic Community, among others. It also lacked any representative of the view that U.S. actions, whatever they were to be, should not ignore the procedures for international consultation that the United States had itself worked painstakingly to develop since the Second World War. In the event, the United States consulted with none of its economic partners before announcing its decisions. The sudden display of U.S. economic nationalism shook the confidence of other nations in the international economic order, and set a risky precedent. It reversed the steady movement toward free trade, contributed to a developing world climate of "neomercantilism," and weakened the practices of international economic collaboration, which most observers believe need marked reinforcement to manage the growing economic interdependence of nations.

President Carter and "the Moral Equivalent of War"

In April 1977, President Carter announced an energy plan designed to fight the "moral equivalent of war." Consisting of taxes on gasoline and gas-guzzling cars, a new natural gas pricing policy, numerous tax incentives, and a grab bag of other items, the package was sent to Congress which, after a year of debate, compromise and intervening "crises" (inflation, unemployment, Panama), remained largely unconvinced. Of President Carter's twelve major proposals only half made it through the congressional process—and many of those only in highly modified form. Despite the original fanfare, the United States in November 1978, was no closer to "solving" its energy problem than it was eighteen months earlier. Many, in fact, would argue that given such factors as deepening domestic inflation, the steady decline of the dollar on international markets, and the deteriorating (though, at that time, as yet unrecognized) conditions in Iran, the United States had moved backward.

What happened? The answer to this question lies, not unlike the previous example from the Nixon administration, in the imbalanced process that produced the president's energy plan. To the dismay of several interested parties, the task of formulating policy was given to a single cabinet officer, Energy Secretary-designate James Schlesinger. Unfamiliar with many dimensions of the issue and lacking any input from his cabinet colleagues, Secretary-designate Schlesinger formulated a relatively narrow set of proposals centered around price increases and mandatory regulation. Unfortunately, the proposals failed to relate energy to any other of the administration's goals or strategies. OPEC, transportation, congressional relations and a myriad of other issues central to energy policy remained untreated. Thus when the going got rough, when other important problems arose or Congress became particularly troublesome on some of the president's initiatives, there was little upon which the administration could fall back. Incoherence reigned supreme as President Carter was forced to jettison large parts of his program—hardly the display of presidential authority and leadership for which the public had been geared with his "moral equivalent of war" rhetoric.

Both cases suggest that a more precise definition of the tasks facing the contemporary president must begin with the proposition that virtually no issue of importance in public policy falls exclusively within the domain of a single department or agency. Categories like "energy," security," "international economics," "domestic policy" and "foreign affairs" do not and cannot describe separable realms. The wide-ranging activities of government tend to jumble agency jurisdictions, cut across lines of authority, and breach the boxes of organizational charts. Plans for a New Economic Policy, for example, could not be handled by Treasury alone, or by Treasury, CEA (Council for Economic Advisors) and OMB. Still less could the energy issue be handled even by the new Department of Energy specifically assigned the problem.

Furthermore, these examples also illustrate the extent to which the day-to-day business of public policy is carried out by separate departments dealing directly with the constituencies to which they are tied. Those dealings are inevitably influenced by the perspectives and functions of the department conducting them and by the concerns of its clientele. Even where appointive officials seek genuinely to serve the president, they must do the business and defend the interest of their departments. Each knows that his influence and effectiveness are gauged—by his subordinates, his department's constituents, the press, indeed by the president himself—in terms of the skill and force with which he advances the department's efforts or argues the department's brief.

This decentralized management of day-to-day business is both inescapable and proper. But it may produce several kinds of problems: the imposition by departments of their own priorities on policy generally; stalemate produced by the disagreement of departments sharing pieces of the problem; logrolling, with compromises meeting the minimum needs of all departments but serving the nation poorly; or unresolved conflict, inconsistency and confusion—still very much the situation with respect to an overall energy strategy.

The difficulties involved with effective decision-making bear most heavily upon the chief executive. As the sign on Harry Truman's desk said, "the buck stops here," for only the president can circumvent, dampen or resolve the problems. Congress lacks the unity, any single executive department (such as State on foreign policy issues, Energy on energy issues, etc.) lacks the perspective and authority. If the policies and actions of the government are to fit a conscious pattern, the president must impose it. Where there are multiple and partially competing objectives it is he who must ultimately make the hard trade-offs, sacrificing some objectives to others. Processes of central decision and coordination must guarantee that no such sacrifice is made without weighing the costs. Thus, the organizational imperative is to devise mechanisms of decision that explore the ramifications and illuminate the complexities of policy through the expertise, perspectives and active involvement of everyone concerned.

III. Why the Collective Cabinet is Not Working

As suggested earlier, when faced with the necessity of organizing their office to perform those tasks, presidents have frequently been inaugurated promising to use the cabinet fully. They have, however, uniformly behaved otherwise.

> With regard to the cabinet as an institution, as differentiated from the individuals who compose it, it is a joke. As a collegium, it doesn't exist. Its members, serving as a cabinet, neither advise the president nor engage in any meaningful considera-tion of serious problems or issues.[5]

The comment is that of Abe Fortas, and it is not a minority view.

The persistent failure of the cabinet as a collegial body reflects two inherent handicaps. Loosely composed of a large number of departments and agencies with their own goals, constituencies, interests and perspectives, it has become too big and too bogged down in special interest to respond effectively to the president's organizational tasks.

Serious work simply does not happen in the cabinet crowd. Since many issues involve only a small number of departments, meetings of the entire group include several irrelevant "participants"—participants who tend to inhibit meaningful discussion. Consequently, cabinet officers are apt to be too reticent to argue hard with their colleagues, especially on issues that only marginally touch on their own concerns. As a result, there is powerful pressure to resolve issues on a "to each his own" basis with blue chip bargaining taking place outside the confines of the meeting. This renders cabinet meetings even less interesting and relevant. The time-pressured cabinet officer is soon forced to wonder why he should attend at all.[6]

Moreover, cabinet meetings force the president to confront the challenge of fragmented power and conflicting objectives, Rapidly socialized to de-partmental roles, cabinet members tend to become spokesmen for the interest groups and congressional committees to which their departments are tied. They often appear to the president, therefore, not as counsellors but as special pleaders. "The members of the cabinet are a president's natural enemies" are the famous words of Charles Dawes.[7]

IV. Assessing Recent Alternatives

Recognizing these inherent difficulties, it has not taken long for recent presi-dents to backslide from their commitments to traditional cabinet-centered processes by the use of other decision-making and coordinating mechanisms.

One series of efforts, characterized by Roger Porter as "centralized man-agement,"[8] is grounded in the desire to shield the president as far as possible from the parochialism of interdepartmental policy bargaining. Relying heavily on formal White House/Executive Office of the President (EXOP) dominated mechanisms to filter departmental recommendations and proposals to the top, it tends to centralize decision-making and coordination functions in the hands of a few individuals with perspectives similar to those of the president. The Nixon administration provided an example of such a process. The dominance of a few advisors and bureaus—of Henry Kissinger and the National Security Council in foreign affairs; of John Ehrlichman and the Domestic Council in domestic affairs, of John Connally in economic matters—created structured lines of White House authority. Participation by others in the policy process was clearly of secondary importance as the White House/EXOP bureaucracy exercised "vise-like" control over the rest of the Executive establishment. In this alternative, the answer to Cabinet size was to eliminate it from the top councils of government.

Such closed systems have undeniable advantages. They provide maximum presidential flexibility, permit *faits accomplis* that foreclose potential opposition, allow novel high-policy conceptions to emerge uncompromised by interagency wrangling, and afford drama that can be turned to domestic political advantage. Nixon's China departure well exemplified all these characteristics. While most presidents find it necessary to hold one or two major issues to a narrow circle of trusted advisers, extensive reliance on a closed system imposes high costs. One is a limited span of control; a very small group can manage only a small number of issues. Another is limited understanding. No small group, however brilliant, can fully comprehend many of the multitudinous issues that affect our foreign relations. It will favor the issues it does understand, ignoring or mishandling others. Reciprocally, the permanent government, while poor at grand conceptions and reluctant to innovate, is an unmatched reservoir of knowledge. When kept ignorant of the issues being considered, its knowledge cannot be tapped. Worse, ignorance and irrelevance destroy morale. Leaks and foot dragging result; implementation goes poorly.

In short, the same principle of exclusivity that succeeds in rationalizing the decision-making and coordination process, rendering it a much less complicated affair, ultimately fails the president by providing him neither of the necessities he requires to be effective: quality and breadth of advice, nor the active engagement of departmental heads.

A second organizational alternative, which Porter terms "adhocracy," is exemplified by the Carter administration's policy of "Cabinet government." Based on the establishment of a series of short-term interdepartmental task forces or "Cabinet Clusters," it is an informal system relying almost exclusively on the president himself for the distribution of assignments and the selection of whom he listens to. Problems like welfare reform, urban revitalization and energy do not flow through set White House/EXOP channels but, rather, are given to cabinet-centered working groups put together by the president on an issue-by-issue basis. In implementing such a system, President Carter sought to counter the problem of cabinet size and superfluousness by restricting the number of participants in policy decisions to those with assignments directly relevant to the issue at hand. At the same time, he attempted to avoid at least one of the pitfalls of his predecessor, exclusivity, by insisting that the participants be broadly chosen from cabinet ranks.

The problems encountered by the Carter Administration stem from a weakness often associated with adhocracy: inattention to the presidential task of overall policy coordination. One aspect of this problem has been stated by a number of high officials who liken the decision-making process to "negotiating complicated multilateral treaties."[9] By decentralizing policy-shaping power to the cabinet while simultaneously downplaying the role of White House and EXOP coordinating mechanisms, the president has created an almost impossible situation: working groups have quickly fallen into quarrels among a series of roughly equal "semiautonomous departmental and agency fiefdoms"[10]— quarrels that can be decided by no one but the president himself. So busy does he become in resolving minute conflictual details that sight of the larger shape and priorities of administration policy is easily lost.

A second, related disadvantage results from the limited ability of adhocracy to engage the president's chief policy makers and implementers in the administration's overall plans and priorities. Ad hoc groups concentrate on individual issues; their membership is rarely continuous across the wide range of topics on the presidential agenda. There exists little incentive for cabinet members to rise above intra-task force frays and sensitize themselves both to the interrelated nature of other issues and to the larger shape of the president's policy—a fact that further impairs the chief executive's already limited ability to create a coherent administration. He simply has no high-powered help. The result? Chaos; or more precisely, a "frequent lack of coordination among some of the agencies . . . disagreements between Secretaries (have) occasionally surfaced, producing a multiplicity of voices that embarrassed the Administration."[11] It is not surprising, therefore, that by November 1978 the president had begun to sound a "retreat from Cabinet government."[12]

Clearly, both alternatives have displayed inherent weaknesses that severely limit their ability to perform the administration-building functions necessitated by the president's central decision-making and coordination responsibilities. Neither has been able to satisfactorily lay out the full dimensions of issues while at the same time ensuring that those charged with key line responsibilities shared the chief executive's broad objectives and strategies.

V. A Modest Proposal: EXCAB

The answer? The strengths and weaknesses of these two alternatives to the full cabinet suggest a third approach that presidents might take in organizing their office for effective decision-making and coordination. This approach calls for the creation of a body that is both more formal and more perspicacious than Jimmy Carter's experiment in cabinet government, and more comprehensive than Richard Nixon's attempt at centralized management. It is a body based on that perennial loser, the collegial cabinet.

The handicaps of the cabinet are serious. The first, that the full complement of executive department heads is simply too large, is unarguable. The second, that cabinet members tend to represent highly varied interests can, if properly managed, readily be turned to advantage; for it can ensure that the full range of interests affected by decisions are weighed before policy is made. Broader use of cabinet members would confer other benefits as well. Presidents need stronger and more responsive performance from key cabinet departments. Strength and responsiveness are not easy to combine. But making key cabinet officers the primary substantive counsellors to the president, and insuring steady face-to-face relations between them and the president, will tend to induce both. The recognized participation of secretaries in presidential decision-making would also sensitize them to presidential perspectives and to interests other than those of their own departments.

Finally, increased involvement of key cabinet members in public policy-making offers a less obvious, but perhaps equally important benefit. Councils and cabinets are not only forums; they are also opportunities for creating staffs. Indeed, no consequence of the National Security Council (NSC) has proven more important than the development of its staff. The use of a cabinet-like body as a forum for decision would facilitate creation of a single integrated cabinet staff. Combining the principal White House staffs that are now autonomous would create a more efficient mechanism for presidential staffwork. Some specialization within a broader and integrated staff would obviously be neces-sary, but a single staff preparing issues for a central forum of broad jurisdiction could address the interacting issues of the future far more effectively than the specialized staffs do now.

It is therefore proposed that an executive committee of the cabinet become the chief forum for high-level review and decision of all major policy issues that combine substantial "foreign," "domestic," and "economic" concerns.[13] Most major decisions about the U.S. economy would fall in this category; so would virtually all key national security issues. Such a committee—it might be called "ExCab"—should surely contain the Secretaries of State, Defense, and Treasury. As the cabinet officer best situated to represent the concerns of domestic social policy, the secretary of Health and Human Services should also be a member. ExCab should probably include an additional representative of U.S. economic interests—ideally, the secretary of a new department created by a merger of Commerce and Labor, although interest-group and congressional opposition have long prohibited such a merger. Barring that possibility, the president might appoint whichever head of either department possessed the larger perspective and greater competence. John Dunlop, George Shultz, and Elliott Richardson are recent reminders that the two secretarial offices have been occupied by men capable of representing larger economic perspectives than those of either department.

These officials might form ExCab's permanent membership, but other cabinet officers and agency heads could be asked join the discussion of issues that concerned them. (Congressional leaders might also occasionally be invited to ExCab meetings, though on a wholly informal basis.) Depending on the issues being discussed, several additional officials might attend: the president's chief substantive staff members and congressional liaison officers; his science adviser, chief intelligence officer, and the director of OMB. At least in the early months of an administration, and at subsequent times of major uncertainty when broad changes in policy are contemplated, issues should be prepared for ExCab deliberation through formal and intensive interagency studies, like those of the National Security Study Memorandum (NSSM) process.

A body like ExCab would yield most of the advantages of the collegial participation of major department heads while avoiding the unwieldiness of the full cabinet. It would also establish an implicit hierarchy of cabinet and "super-cabinet"[14] positions, a means of improving the integration of policy which has attracted many presidents but proven impossible to achieve through formal reorganization in the face of congressional opposition. ExCab would possess no formal authority of its own, but might still prove a powerful innovation. It would give the president a wide circle of advisers to normally consult before taking major decisions, thus improving the odds that major decisions would be taken with an eye to both their domestic and foreign effects. It would put those advisers directly in touch not only with the president but with each other, helping to generate a collegial comprehension of the varied dimensions of the issues confronting the president. And it would reinforce the standing of cabinet officers as the primary substantive counsellors to the president. The size, formality, and title of the forum used to accomplish these purposes are quite secondary. What is essential is that some such forum regularly bring together for substantive discussion and decision the senior line officials of the government, the officers who together can best assess the full implications of major issues and who individually and jointly must understand, support, and manage the processes by which decision becomes action.

ExCab would clearly have to be supplemented by an integrated series of cabinet subcommittees modeled after the Ford Administration's Economic Policy Board (EPB)[15] and by ad hoc task forces. Such task forces would utilize small numbers of subcabinet officials, together with White House staff members, in addressing particular issues—in some instances providing staff work for presidential decision, in others managing continuing processes of im-

plementation, review, and redecision. Presidential assistants might appropri-
ately chair groups engaged in the first process; departmental officers, selected
for personal competence as well as departmental position, would normally be
designated "czars" for issues of enduring concern—nuclear proliferation, for
example. The actual operation of any arrangements for high-level policy-
making will obviously depend on the larger context in which issues arise, and
on the personal characteristics of the president and other key officials. Nonetheless, a speculative replay of the two cases discussed above may suggest how
the changes we have proposed might importantly affect the information and
perspectives brought to bear on the issues, and alter the weights accorded to
them.

Consider first August 1971. It had been clear for several years that the U.S.
dollar was overvalued relative to other currencies and that this could not be long
sustained. Under the organizational arrangements we have proposed, an interagency task force would likely have been established well before summer 1971
to consider alternatives. Operating before a crisis had developed, the group
would almost surely have produced a map of the issue that not only identified
alternative courses of action but assessed the probable impact of each on the
international economic system and on U.S. relations with key allies. Even if
early action had not followed and the August crisis had occurred, deliberation
of the U.S. response in ExCab would have involved both Secretary Rogers and
Presidential Assistant Kissinger. Even assuming no change in the personal
interest or economic competence of either, Rogers would nonetheless have
been backed by a well-staffed Under-secretary of State for Economic Affairs,
for whom the issue would clearly have been first-order business, and Kissinger
by a professionally competent deputy for foreign economics. Under these
circumstances, it is hard to imagine that one or both would not have strongly
advanced the arguments championed by Arthur Burns. Given Secretary Connally's forcefulness and the fact that he was telling the president what he wanted
to hear, Connally might still have prevailed. Yet such strong support for the
Burns position would have forced sharper recognition of the ultimate costs of
the Connally proposal and might well have produced a less heavy-handed
strategy for achieving the basic objectives. At a minimum it would have
ensured that allies were consulted in advance of unilateral U.S. action.

With regard to the Carter energy package, an ExCab presence would have
substantially altered both the substance and scope of the administration's
response to the pressing energy problem. Charged with the responsibility of
collectively working with the president to shape and coordinate the overall
course of the administration, this high powered group of cabinet-officers would
have been meeting on a regular basis from the start of the Carter presidency.
Together they would have fleshed out the four or five major problems (of which
energy would undoubtedly have been one) on which the president should

concentrate, explicitly recognizing the interconnections between them and establishing a sense of operational priorities. The general shape of an energy policy would therefore have emerged with its many dimensions fully discovered and felt by the administration's key actors. With the active presence of the secretaries of state and treasury, fundamental questions including: "what policies can the United States pursue internationally, in, for example, Iran and Mexico, to assure itself of necessary external supplies?" and "what will be the effects on inflation of alternative energy pricing and taxation policies?" would have been asked and answered. In such a situation, the president and ExCab would be forced to weigh the relative costs and benefits of, and therefore coordinate, major policy initiatives on all fronts. By directly addressing the tensions between priorities such as security of supply and human rights violations in Iran and other oil producing nations or between domestic conservation and inflation, the administration would likely have been led to programs very different from those promulgated by Secretary Schlesinger—programs that would have given the president a clear, consistent and comprehensive energy policy.

VI. Conclusion

Contemporary presidential experience has found that, while historically and theoretically attractive, the cabinet meeting is, in practice, an ineffectual mechanism around which to organize a modern administration. It has become too big and cumbersome to fulfill the functions for which it was originally created: to give the president a full display of the issues and to extend his control throughout the executive branch of government.

Consequently, recent presidents have felt it necessary to develop alternative mechanisms to aid them in carrying out their decision-making and coordination responsibilities. The evidence suggests, however, that these alternatives contain numerous problems of their own, leaving the president at least as organizationally deficient as the traditional cabinet-centered system.

The solution, it has been argued, is to recognize that our presidents' original instincts about the potential effectiveness of the collegial cabinet are essentially correct. Collectively, it does indeed possess both the breadth and depth of expertise and authority the president needs to create a coherent administration. What is needed now is a plan of action that can counter the cabinet's present drawbacks of size and special interest, shaping it into the lean, modern, and manageable institution it can and must become.

Such a plan is attempted in the proposal for ExCab. Involving intensive interaction among the president and the key line functionaries of the executive branch, it provides a first cut at the kind of serious administration-building mechanisms the presidency so desperately lacks.

Notes

*The author wishes to acknowledge the assistance of Paul Zigman. This article builds upon an argument first presented in Graham Allison and Peter Szanton, *Remaking Foreign Policy: The Organizational Connection* (New York: Basic Books, 1976).

1. Much of the historical material in this section is based on Richard F. Fenno, *The President's Cabinet* (Cambridge, Mass.: Harvard University Press, 1963), pp. 3–50.
2. Ibid., p. 14.
3. Quoted in Ibid., p. 29.
4. Ibid., p. 5.
5. Quoted in Emmet John Hughes, *The Living Presidency* (New York: Coward, McCann and Geoghegan, 1973), p. 335.
6. Based on Testimony of Francis M. Bator before U.S. Congress, House, Committee on Foreign Affairs, Subcommittee on Foreign Economic Policy, *U.S. Foreign Economic Policy: Implication for the Organization of the Executive Branch*, 92nd Congress, 2nd session, 1972, pp. 115–17.
7. Quoted in Richard E. Neustadt, *Presidential Power*, 3rd ed. (New York: John Wiley and Sons, 1976), p. 107.
8. The insights of Roger B. Porter were particularly helpful in preparing this section. For a more detailed discussion, see his forthcoming book, *Presidential Decision Making: The Economic Policy Board* (Cambridge University Press, June 1980).
9. Timothy B. Clark, "The Power Vacuum Outside the Oval Office," *National Journal* (February 2, 1979), p. 296.
10. Ibid., p. 296.
11. Dom Bonafede, "Carter Sounds Retreat from 'Cabinet Government,'" *National Journal* (November 11, 1978), p. 1852.
12. Ibid., p. 1852.
13. A similar body was proposed by former chairman of the Joint Chiefs of Staff Maxwell D. Taylor in "The Exposed Flank of National Secutiry," *Orbis* (Winter, 1975): 1011 ff.
14. Unlike the "Super Cabinet" proposal put forward by President Nixon in 1971, these "Super Cabinet" positions would be filled not by White House Staff but by cabinet members themselves.
15. For further details, see Porter, *op. cit.*

The Rise and Fall of Presidential Economic Stabilization Policy

Ronald A. Krieger

Americans tend to attribute the overall state of economic well-being in the society to the discretionary stabilization policies pursued by presidents. Thus, in the popular mythology, we have had the "Hoover" depression, the "Eisenhower" stagnation, the "Kennedy-Johnson" prosperity, the "Nixon-Ford" recessions, and the "Carter" inflation. More sophisticated versions of this viewpoint recognize that economic events are not self-contained within a presidential term and that stabilization policies often have a delayed impact, making the economic situation in one president's term the partial captive of policies undertaken by his predecessors. Nevertheless, responsibility for the level of economic activity in the country is still widely attributed to past or present presidential stabilization policies, directed at countering cyclical fluctuations.

Virtually all countercyclical stabilization efforts fall into one of two familiar categories: fiscal policy or monetary policy. Fiscal policy, usually initiated by the president but requiring congressional action, involves the use of federal taxing and spending to influence the level of aggregate demand in the economy. Fiscal deficits are thought to stimulate output and employment while surpluses are contractive. Monetary policy, engineered by the Federal Reserve Board (appointed by the president) and the larger Federal Open Market Committee, attempts to manage aggregate demand through manipulation of interest rates and the growth of bank reserves and the money stock. A stimulative posture typically includes lower interest rates and faster growth of the monetary aggregates. While the president exerts no direct control over monetary policy, he is usually successful in persuading the Federal Reserve to reinforce or at least accommodate his fiscal thrust with the appropriate monetary actions. In fact, apart from isolated disputes over timing, the Federal Reserve seldom requires much persuasion to "lean against the wind" in the same countercyclical direction as administration fiscal policy.

Although presidential responsibility for economic growth and stability is widely accepted, it is doubtful that there has ever been a prolonged period in the nation's history when presidents really exerted significant control over the level of economic activity, production, and jobs. And, to the extent that they did—perhaps for a few years in the mid-1960s—the very use of activist stabilization policy contained the seeds of its own destruction as a useful policy tool. Its application touched off a sequence of events that crippled the mechanism and rendered subsequent presidents impotent in their handling of fiscal and monetary actions to manage the economy.

Economic Theory and Presidential Power

The rise and fall of presidential stabilization policy has coincided, to a remarkable degree, with developments in macroeconomic theory and the application of this body of theory to questions of federal policy. The ascendancy of Keynesian ideas during and after the Great Depression set the stage for the emergence of activist fiscal policy in the 1960s. Subsequent failures of fiscal policy led to theoretical reevaluations that resulted, for a time, in a misplaced reliance on activist monetary policy. As both of these tools have been found wanting, a radical new body of theory has emerged that indicts virtually all activist stabilization policies as useless at best and actually *de*stabilizing in many instances. If these new ideas are correct, then twilight has most certainly fallen on the day of presidential economic management, if indeed it had ever really dawned except in the euphoric fantasies of economists and politicians.

Contrary to popular myth, the conscious use of fiscal policy to stabilize the economy did not begin with President Roosevelt in the 1930s. Lacking the theoretical foundations that would later be provided by John Maynard Keynes in *The General Theory of Employment, Interest and Money* (1936), Roosevelt campaigned in 1932 on a commitment to balance the budget. Even after the publication of the *General Theory*, the budget deficits that arose during his first two terms were largely the passive product of depression-induced revenue shortfalls, rather than the conscious result of activist, deliberate fiscal stimulation. It was the massive spending undertaken for wartime mobilization—rather than for stabilization purposes—that pulled the economy out of the Great Depression.

Keynesian prescriptions were enshrined as official policy by the Employment Act of 1946, by which the government accepted responsibility for maintaining prosperity. But it was not until fifteen years later, during the Kennedy Administration, that the discretionary use of stabilization policy really became the order of the day. Although Kennedy started his term as a traditional budget-balancer, his Keynesian advisers apparently were successful in educating him to the "New Economics." Buoyed by the apparent success of the tax cut initiated in 1963 and implemented under President Johnson in 1964, presidential economic advisers boasted of their ability to "fine-tune" the economy. The 1965 *Economic Report of the President* spoke of the desirability of having fiscal and monetary policies "continuously adjusted to keep the aggregate demand for goods and services in line with the economy's growing capacity to produce them." In their fantasies, the Washington economists apparently saw themselves in a position analogous to flight controllers in a land-based space center, twiddling dials to correct the course of a space vehicle as it sped toward the moon. The president commanded, the economists spun the dials, and the economy glided upward and onward on a precise, stable journey.

The euphoria did not last long. The successful 1964 application of deficit spending in a period of sluggish economic growth has been followed by a fifteen year orgy of push-pull, stop-go monetary and fiscal manipulations that have grown ever more inflationary while exerting ever less power to control the real level of economic activity. When the soaring fiscal deficit finally overheated the economy in 1968, economic fine-tuners persuaded the president to reverse directions by imposing an income tax surcharge. The failure of that surcharge to cool the economy was the first of what has become a continuing nightmare of setbacks for stabilization policy activists. With Richard Nixon's ascendancy to the White House in 1969, restrictive monetary policy quickly led to the first recession in almost a decade. Futile attempts at a quick expansionary fix were followed by a long succession of boom-bust manipulations that put the economy on a perpetual seesaw, teetering precipitously from inflation to recession and back again. The fine-tuners despaired as the same stimulative policies that had spurred employment in the past now failed to stimulate anything but higher prices.

In the mid-1970s, the emergence of "stagflation"—roaring inflation in the face of stagnating economic activity—convinced more and more economists that the era of fine tuning was over. Activist presidential economic stabilization policies lay in ruins, and hand-wringing economic policy-makers mourned that the "old rules" no longer seemed to apply to the U.S. economy. In a very real sense, they were absolutely right. Repeated doses of fiscal and monetary stimulus had been applied to the economy so often that it had became virtually immune to policy action. The depression-era theories that had informed economic policy for forty years—and created the illusion of presidential power over economic activity—were in full retreat. But something new was emerging to take their place.

Economic Theory and Presidential Impotence

The decline and fall of activist stabilization policy came as no surprise to economists who had followed the progress of a new area of economic theory known as "rational expectations," one of the least understood but most promising developments in economics in recent decades. Although first cited in the professional journals as early as 1961, it attracted little attention until the economic disturbances of the early 1970s brought a new urgency to macroeconomic research. Since then, there has been an explosion of technical studies of the rational expectations hypothesis and its consequences, including a considerable amount of empirical verification.

For the most part, the literature of rational expectations has been highly abstruse and mathematical, putting it well out of the reach of lay policy-makers and even of less technically adept members of the economics profession. Its acceptance has been far from universal, in part because of its inaccessibility, but also because of the extreme nature of its assumptions. Another roadblock may even be the very real threat it poses to the vested interests and cherished beliefs of a whole generation of economists, who have prospered as government advisers and public and private forecasters over the past two decades. It certainly turns upside down much of the theory of macroeconomic policy that this author was taught in graduate school in the early 1960s. It is therefore no surprise that it has caught on so far only with a minority of the profession.

But the roll call of adherents is growing, especially among younger, technically sophisticated academic economists with few emotional or commercial ties to past conventional wisdom. Within that group, its acceptance has been dramatic and rapid—and not without reason. At the time of this writing (spring 1979), the theory of rational expectations appears to offer the most coherent explanation now available of the current economic situation, of recent stagflation, and of the failures of macroeconomic forecasting and stabilization policy. While its assumptions are extreme, its predictions—the ultimate test of any scientific theory—are more consistent with the empirical evidence than are those of any available alternative hypothesis.

Its proponents do not deny that the assumptions of the theory seem heroic. For example, when applied to inflation, the purest form of the hypothesis flatly asserts that information about a new rate of monetary expansion, or anything else that can generate inflation, will be incorporated instantly and correctly into inflationary expectations. In fact, "rational" individuals will learn to anticipate almost any government actions that are systematically related to economic conditions, fully discounting them (i.e., taking them into account and acting accordingly) *in advance* of the policy actions. Under the hypothesis, all this information will have an immediate effect on the spending behavior of businesses and individuals, and hence on present and future rates of price increase.

Although it does seem extreme to posit the instant and correct incorporation of all relevant information into economic decisions, the assumption rests on a common-sense interpretation of rational behavior. In essence, the rational expectations theory merely asserts that people tend to act intelligently in their own self-interest when they anticipate change. If that is true, then it is not unreasonable to suggest that they will take into account whatever information available to them that seems relevant, using that information to avoid repeating past mistakes. Among the data they are likely to include in economic decisions is knowledge about past government policy actions and about the predictable response of policy-makers to changing economic conditions. They use this information as efficiently as possible because their economic well-being is at stake. Even though they will invariably be proved wrong by the inherent uncertainty of random economic events, their expectations will be "statistically unbiased" in the sense that they are just as likely to be too low as too high. That is, the theory maintains that rational individuals will avoid *systematic* errors. To keep making the same mistakes about the response of the economy to policy, and of policy to the economy, would be to behave irrationally. In short, the basic assumption of the theory is simply that people learn from experience—not a terribly startling assertion about human behavior.

What has set the economics profession on its ear, however, and perhaps irrevocably altered the fields of macroeconomic policy and forecasting, is the dramatic implication of this assumed rational behavior. Followed to its logical conclusion, the theory implies that by adjusting behavior to take into account the likely impact of anticipated government policies, the public effectively nullifies the policy actions. To a generation of economists wedded to the optimistic possibilities of macroeconomic fine tuning, this conclusion is totally devastating. It obliterates any illusions that a U.S. president, with his wizards and soothsayers by his side, can substantially influence the level of economic activity through discretionary fiscal and monetary policy. According to the theory, the collective effect of rational responses by millions of individuals and businesses to interventionist economic policy is to render such action impotent in bringing about the desired results. Monetary and fiscal policies are still powerful, but their effects are likely to be quite different from those intended by the policy-makers.

Scenarios of Futility

To understand the mechanism by which rational expectations frustrate government attempts to manage aggregate demand, it is useful to review the conventional model of fiscal and monetary policy actions (loosely following scenarios suggested in the 1977 *Annual Report* of the Federal Reserve Bank of Minneapolis). Take, for example, the case in which fiscal stimulus is applied by the government to lift the economy out of a recession. The president programs a deficit into his annual budget, and Congress adopts his recommendations of increased spending and perhaps lower taxes. The Treasury borrows to make up the difference, with the president putting pressure on the Federal Reserve to finance the action by stepping up its purchases of government securities—in effect printing new money. Under the typical modern macroeconomic scenario, prices rise as the government hikes its spending on goods and services, and producers erroneously believe that the demand for their products has grown relative to demand in general and that their prices will rise more than their costs. Thus anticipating greater profit opportunities, business expands its output and bids up wages to hire more workers. In turn, members of the labor force, erroneously believing that the higher wages represent greater purchasing power, take more jobs, work longer hours, and reduce their leisure time. Unemployment is down, production is up, and presidential economic stabilization policies have won the day.

The problem with this scenario, according to the rational expectations view, is that it will work only so long as business is deceived by the illusion of higher profit opportunities, while labor is similarly fooled by illusory money wages that rise no faster than prices. In the scenario above, both business and labor misinterpreted a general increase in aggregate money demand as a specific rise in the relative real demand for their products or services. Once they catch on, their response will be quite different and the policy action will no longer have its intended effect. For example, if workers refuse to allow their ''real'' incomes to lag behind and insist on indexing their wages to changes in consumer prices, the fiscal stimulus will fail. Wages will rise by at least as much as prices, business will not perceive any greater profit opportunities, and the expansion will never occur.

Thus, according to the rational expectationists, the ''expansionary'' fiscal policies will stimulate output and employment only if they take people by surprise—an unlikely occurrence after the initial application of the policies. Once labor leaders get wise to the erosion of real wages occasioned by stimulative government actions, they begin to work inflationary expectations into labor contracts whenever fiscal permissiveness seems likely to overheat the economy. Eventually, they will come to do so even in slack periods, anticipating future stimulative fiscal actions by the president and Congress. Therefore, as they continue to learn from unhappy experience, they will insist on provision for higher wages even in advance of the expansionary policy actions. Labor contracts will be made for shorter and shorter terms, and more and more contracts will build in cost-of-living escalators. In fact, the number of American workers covered by such clauses has more than doubled since 1970 as unions have grown more sensitive to inflation and have acted accordingly. In such a situation, business has no incentive to increase production when policy is expansive. The only predictable effect of fiscal stimulus backed by monetary expansion is accelerating inflation. Output and employment remain flat while the greater nominal or money level of aggregate demand stimulates only the movement of prices and wages.

A second casualty of rational expectations is the conventional use of monetary policy to stimulate business investment and consumer spending through lower interest rates. Traditionally, the Federal Reserve eases monetary policy by purchasing more government securities. This is the classic posture taken by the Federal Reserve in a recession as it attempts to "lean against the wind." According to the usual analysis, the monetary expansion drives up security prices and forces down interest rates. To a minor degree, this leads consumers to borrow more for purchases of such durable goods as autos and household appliances. But the major thrust of the policy is to stimulate capital spending by business, as the interest costs of new plant and equipment are reduced. Bank reserves expand, demand soars, prices rise, profit opportunities increase, production grows, more workers are hired, and unemployment falls. The expansion will take place even in the face of wages rising as fast as prices, unlike the fiscal-stimulus case, as long as new investment spending is attracted by the lure of lower interest rates.

Once again, however, the policy action is thwarted by rational expectations. The purchases of securities by the Federal Reserve serve to increase the rate of growth of the money supply and hence to drive up the rate of inflation. As they come to anticipate future price hikes, both borrowers and lenders perceive that loans made in the present will be paid back in future dollars of depreciated purchasing power. Lenders therefore come to insist on building an "inflation premium" into the interest rates they charge, while borrowers are willing to bear such a burden because they realize that they will get to pay back cheaper dollars. Thus, interest rates, especially on the longer-term instruments that finance capital spending, rise to reflect inflationary expectations on top of the real return to capital. Once this starts to happen, the higher profits that would have resulted from lower interest costs are no longer on the horizon; therefore, the monetary expansion generates no further business investment, but serves only to accelerate inflation. Expansive monetary policy will stimulate production and jobs only when it comes as a surprise, and it is not likely to do so once people begin learning the lessons of previous experience. As in the fiscal scenario, stimulative monetary policies ultimately affect only the price level and inflation rate, with a minimal impact on real output and employment.

Challenge and Response

This is a damning indictment of discretionary economic stabilization policy, and it has not gone without challenge in professional dialogue among economists. The critics will often accept the logic of the rational expectations argument, but they vehemently deny its relevance. They claim that it is wildly unrealistic to assume that all individuals and businesses will fully and instantly incorporate all available information into their anticipations of future economic events and then act on this information correctly. People just are not that smart, worldly, and farsighted. Furthermore, long labor contract periods prevent the instantaneous adjustment of wages to new expectations. And if all labor and product markets do not "clear" in every time period, monetary and fiscal policy can still have a short-run impact on output and employment.

Proponents of the theory reply that the process they envision requires only the intelligent foresight of a few key economic actors, not the omniscience of everybody in the marketplace. They insist that *on the average*, people collectively learn from experience, process information efficiently, and act on it rationally, even if many individuals do not. The relevance of the theory does not depend on all workers, businesses, and consumers having perfect foresight, they argue. It simply means, for example, that key union leaders must be concerned with real wages as well as nominal wages, which they demonstrably are; this is showing up in shorter union contract periods and more frequent cost-of-living adjustments within contract periods. Further, it means that small borrowers and investors must trade in the same efficient commodity, security, and money markets as their larger and more sophisticated counterparts, which they usually do. It also means that a certain number of small businesses and consumers must be aware of what the experts are predicting, but this is no problem for anyone who reads a newspaper. And with anticipations being incorporated into economic activity more and more automatically, through the workings of futures markets and escalator clauses, the rational responses to policy of just a few knowledgeable economic agents will quickly ripple throughout the economy. Thus, the rational expectationists claim that their theory is actually *more* realistic than the conventional viewpoint on stabilization policy, which, they say, implicitly assumes that the public, on average, is too dense or irrational to learn from experience.

Rational Expectations and Irrational Forecasts

One vivid demonstration of the limitations of the traditional approach is the dismal forecasting record in recent years of conventional macroeconomic models, whether Keynesian or monetarist. Econometric models of the economy are composed of sets of equations relating economic variables to one another on the basis of historical data. They assume that past relationships will continue into the future, and that people form expectations by naively extrapolating past experience. In other words, these models assume that businesses, consumers, and workers change their behavior sluggishly, if at all, in response to policy changes, and therefore can be fooled for long periods of time into acting against their own best interests.

But if this assumption ever was correct, it surely is no longer the general case. People who have been deceived in the past have indeed learned from experience. They consume, save, invest, and bargain much differently in the face of past mistakes. Their inflationary expectations take into account current and expected government stabilization actions in addition to historic rates of price increase. And their resulting behavior has eroded the old relationships among such variables as personal income and aggregate consumption, or monetary growth and national product, on whose stability many of the models depend. Small wonder that the models no longer predict well.

Without reliable forecasting models with which to simulate proposed economic policy initiatives, discretionary stabilization policy becomes even more hazardous and unpredictable. For example, a standard relationship built into most forecasting models is the Phillips Curve. This handy tool purports to demonstrate that there is a stable trade-off between unemployment and the rate of inflation. Developed in the late 1950s, it quickly became indispensable for presidential economic stabilization policy. According to a well-known interpretation, it allowed the president a "menu of choice" among national economic objectives, from which he could select, say, higher inflation with lower unemployment, or stable prices with more workers out of a job. But in a world of inflationary expectations, this trade-off is rapidly vanishing. The traditional Phillips Curve depends upon workers being fooled by higher money wages into offering more labor, and upon businesses being fooled by the illusion of higher profits into expanding output and employment opportunities. Its assumptions are the same as those of the fiscal-stimulus scenario described earlier. But now, expectations are growing more rational. As workers and businesses learn from experience and shed their illusions, expansive monetary and fiscal policies are translated more and more rapidly into higher inflationary expectations. The resulting behavior leads to intensified inflation without any lasting effect on unemployment or the real level of economic activity.

The recent experience of the United States suggests that the Phillips trade-off has virtually disappeared. The president no longer can select his priority choice from the policy "menu" at the expense of a lower-priority variable. For high inflation now walks hand in hand with high unemployment. Any trade-offs that still exist are strictly temporary and are getting shorter and shorter as the public gets more knowledgeable. The president can still attempt to stimulate the economy in order to reduce unemployment, but it will have no more than a transitory effect on the unemployment rate. He will get little from his efforts except an acceleration of inflation. Models that still posit a Phillips trade-off provide an erroneous guide to policy. Unfortunately, they are still widely used, just as if nothing had changed since 1965.

Living with the New Limits to Policy

In this situation, what options remain for presidential economic stabilization policy? There are at least four ways to go: (1) ignoring the evidence and continuing as before, (2) shifting the emphasis from aggregate demand management to direct controls, (3) using unpredictable policy "surprises" to get the desired results, or (4) abandoning countercyclical stabilization attempts in favor of a steady, consistent policy throughout the business cycle.

Little need be said about the first two options. Further attempts at fine tuning, ignoring the environment of enlightened expectations that now permeates the U.S. economy, would serve only to destabilize the economy and accelerate inflation. As for wage-price controls, whether mandatory or "voluntary," experience teaches that guidelines cannot long withstand the pressures of inflationary anticipations built up by earlier doses of excess demand. But to the extent that they "work," three results are almost inevitable. First, they will cause black markets, shortages, and production disincentives, creating so many strains and distortions in the economy that they will eventually have to be rescinded. Second, the price level will be as high or higher after the controls are lifted than it would have been had controls never been imposed. Third, the bout with controls will leave the economy weaker, less productive, growing more slowly, and more susceptible to inflationary shocks.

Suppose, then, that the president and his advisers accept the presence of rational expectations but still wish to influence economic activity. They could opt for "unpredictability" and attempt repeatedly to catch the public off guard with unexpected policy actions. For example, they could perpetually try to surprise the people with tax cuts, government spending sprees, or sudden additions to the rate of growth of the money stock. For a time, they might even get the desired results, although that is problematical. But they could not continue a series of surprises forever. And even if they could, it would probably make matters worse in the long run as economic activity became paralyzed by the constant state of uncertainty. Eventually, erratic policy would either become ineffective or, more likely, put the economy on a permanent boom-bust roller coaster that would seriously inhibit long-term economic growth.

This leaves the fourth approach to policy, steady rather than countercyclical, as the least unsatisfactory option. A few years ago, it would have been traumatic for most economists and political leaders to accept the notion that they could not successfully manipulate the economy. But the repeated failures of presidential stabilization policy have been humbling, and they should make for a more modest attitude in the future. It is not the policy *tools* that are impotent, but the policy-*makers*. Monetary and fiscal policies still have great power to shock the economy off its previous course. The problem is that the effects of these powerful tools cannot be controlled. In fact, rational expectationists maintain that the economy is basically stable in the absence of government intervention, and it would remain on a smooth, predictable course if it were not subjected to repeated shocks by government policy.

Of course, even a steady hand on the policy tiller would not put an end to the ups and downs of the business cycle. Cyclical fluctuations are inherent in the economic process, and such random shocks as the OPEC oil price hikes will also continue to destabilize the economy in the short run. But at the least, the absence of government intervention would permit natural recoveries from these shocks and fluctuations, without the magnification of cyclical swings that results from attempts at fine tuning. And the reduction of uncertainty would surely foster more business confidence and promote some badly needed investment in plant and equipment.

A steady, predictable policy would mean an end to attempts to counter short-run cyclical swings by expansive and contractive government measures. It would have two basic elements. On the fiscal side, it would strive for a ''neutral'' budgetary stance, with deficits and surpluses arising only in passive response to changes in the level of economic activity. In monetary policy, it would mean adhering to a steady rate of monetary growth consistent with the long-run noninflationary growth rate of potential real output.

The benefits of maintaining steady policies over the long run would be solid but unspectacular. They would provide a predictable environment to encourage a high level of economic activity, and they would promote a gradual reduction of inflationary expectations—and the inflation rate—as the new policy stance gained credibility. The promises of steadiness pale in comparison with the extravagant claims once made for discretionary stabilization policy. But in a world of rational expectations, it is the only realistic course and the best hope for an eventual return to a stable, growing economy.

An Imperiled Presidency?

Thomas E. Cronin

''Who would have thought five years ago that we would today be calling for new measures to strengthen the American presidency?'' That is how not one but two activist liberal friends of mine put it in some meetings a year ago in Washington, D.C. A mere seven years after Watergate there is again an intensified call for vigorous presidential leadership. If our two most recent presidents have been a welcome relief from the profound tragedies of the Watergate period, they have nonetheless not regularly lived up to our expectations of presidential leadership. Plainly, our expectations are always too high. No doubt we give presidents more than they can do, more pressure than they can bear, we abuse them often and seldom praise them, wear them out, use them up, and yet we keep asking them for more.

As President Jimmy Carter passes the three-quarter mark of his first term it seems an appropriate time to ask about the presidency in general. How is it doing since Watergate and Richard Nixon's inglorious departure? Have post-Vietnam and post-Watergate ''reforms,'' such as they are, really weakened the presidency? Are the problems Gerald Ford and Jimmy Carter have had with Congress problems of their own making or those of institutional weakness? It is the aim of this essay to evaluate the problems our two recent presidents have had with Congress and to offer some discussion about the state of the institutional presidency at Carter's midterm point.

Ford and Carter have been sensitive to most of the complaints Americans had about how the presidency was run in the late 1960s and early 1970s. For example, students of the presidency kept saying things would be well if only we had a president who didn't have an enemies list. Or things would be well if we could finally get this war over and no American boys were dying overseas. Or things would be well if only our presidents regularly met with the press, regularly met with their cabinets, and if only they would treat their vice-presidents humanely. There was also, of course, a widespread feeling that presidents should "depomp" or "deroyalize" the ceremonies and status symbols at the White House. And during the Nixon and Ford years we heard repeatedly that presidential-congressional relations would be much improved if only these two branches were under the control of the same political party.

All these things have come to pass. The war is over. The era of the manipulative and imperial presidency has thankfully passed. Ford and Carter have upgraded the status of the cabinet and appointed reasonably strong activist persons to the vice-presidency. If anything, these two presidents have bent over backwards in an effort to restore as much integrity and openness to the office as possible. They have, to their credit, achieved most of the objectives that critics had called for eight and ten years ago.

But save for President Carter's notable achievement in arranging for and helping to achieve the Middle East peace accords, both Ford and Carter have had very rough troubles with Congress. Their seeming inability to get Congress to pass much of their programs has contributed to a general impression of ineffectiveness. Why then have they been ineffective—or at least appeared ineffective? No single explanation will suffice. Clearly, Congress has strengthened itself in some respects and it is enjoying asserting itself in both policy-making and policy-thwarting activities.

Congress may have reorganized and revitalized itself in many ways, but many of its reforms have also had the effect of diluting the ability of congressional leaders to obtain action. Power in the Congress has been decidedly decentralized. Also, fringe benefits for members of Congress have had the effect of making it easier for members to engage in constituency services and spend more time on reelection chores—developments that make members of Congress less dependent on presidential patronage or election support.

Several "system" factors are doubtless also at work. Thus our national and international problems are more complex than they used to be. Our economy is vastly more interdependent with those of other leading nations around the world. Our dependence on imported raw materials is much greater now than a decade or two decades ago. We used to concern ourselves almost exclusively with the *demand* side of the economic equation while now we have to worry about the *supply* side of the equation.

But for the other reasons that have given Ford and Carter their problems we shall have to take a close look at these presidents and their relations with Congress.

Ford and Congress

"I do not want a honeymoon with you. I want a good marriage," said Ford to Congress as he started his presidency. "As President I intend to listen . . . ." Ford said his relations with Congress would be characterized not by confrontation but by "communication, conciliation, compromise and cooperation." But his hope for holy wedlock soured and an unholy deadlock set in as he proceeded to veto 69 legislative measures.

Congress did give Ford a hard time. Having shaken off years of inertia, Congress took advantage of an appointed president to regain some of its own lost authority. Thus it rejected some of his nominations, took four months to confirm Nelson Rockefeller, rejected his foreign-aid bill, trimmed his defense appropriations, curtailed military aid to Turkey, denied him the means to conduct open or covert operations in Angola, and so on.

Some of Ford's aides warned of a new period of congressional government. Ford himself said:

> "Frankly, I believe that Congress recently has gone too far in trying to take over the powers that belong to the president and the executive branch.
>
> This probably is a natural reaction to the steady growth of executive branch power over the past forty years. I'm sure it is a reaction to Watergate and Vietnam. And the fact that I came to this office through a Constitutional process and not by election also may have something to do with current efforts by the Democratic Congress to take away some of the powers of the president.
>
> As a member of Congress for 25 years, I clearly understand the powers and obligations of the Senate and House under our Constitution. But as president for 18 months, I also understand that Congress is trying to go too far in some areas."

Why did Ford have such troubled relations with Congress? Reaction to Vietnam and Watergate obviously played a role in his difficulties. Congress was a more democratic institution now, with power much more dispersed among its members. Subcommittee chairmen were now especially important. It had streamlined some of its procedures, and it was more conscious of its responsibility to the people. But there were additional factors that explain Ford's difficulties with the Congress. Perhaps the major problem was that he was decidedly more conservative than Congress as a whole. This should have come as no surprise to those who had looked at Ford's voting record as a congressman. He had voted against medicare, opposed the creation of the Office of Economic Opportunity, opposed aid to education, and opposed federal help for state water pollution projects. He had, however, always been a strong supporter of Defense Department spending.

Moreover, he was an appointed president. As our first 25th Amendment president he also bore "the stigma of illegitimacy," as Arthur Schlesinger, Jr. put it. He had absolutely no mandate from the people. He had to deal with a Democrat-controlled Congress. He came to office right in the midst of a mid-term congressional election. At the State Department he had the always secretive Henry Kissinger who had by then acquired strong opponents in both parties. And he had to contend with a strong attack from the right wing of his own already minority party. The Ford presidency experienced additional troubles because it came during the seventh and eighth years of the Nixon-Ford administrations. Their top people were tired and had run out of imaginative ideas and solutions. And finally, Ford suffered from the disillusionment that invariably sets in toward the end of an eight-year hold on the presidency. The same thing had happened in 1960 and 1968.

In fact, the Ford presidency was neither as weak and constrained as it wanted people to believe (the White House liked to convey the impression that the press, the courts, and Congress were literally undermining presidential powers). Ford himself may have been vulnerable but the presidency was not weakened during this period. The major powers of the office available to presidents were still impressive. Of course, the effective use of those powers required shrewd use and especially clear communication of intent.

Carter and Congress

Carter's relations with Congress in his first two years in office were turbulent. He suffered setbacks on his energy package, tax reforms, welfare reforms, election reforms, the proposed consumer protection agency and countless other measures. He scored victories too (i.e., B-1 bomber, and especially with his Middle East peace initiatives) but these often seemed to be the exception to the rule and very often these victories were on policy matters where Congress has historically deferred to the executive branch.

Carter's difficulties with Congress were also partially due to the post-Watergate efforts to constrain the American presidency. But *only partially*. To be sure, Congress did not want to become a rubber stamp for a Democratic president. For eight years (1969-1976) the Democrats in Congress had grown accustomed to opposing the White House. And Congress was enjoying its struggle to reassert itself. Also, the dispersion of influence (i.e., power to the subcommittees and subcommittee chairmen) in the House of Representatives made it more difficult for a president to deal with Congress. Gone were the days when the White House could deal with a handful of "whales" who really ran the show. But Carter's difficulties stemmed from a number of other factors as well.

Early Resentment

Carter ran for the White House as a Mr. Pure, a Mr. Integrity, and as a Mr. Outsider. He sold himself almost like a detergent who would go to Washington and clean things up. That could only breed resentment. Many of his campaign slogans were viewed as a "put down" to Congress. He talked too much of *the mess* in Washington to win friends there. He said Congress was "inherently incapable of leadership," and added that "in the absence of strong presidential leadership . . . there is no leadership."

His personal style of campaigning stressed confrontation more than negotiation. He seemed righteous and almost too good to be true. He stated that his administration would be guided by only the highest moral standards and that he would only appoint "the best" as in "why not the best?" So when the Bert Lance affair occurred, he was judged all the more critically. Congress and others resented Carter's pious style. As one person put it, "[Next] time, I'd like someone who doesn't talk so high and mighty before he gets in and does more of a job after he's elected."

Weak Democratic Base

Much was made of the idea in 1976 that most of the problems in presidential-congressional relations could be overcome if only both branches were held by the Democrats. That came to pass in January 1977, but the promised harmony did not ensue. Part of the reason is that the Democratic party is in many ways several parties in one. Any party with both a Congressman Ron Dellums (D-Calif.) and a Senator James Eastland (D-Miss.) is a party either split or very strained.

Moreover, Carter really has no political base within the Democratic party. He is not really a southern old-boy conservative. Some have suggested that the toothful southerner is more of a Yankee puritan. In many ways, the mere fact that he is a southerner in the White House makes him a novelty. Ironically, although Carter enjoys his highest popularity in the southeastern section of the nation, the members of Congress from that region give him the lowest rates (about 30 percent) of support for his programs in Congress.

Activist without Mandate

Carter is an activist who wants to achieve countless comprehensive policy and process changes but he has no mandate to do so from the 1976 election. Forty-seven percent of the voters stayed home. He lost nearly 30 points in the polls between August and election day as his election campaign stumbled haphazardly to a narrow victory. White voters, and even white southerners, preferred Ford over Carter. The 1976 election was hardly an issues-election the way 1936 and 1964 or 1972 were.

Carter, moreover, ran well behind almost all of the Democrats who won election to Congress and the state houses in 1976. His election seemed to be due more to the public's lack of confidence in Gerald Ford than to any program Carter put forth.

Yet Carter in office acted as if he has some direct mandates to reshape domestic and foreign policy. While he is not a populist, he tries nonetheless to be assertive, bold, and sometimes brash. He is clearly a Democrat in the activist "Don't just stand there, do something" tradition. He strives to be "a take charge guy'' who wants to set standards and establish policy guidelines. His statements on human rights, environmental protection, and energy conservation have often been unusually aggressive.

The Hill is not accustomed to handling so many initiatives at one time. The vast majority of its members weren't around for the 89th Congress. And even then most of Lyndon Johnson's programs had been incubating in the Congress for several years before they were passed. So, many of Carter's problems arise either because he is in advance of his times or he is unable to communicate why his so-called "comprehensive policy changes" are needed.

Carter Isn't Political Enough

Some of Carter's early difficulties stem from the fact that he does not enjoy the politics of dealing with members of Congress. He gave the impression that he was the rational man and that Congress should deal with him and his programs completely on their merits. The idea that deals will be made and favors will be dispensed seems quite alien to Carter. Similarly deals and horse-trading must go on, at least to some extent, with various interest group leaders. That may be how politics works, but Carter has set out, often in vain, to establish a new model.

Reporters covering his trips around the country say he is almost incapable of saying nice things about members of Congress even as he travels among their constituents. One U.S. senator's office had arranged for Carter to say a few words of endorsement for the senator when Carter was in the senator's home state. Expensive television and video machinery had been rented and set up to capture Carter's few words of praise, hoping that they might be usable in the 1978 election race. But Carter came and talked and went but never uttered the expected words of praise. Washington is full of such anecdotes. It is as if he doesn't like politics, and yearns to be above both politics and politicians.

Members of Congress complain too that he does not consult them enough. Unlike Lyndon Johnson, he seldom invites them in to go over the drafts of prospective bills. Carter seems often to prefer a government by surprise. He also has a penchant for bypassing Congress and going to the country. Of course, most presidents do this, but his style of doing it coupled with his reputation as an ''outsider'' come back to weaken his ties to Congress.

One scholar who has studied Carter's legislative relations staffs offers an additional explanation that since Carter won the nomination and then the presidency itself largely without having to build coalitions with the left, right, and center of the Democratic party, so also his congressional relations teams did not build these needed coalitions to get things passed. Political scientist Eric Davis puts it this way:

Since they did not have to engage in bargaining to get the nomination or to win the election, they would not have to engage in bargaining or exchange to get their programs passed on Capitol Hill. Because they did not recognize the importance of coalition-building through brokerage, they did not, at the very outset of the Administration, make an effort to establish cooperative lobbying relationships with the other important participants in the legislative process . . . . Since these relationships were not established, the White House had to rely on its own resources to obtain legislative successes. Therefore, legislative defeats resulted. And these defeats fed upon themselves, creating the image of ineptitude on the part of the White House. This image of ineptitude, in turn, has led to members of Congress being less willing to rely on White House judgments and to accept White House analyses of issues.

Different National Mood

In the early 1960s the mood of the country embodied a seemingly boundless self-confidence in itself and in what its government could achieve. The mood was one of feeling we could go anywhere and do anything from conquering outer space to effecting land reform in Latin America and political reforms in Indochina. We believed government could end poverty in America and achieve countless other things.

John Kennedy became our president during this era of good feelings, this era of confident and sometimes reckless adventuresomeness. Optimism and idealism aided both him and Lyndon Johnson in their efforts to deal with Congress.

But that era is over. Today we dwell on the scarcity of our resources. We acknowledge that we overextended ourselves abroad. We salute the slogan of "Small is Beautiful" and read study after study predicting the limits to growth.

President Carter would doubtless like to provide leadership of the Roosevelt, Wilson, and Kennedy kind but he doesn't have the appropriate climate of expectations. There is neither the trauma of a depression nor the crusading spirit of a world war, nor the bouyant national optimism of the early 1960s.

The presidency is obviously hedged in by the national mood. The mood today is one of profound disillusionment with federal programs. Moreover, this is certainly not the age of the hero. We may long for leadership, but we are skeptical of our leaders. Carter's difficulties with Congress arise in no small measure from his desire to offer strong and inspiring leadership to a nation that has turned inward, introspective and neo-narcissistic as opposed to nation-centered. The people are acting as if this is a second Ford administration while Carter often wants to act as if the year is 1933 or 1943 or 1963. In a sense Carter's chief handicap arises because he is a strongly activist "doer" who came along at a time when passivity and tax cutting are what many, and perhaps most, Americans want.

So Carter is having his problems with Congress, but most of his problems are due to factors other than the post-Vietnam, post-Watergate, anti-imperial presidency reforms.

Resurgent Presidency?

Even as the presidency was being soundly criticized for abuses of power in the late 1960s and early 1970s, it was simultaneously portrayed by many people as alarmingly weakened by Vietnam and Watergate. The ranks of the defenders of presidential government may have been temporarily thinned in 1973 and 1974, but today the cult of the strong presidency is alive and well.

As Michael Novak once observed, the Right worries about the imperial presidency at home and the Left worries about the imperial presidency abroad. What he didn't say is that the Right doubtless wants a near-imperial presidency abroad and the Left often wants something approaching an imperial presidency at home.

There are compelling indications that the experiment of trying to curb presidential power and relying more instead on the Congress for national leadership has ended.

The American public may have lost confidence in its leaders, but it has not lost hope in the efficacy of strong purposive leadership. Thus the Gallup organization in 1979 asked a national sample: "Do you think what the country needs is really strong leadership that would try to solve problems directly without worrying about how Congress or the Supreme Court might feel or do you think that such leadership might be dangerous?" By a 63 percent to 30 percent margin the respondents indicated a preference for a strong government over a constitutional one.

Fears of another Watergate presidency are rapidly disappearing. Perhaps all the revelations about the crimes of Watergate and the dramatic resignation of a president have lulled most people into believing that "the system worked," that the checks checked and the balances balanced. Perhaps the very cataloging of the misuses of presidential powers seemed to solve the problem. Obviously, it was not right, but the very revelations may have appeared the same as remedies.

Moreover, if the nation worried about an imperial presidency, it worried also—alas even feared—an imperial Congress. Few could object to the efforts of streamlining, democratizing, or better staffing the Congress. But few informed people wished to rely only, or even primarily, on Congress for national leadership.

In the wake of the wounded or imperiled presidency of the Watergate era, could Congress furnish the leadership necessary to govern the country? Most scholars and writers who comment on the presidency said no. The conventional answer heard in the late 1970s is that "we will need a presidency of substantial power" if we are to get on top of the energy problem and maintain our position in foreign affairs. The Iran and Afghanistan crises merely heightened this sentiment.

The president's primacy, they would add, has been founded in the necessities of the American condition. Today, the federal government has become committed to burdens of administration that demand vigorous, positive leadership. We live too in a continuous state of emergency, where instant nuclear warfare could destroy the country in a matter of minutes and where global competition of almost every sort highlights the need for swiftness, efficiency, and unity in our government. Further, today's social and urban and environmental problems require a persistent display of creative presidential leadership. Any reduction in the powers of the president might leave us naked to our enemies, to the forces of inflation and depression at home, and to the forces of unrest and aggression abroad.

Former President Gerald Ford scoffed in 1977 at the idea that Congress had improved things in recent years. Speaking for the repeal of the War Powers Resolution of 1973, Ford said "when a crisis breaks out, it is impossible to draw the Congress into the decision-making process in an effective way." Ford cited these reasons for this claim: (1) legislators have too many other concerns to be abreast of foreign-policy situations; (2) it is impossible to wait for a consensus among scattered and perhaps disagreeing congressional leaders; (3) sensitive information supplied to legislators, particularly via the telephone, might be disclosed; (4) waiting for consultation could risk penalties for the president "as severe as impeachment"; and (5) consultations with congressional leaders might not bind the rank and file, particularly independent younger members.

Defenders of a powerful presidency such as Samuel Huntington and columnist Robert Novak wondered how a government could conduct a coherent foreign policy if legislative ascendancy really meant the development of a Congress into a second United States government. Could the U.S. afford to have two foreign policies? A nation cannot long retain a leadership role in the world unless its own leadership is both clear and decisive. They argued, too, that congressional decisions—including foreign-policy decisions—must be based almost entirely on domestic politics, which is why Congress cannot conduct foreign policy.

More specifically, Robert Novak in 1976 charged: "Congress by its headline hunting investigations, has destroyed the Central Intelligence Agency as an effective means of national policy for the United States." Elsewhere he writes: "In the . . . Angola episode . . ., Congress has served notice that the President of the United States cannot conduct the foreign policy of his country to confront brush fire occurrences, to confront Soviet expansionism."

Political scientist Huntington, writing in 1975, urges readers to recognize the legitimacy and the necessity "of hierarchy, coercion, discipline, secrecy, and deception—all of which are, in some measure, inescapable attributes of the process of government." "When the President is unable to exercise authority . . ." writes Huntington "no one else has been able to supply comparable purpose and initiative. To the extent that the United States has been governed on a national basis, it has been governed by the President."

The same verdict is heard from those who yearn for strong creative leadership in domestic or economic matters. Thus, Arthur Schlesinger, Jr.—even as he condemns the imperial presidency—says that "history has shown the presidency to be the most effective instrumentality for justice and progress." Time and again, people caution against overreacting to Watergate. Do not be ahistorical, they say. Quoting Harold Laski, they say "Great power makes great leadership possible."

Supporters of a strong, powerful presidency worry that a president has too little power today to tackle economic and energy resource problems effectively. For example, he has very little influence over the Federal Reserve Board's policies on credit and money. He has few tools for effective, long-range economic planning. And, as President Carter learned in his first two years of office, his authority over government reorganizations is puny compared to our expectations of him as the so-called "chief executive."

Without strong presidential leadership, the parochialism in Congress, they contend, is so profound and insidious and unremitting that Congress is not a good institution in which to place our hopes for the future. Advocates of national planning are especially fond of looking to the White House for leadership because they believe that *only the president* has the national perspective to plan coherently, to plan comprehensively. Sure, they say, Congress has its role. But Congress, rather than balancing presidential powers, has often simply blocked needed presidential actions because of localized self-interest.

People cite President Carter's rational call for the end of Congress' pet water projects that cannot stand the test of any kind of economic analysis. "It is at this point that congressmen are transformed from people who occasionally do perceive and pursue national interests into people who are actuated by the narrowest of local interests. And you find Morris Udall, of all people, leading the pack to roll back those nineteen cancellations."

Thus, as almost always during the twentieth century, advocates of a strong presidency lament that presidential powers are not stronger. For the presidency is America's strongest weapon against those banes of progress: sectionalism, selfish or over-concentrated corporate power, and totalitarianism abroad.

Americans still long for dynamic, reassuring, and strong leadership. Watergate notwithstanding, we still celebrate the gutsy, aggressive presidents, even if many of them did violate the legal and constitutional niceties of the separation of powers. It is still the Jeffersons, Jacksons, Lincolns, and Roosevelts that get placed on the top of the lists of great presidents. As James Sundquist put it in 1974, "The day of the strong President is here to stay. It is a necessity of the times. People want it that way . . . . The great presidents are the men who built the Presidency and made a practice of kicking the Congress around . . . . I don't mean to be happy with this, but I think it is realistically what the situation is."

President Carter is criticized for not growing fast enough in the job. He has been taking crash courses in foreign policy and in how to work in Washington, but only recently has he seemed to catch up enough to appear in charge. He still reverses himself and a little too often. And if he earlier tried too frequently to be all things to all people, he now seems too willing to capitulate to the special interest lobbies. Thus he lost complete control of the recent tax-cutting package and appeared to cave in too readily. Also his hospital cost containment program, defense-budget spending, and most of his urban policies have all been closer to the Right. Perhaps he is letting himself be shaped by the times rather than trying to be an educator and mobilizer behind that which he believes to be in the best interest of the nation.

Although Carter of late has enjoyed enhanced public approval ratings and praise for his on-the-job learning, there remains widespread questioning about whether he is as potent a leader as the times demand. It may be altogether wrong, but there remains a fixation with a storybook-charismatic kind of presidential leadership.

Newsweek columnist Meg Greenfield puts it well:

> Even in a city that has known at firsthand the horrors of an overblown Presidency, there is a remarkable degree of unanimity now that what is needed is a little more Presidential size: a sense that though he may not be the daddy of us all, the President does not control his destiny (and ours) to some extent, that he is not just one among equals; that he knows, in ways beyond our grasp, exactly what he is doing . . . . It will be the ultimate revenge of the imperial presidents and their imperious aides if the legacy of their misuse of Presidential power is fear of using it at all.

In sum, more and more people think the nation in the mid-1970s entered a period of overreaction to Watergate, Vietnam, and the Nixon presidency. Some rebalancing was needed, but many in Congress and elsewhere embarked upon a course that endangered the effectiveness of the presidency. Those who hold to this overreaction thesis say the White House today is enmeshed in a complex web of constraints that hobbles presidents and that would have prevented an FDR or a Lincoln from providing vital leadership. Fears of presidential dictatorship, they say, are much exaggerated. It is unfortunate that people dwell so much on Richard Nixon and his abuse in office. The Nixon presidency, they contend, was one of a kind and it was dealt with effectively by the impeachment provisions of the Constitution. The central challenge, then, is not to reduce the president's power to lead, to govern, or to persuade but to check the president's power to mislead and corrupt.

Resurgent Congress?

There are still many, though clearly now a minority, who insist that the reassertion of congressional power is a much needed corrective and that it hasn't gone far enough. Supporters of a truly strong and tenacious Congress question the depth, sincerity, and staying power of congressional assertiveness. They point to President Ford's failure to comply with the War Powers Resolution of 1973 when he ordered military action and bombings in connection with the 1975 rescue of the merchant ship Mayaguez. They note that the Defense Department's budgets continue to grow and to pass through Congress with minimum changes. They point to President Carter's penchant for surprising Congress or for bypassing it entirely with appeals to the public. They contend too that despite all the talk about more and better program oversight, most members of Congress find this type of work the least glamorous, least appealing, and least rewarding—especially in terms of winning reelection. Hence they wonder whether Congress will really maintain its interest in this vital work.

Those who want more reform point out that the imperial presidency was at least as much the product of an unassertive Congress as it was of power-hungry presidents. They contend too that although Congress may have asserted itself in response to the events of Watergate, the more distant those events become, the less motivated Congress will be to challenge the presidency. This reasoning leads them to say: It is the Congress after Watergate that bears watching, and it is Congress that needs to develop a leadership strength of its own.

There is also the view that the presidency, as Watergate and the Ford presidency have verified, is an indestructible office, tough and resilient. It readily survived, and Watergate may have actually strengthened it. That is, Watergate had a kind of purifying effect on the office, for after the trauma of 1973-1974, many people found a false comfort in the claim that "the system worked." Once Nixon was removed, the problems of the office were assumed to have been removed. But to those who still worry about a too strong presidency, this attitude is very dangerous. We should have been more alarmed than we were—or than we are. The seeds of the imperial presidency are still there. The office still needs to be cut down to size.

But the period of post-Watergate reforming has just about run its course. Few new "reform" ideas are being heard these days. The call for strengthening the presidency—or at least leaving the presidency alone—is the dominant one these days and likely to be so for the next few years. Fears of another era of congressional government are unfounded. Plainly, the pendulum has already swung back in the other direction, although how far it will swing and what consequences will follow cannot yet be determined.

Reassertion and Balance

After debating the merits of congressional reassertion as opposed to the dominant presidency, most Americans recognize that our choices are few. First, we could really cut the presidency down, even to the point of crippling it. Second, we could leave it almost entirely alone, as Clinton Rossiter, Richard Neustadt, and most mainstream historians and political scientists have so often advised. Finally, we could try to regulate the presidency and at least in some moderate, incremental way, try to protect against abuses that will inevitably arise from the accelerating rate of centralization of authority and power in its hands.

Few people seriously advocated recommendation number one. To weaken the presidency, upon closer inspection, really meant that the bureaucracy and the special interests would be strengthened. A weakening of the presidency would not mean the turning back of power to Congress and the people.

The idea of leaving the presidency entirely alone and not heeding the lessons of the Watergate period was not a very satisfactory solution, though it was sometimes adopted as the lesser of various evils by those who believed that nearly every proposed remedy has an ill of its own.

Most settled for the third choice. Recognize that the presidency has become the dominant political institution in our system, but do everything possible to keep it within the Constitution and guided by the doctrines of constitutionalism. Most would agree with Larry Tribe when he wrote that "We are and must remain, a society led by three equal branches, with one permanently 'more equal' than the others: as the Supreme Court and Congress are preeminent in constitutional theory, so the President is preeminent in constitutional fact." The goal should be a system of checks and balances that leaves the presidency strong enough for effective leadership, while dispersing power enough to enhance and protect liberty.

The balance is delicate, and rebalancing efforts such as the congressional reassertion of the 1970s will often be necessary. The reaction to the imperial or Watergate presidency has been significant, although perhaps not lasting. There is a healthy skepticism toward presidents. There is less glorification of presidents and their policies. There is a new spirit of independence among congressmen. They say: "We want a strong and intelligent president, but he has to bear one thing in mind—we got elected too." Or as former U.S. Senator Mike Mansfield put it, "The people have not chosen to be governed by one branch of government alone."

There have been campaign-finance reforms, open-meeting laws, and a rash of congressional reorganization efforts. There is also a new emphasis on accountable and responsible leadership. We know now that a strong power-maximizing presidency need not be an accountable one. We also know now that a strong and responsible president is not one who holds himself above the law, who disregards the Constitution, who misuses the intelligence agencies, who intimidates the press. Strength in the White House these days is judged more on the quality of ideas, on a president's integrity, know-how, and negotiating skills, and on the quality of the staff and cabinet he can assemble to help him.

Congress has most of the tools it needs to become a reasonably effective partner in shaping national policy. Whether it chooses to use them is another matter. The reassertion most needed in Washington is the reassertion by Congress of its traditional powers such as the power of the purse and the powers to confirm, to investigate, and to oversee the implementation of national programs. Congress will probably achieve very little by passing symbolic "reform" measures such as the War Powers Resolution of 1973. And excessive legislative veto provisions written in an effort to control all departmental regulations will make the implementation of some laws an administrative nightmare.

However much the public may want Congress to be a major partner with the president and a major check on the president, the public's support for Congress will always be subject to deterioration. Power is much dispersed in Congress. Its deliberations and quarrels are very public. After a while, the public begins to view Congress as "the bickering branch" or the policy-thwarting branch, especially if there is an activist in the White House. The public generally realizes too that Congress and its committees could not have conducted the negotiations with Anwar Sadat and Menachem Begin that led to the Middle East peace accords early this fall.

Congress is a splendid forum that represents and registers the diversity of America. But this very virtue makes it difficult for Congress to provide leadership, and difficult for it to challenge and bargain effectively with presidents. Not surprisingly, a weary public dissatisfied with programs that do not work and policies that do not measure up to the urgencies of the moment will look somewhere else—and that somewhere else will usually be the president, or an aspiring presidential candidate offering himself as an alternative to the president.

How you stand on the question of a strong presidency depends in large part on what policies you favor and how those policies are advanced or hampered by the president or by Congress. It matters too, of course, whether you like the person in the White House. If you approve the president and most of his policies, the tendency is to believe with Woodrow Wilson that the president should be "free to be as big a man as he can be."

The cycle theory of presidential-congressional relations has long been fashionable. It holds that there will be periods of presidential ascendancy followed by periods of congressional reassertiveness. Usually these periods have been a decade or more, and sometimes a generation in length. The responsibilities of the presidency nowadays coupled with the complexities of our increasingly interdependent foreign and economic policies do not really permit any serious weakening of the presidency. Congress has tried to offer constraints to curb the misuse and abuse of power—but it has not really weakened the presidency.

The American presidency as an institution is still very strong. Its powers are such that the country will rally behind a president if the nation's vital interests are threatened. A president has a greater obligation today to communicate more persuasively than in the past about when and why the national security of the nation is threatened. But Congress and the people will follow persuasive presidential leadership when it is linked with purpose.

Defenders of the presidency argue that Congress and the reformers have overreacted to Watergate and Vietnam and thus they call for the repeal of the War Powers Resolution of 1973, restricting the use of legislative vetoes, restraints on the oversight of the intelligence agencies, independence for the executive's use of executive agreements, and in general a word of caution to Congress not to interfere too much in executive branch negotiations in foreign policy and security matters.

Many will continue to worry about future imperial presidents and about the possible alienation of the people from their leaders as complex issues continue to centralize responsibilities in the hands of the national government and in the executive. Those who are concerned about these matters will not content themselves—nor should they—with the existing safeguards against the future misuse of presidential powers. The difficulty is that few of the safeguards suggested seem to be politically acceptable or practicable. It is not easy to contrive devices that will check the president who would misuse powers without hamstringing the president who would use the same powers for purposive and democratically acceptable ends. There are some proposals heard these days that might assist in achieving that goal. An example is a provision that either the attorney general or a panel of federal judges could trigger the appointment of a special public prosecutor who would function for a specified time outside of the executive branch to investigate and prosecute alleged wrongdoing or conflicts of interest or cover ups and so on.

In the end, both the president and Congress have to recognize they are not two sides out to "win" but two parts of the same government, both elected to pursue together the interests of the American people. Too much was made by too many presidents and by too many scholars of that long-standing but partial truth that *only the president* is the representative of all the people.

Was Nixon Tough? Dilemmas of American Statecraft

Aaron Wildavsky

The one thing about which former President Richard M. Nixon and his critics appear to agree is that he was tough. The chief claim Nixon makes for himself in *The Memoirs* (1978) is that he was tough in foreign policy. When they do not merely use the term as a noun rather than an adjective (i.e., a tough, a ruffian, or hooligan), Nixon's opponents are likely to say that he was too tough, implying some concatenation of secondary meanings such as harsh and unyielding. No one, so far as I know, has asked whether either characterization was correct—Nixon the strong or Nixon the stubborn—or even relevant to discussions of leadership in general or foreign policy in particular. Yet the basic materials exist—Nixon's own reflections before and after the event. By limiting ourselves to *The Memoirs* alone, we can assure that every instance and interpretation favoring Nixon's self-image will have been reported.

Loading the dice in favor of a hypothesis of toughness is important if this essay is not to be about Nixon alone (his personality has preoccupied us long enough) but about efforts to practice statecraft. For similar issues face us today, issues about which we can learn from the experience of the Nixon administration, whether or not we approve of what it did. What is President Jimmy Carter to do, for example, when faced with challenging action by the Soviet Union? Opinion polls suggest that most citizens feel he is not tough enough but that they would welcome a treaty limiting strategic arms. Should Carter insist on what Henry Kissinger called linkage, tying arms to other actions, from Soviet armies in Afghanistan to Cuba's armies in Africa? Nixon spoke the language of linkage but he was not often in a position to practice it. By asking whether and under what conditions Nixon acted tough towards which countries, we may not only arrive at a more complex (and more interesting) appraisal of his role but also gain insight into recurrent dilemmas of American statecraft.

Layers of Toughness

When *Webster's Seventh New Collegiate Dictionary* defines tough as "firm . . . but flexible" the adjective itself may not indicate an unambiguous line of action so much as an unresolved conflict. Proverbial advice—look before you leap but he who hesitates is lost—is not useful without a statement of the conditions governing applicability.

Acting tough under any and all circumstances (I will distinguish various meanings and degrees of toughness as we go along) is not a commendable course of conduct. As Kissinger said about "the toughness of [South Vietnamese President] Thieu's position . . . His demands verge on insanity." Thus it becomes necessary to ask when to be tough, to what degree, toward whom, for how long. Nixon's behavior, as we shall see, admits of degrees of toughness according to circumstances. His theory may be monolithic but his practice was not.

Being tough is presumably an instrumental relationship. It does not—or ought not in a statesman—exist for its own sake. Its purpose, presumably, is to secure a better outcome for the country (including possibly a better reputation for the statesman) than acting otherwise. How, then, are the rewards of toughness to be appraised? Any football coach knows that victories are a function of scheduling. It's easier to be tough toward the weak—namely, South Vietnam—than the strong. It may be tougher to take punishment, than to dish it out. A number of times Nixon eschewed talking tough in public because he thought an open display would make it difficult for his adversaries to back down. President Carter has played the game differently in respect to Soviet dissidents. Which approach is better, wiser, tougher?

What kind of action accounts as tough? Consistent action apparently. "It will be my policy as President to issue a warning only once," Nixon said at a press conference, "and I will not repeat it [an earlier warning to the North Vietnamese] now." As Kissinger put it when, as often happened, he thought the Russians were not pressing the North Vietnamese hard enough to settle, "It is not President Nixon's style to threaten." "You will find I never say something I cannot do," Nixon told Chou En-lai, "and I always do more than I say." To make good on these promises, statesmen would need, first, total self-control, and second, complete control of others. Being neither perfect nor omnipotent, Nixon necessarily fell short.

Just as he expected to make good his threats and promises, so the president emphasized to the Chinese that "Richard Nixon would turn like a cobra on the Russians, or for that matter on anyone else, if they break their word with him." Bringing this point home to Prime Minister Golda Meir of Israel when she was warned about détente with the Soviet Union, Nixon said, "Our Golden Rule as far as international diplomacy is concerned is 'Do unto others as they do unto you'" and Kissinger injected, "Plus ten percent." But, in fact, no such single instance is recorded. President Nixon remained wholly within the framework of defensiveness that came to characterize American foreign policy since the end of World War II.

Is tough talk bravery or bravado? Is it desirable to threaten at all or to threaten only once? Presumably, the purpose of issuing a warning is to signal the other side to avoid behavior that is regarded as so undesirable as to call forth some sanction. Threats ward off direct confrontation by informing adversaries in advance of undesirable behavior. Suppose, however, that the warning does not deter the action either because it is ambiguous or belated or because the threatened party cannot do what is required. Might one not wish to warn again, because of ambiguity, or forget it, in case of incapacity, or withdraw it in the event the consequences of direct action are, upon renewed inquiry or changed circumstance, likely to be unfortunate. All these conditions (and more) prevented Nixon from matching deeds to words.

Consistency could be achieved by concentrating on sure things, but that is more like talking to hear one's own words, whistling in the light, so to speak, when the outcome is so obvious one doesn't have to threaten at all. Were toughness to depend on tenderness, weak friends would be a more tempting target than strong enemies. Credibility, which is what Nixon is seeking by consistency, cannot be gained at the expense of the weak, where it is immediately discounted, but must be hard won from worthy opponents.

Standing Up

Nixon writes of his "instinctive belief that the only way to deal with Communists is to stand up to them." In a memorandum to Kissinger, Nixon reiterated this familiar litany: "We are going to stand up in Vietnam and in NATO and in the Mideast, but it is a question of all or none." Is it really? Standing up everywhere all the time is bound to be tiring. What is worse, since conditions change, it cannot always be successful.

Consider "a very painful personal decision." Like any father, Richard Nixon wanted to attend his daughter Julie's college graduation and she wanted him to go. But he knew that after the Cambodian invasion there would be demonstrations. Should he stand up? In a speech in California, the president drew cheers when he said, "As long as I am President, no band of violent thugs is going to keep me from going . . . wherever I want to go . . . . This President is not going to be couped up in the White House." But in the end, out of concern for an "ugly incident," he did not go. As lawyers say, circumstances alter cases.

Consider, on a much larger scale, the president's efforts to drive North Vietnam out of the war. He was determined to "go for broke" as he put it in a memorandum to his secretary of state. First the language of toughness: "I think we have had too much of a tendency to talk big and act little. This was certainly the weakness of the Johnson administration. To an extent it may have been our weakness where we have warned the enemy time and time again and then have acted in a rather mild way when the enemy has tested us." Then comes the threatened action: "I intend to stop at nothing to bring the enemy to his knees," somewhat vitiated by his plaintiff cry to get the military "off its backside and give me some recommendations as to how we can accomplish that goal . . . ."

To Nixon toughness was not a question of resources but of resolve. "The only question is whether we have the will to use that power," said Nixon. "What distinguishes me from Johnson is that I have the will in spades." Knowing the outcome, we also know that will was not enough.

It would be easy, because true, to say that President Nixon was hung-up on trying to be tough. Some of the never-ending threats to his manhood were self-made. Vietnam, after all, did not have to be a test of Nixon's toughness; he made it so. If this picture is accurate, however, it is also incomplete. For if we put the question another way—Why have all post-World War II presidents been concerned about toughness?—simply saying they were all men would not provide an acceptable answer. The utter ubiquity of the phenomena in recent American history, from John F. Kennedy's concern over being pushed around by Nikita Khrushchev to Carter's care to talk tough on Soviet dissidents, suggests that it taps a deeper dimension of foreign policy with which every president, whatever his personality, must grapple.

Every presidential act, except possibly at the end of the president's term in office, is part of a sequence of actions, not just an isolated event. Hence the influence of this act on those that follow has to be taken into account. The rationale for any action, therefore, may be of two kinds: (1) substantive rationality, which depends on appropriateness under the immediate circumstances; and (2) indicative rationality, which serves to signal the likelihood of similar responses in the future. The importance of acting tough and standing up in this context is that it send the right message: Don't try this sort of thing again! Even if the action itself lacks substantive merits, is inappropriate or excessive or unjust, the argument may be heard that it must be supported so as to save trouble in the future by indicating that one is not to be trifled with—i.e., is tough.

Now all these abstractions might not matter if they did not delve directly into the purposes of American diplomacy, namely, as it was once put, to jaw instead of war. The overriding objective of the United States is to create a world order in which decisions will be made by consent informed by debate not violence deformed by the threat of a nuclear conflagration. If the United States wants conflicts settled at the symbolic level by words, not by deeds, however, its threats must be credible. That is what talking tough is about. A reputation for being tough is sought as a substitute for constantly having to act tough. Whether one can have the one without the other is the question.

Not long ago all a foreign policy had to be was for or against the war in Vietnam. Now, willy-nilly, it is time to see if we can find a foreign policy whose new dilemmas are preferable to those we face now. Instead of disowning the Nixon experience, Americans would be better off using it to explore their common and continuing dilemmas. To be fair, let us begin with those episodes in which Nixon's threats appeared to deter action and his success was measured by not having to fight.

Not Having to Fight

On September 18, 1970 President Nixon learned that the Soviet Union was building a submarine base in Cuba in apparent violation of the understandings reached to end the Cuban missile crisis. Nixon felt that President Kennedy, by making public the installation of missiles, had threatened Khrushchev's prestige, thus making it difficult for Khrushchev to back down and giving him reason to require concessions to save face in the cessation of anti-Castro guerrilla activity. So Nixon decided to keep quiet. And the Soviets, claiming there was no construction, accepted the president's insistence that the base be dismantled.

As usual, the Middle East was more complicated. At the end of January 1970 in the midst of border raids into Israel and Israeli reprisals, Nixon received what Kissinger called "the first Soviet threat" of his administration. A letter from Soviet Premier Kosygin declared that if Israel continued its bombing, the Soviet Union would make "a due rebuff to the arrogant aggressors . . . ." Of such stuff is modern diplomacy made. Replying in a low key, Nixon suggested that the two countries consider limiting arms shipments to the Middle East. Thus the president's first action in the Middle East was anything but tough: postponing the delivery of phantom jets to Israel. In this way, he hoped to renew diplomatic relations with Egypt and Syria. Half a year later, when Palestinian guerrillas held American airline passengers hostage, Nixon decided to deliver the jets.

In mid-September Palestinian refugees in Jordan, backed by Syria, encouraged by the Soviet Union, rebelled against King Hussein's government. "We could not," Nixon recalls, "allow Hussein to be overthrown by a Soviet-inspired insurrection." President Nixon began his diplomacy by telling reporters that the United States might have to intervene if Syrian tanks crossed into Jordan. He got the headlines he wanted: "Nixon Warns Reds Keep Out." Then Syrian tanks appeared in Jordan. "They're testing us," Nixon told Kissinger. So the president called on the Syrians to withdraw. And he had Kissinger call the Israelis saying, if there were no other way, the United States would support Israeli air strikes against the forces of Syria in Jordan. In addition, the president placed American troops on alert and moved naval forces into the Mediterranean. By then, however, King Hussein had rallied his troops and the Syrians went back home.

While Indira Ghandi, the prime minister of India, was in Washington telling the president her country had no designs on Pakistan, her armies were preparing to enter East Pakistan. "I wanted to let the Soviets know that we would strongly oppose the dismemberment of Pakistan by a Soviet ally using Soviet arms," Nixon writes. So he had Kissinger inform the Soviets that "promoting a war on the Indian subcontinent was incompatible with improved relations between us." Now it was Nixon's turn to ask Leonid Brezhnev for a cease-fire, urging him "in the strongest terms to restrain India with which . . . you have great influence and for whose actions you must share responsibility." The Soviets delayed. Nixon insisted. The Soviets replied that India was recalcitrant. Nixon insisted that was no excuse. The Soviets said they could guarantee there would be no Indian attack on West Pakistan but would not speak for another country in public. Without Soviet support, Nixon concluded, India could not attack and "by using diplomatic signals and behind-the-scenes pressures" another confrontation between the super powers had been avoided.

On the record before us, President Nixon, by a combination of verbal threat and movement of troops, but without armed conflict, warded off three potentially dangerous states of affairs. No doubt Nixon concluded from these episodes that a tough line paid off. But it is worthwhile exploring other forces at work. One is the disposition of relative forces. As in the Cuban missile crisis, the Soviet Union was not in a position to resist determined American action close to the United States' own shores. The presence of a strong ally in Israel and a resolute defender in King Hussein created conditions where American warnings might be taken seriously. And always, in back of Pakistan, there was China. But who was in back of South Vietnam or of Israel?

South Vietnam and Israel

As support for the war decreased within the United States, President Nixon decided he had to end it by a peace treaty before Congress cut off the money. So he told South Vietnamese President Thieu that his strongest supporters in Congress "had unanimously avowed that if Thieu alone were standing in the way . . . they would personally lead the fight against him . . . ." Now that's tough. To put it mildly, President Thieu, in Nixon's words, "was naturally skeptical of any plan that would lead to an American withdrawal without requiring a corresponding North Vietnamese withdrawal."

Thieu countered with proposed changes in the peace accords, of which three were critical: (1) the removal of North Vietnamese troops; (2) making the demilitarized zone (DMZ) into a secure border; and (3) no coalition government, even in appearance. Nixon said "no." If Thieu were to persist, Nixon wrote to him, "your decision would have the most serious effects upon my ability to continue to provide support for you and for the government of South Vietnam." In his diary Nixon wrote about Thieu as he never did about Brezhnev: " . . . If he doesn't come along after the election we are going to have to put him through the wringer." To be sure, Thieu tried to manipulate the situation to his own advantage. The point is that the United States had all the cards and used them. Nixon threatened publicly to accuse Thieu of obstructing peace while cutting off all economic and military assistance. Thieu gave in. And when their turn came, so did the Israelis.

"It was hard for me to believe," Richard Nixon wrote after Israel was attacked on the Day of Atonement in 1973, "that the Egyptians and Syrians would have moved without the knowledge of the Soviets, if not without their direct encouragement." Nevertheless, he waited. When it became apparent Israel might lose without resupply, he decided to replace its losses. As the airlift of weapons grew, Israel turned the tide on the battlefield, the Soviet leader wrote of a mutual interest in maintaining good relations, and asked Kissinger to come to Moscow. Here was a time to consider acting tough: Soviet allies were losing; Kissinger could have stayed home or asked the Soviets to go to Washington. Instead, he went to Russia where a cease-fire was agreed upon that stopped Israel from pressing its advantage. Within a few days Egypt requested a joint American-Soviet peace-keeping force. The United States did not want the Soviet Union to re-establish its military presence, so President Nixon told the Egyptian president this would only increase rivalry among the great powers. Immediately Brezhnev accused Israel of continuing to fight, suggesting a joint force, though, if the United States refused, the Soviet Union might act alone. To Nixon "this message represented perhaps the most serious threat to U.S.-Soviet relations since the Cuban missile crisis eleven years before." Aware that the Soviet Union was moving ships and had put troops on call, Nixon, upon the advice of his major advisers (though not apparently the secretary of state) declared an alert of all American conventional and nuclear forces.

It is possible to be too tough. While the Soviets may have been temporarily deterred by this display of irrationality (defined as lack of fit between means and ends), the value of a nuclear alert in signalling a life and death encounter had been compromised. The same sort of signal could hardly be used again. And the inevitable loss of credibility at home—nuclear alerts should be above suspicion—outweighed any temporary shock value.

American reaction to the attack on Israel has a rationale but not one that would commend itself to future allies who might realize that being tough has a double edge, applying not only to opponents but to them as well. An ally of the United States was attacked by surprise, suffered severe casualities, and was almost overrun. The United States waited until its ally grew desperate before sending arms. This certainly made the Israelis aware of their dependence. When Israel appeared to be victorious, the United States intervened to help its attackers, so Egypt would also recognize its dependence. The true test of toughness, to be sure, remained American ability to obtain concessions not from its dependents but from its adversaries.

Leaning on the Russians

The major effort to put pressure on the Soviet Union in order to encourage it to change the behavior of another nation—perhaps *the* hallmark of Nixon diplomacy—took place in regard to North Vietnam. The idea was that, for fear of losing American favor in trade arrangements, or strategic arms agreements, or whatever it was thought to desire, the Soviet Union would stop or limit arms shipments or would encourage or coerce the North Vietnamese to accept peace terms. To all this the invariable Soviet response was that they could not control a sovereign nation, that they would never abandon a socialist ally, but that they would forward American proposals.

In view of the fact that Vietnam was a debilitating experience, gravely weakening American defense, it might be thought the Soviets would just as soon have it drag on. And, unless the Nixon administration was willing to continue not only a controversial war but an unrestrained nuclear arms compet-ition (as well as having other foreign policy fish to fry), it could hardly withhold all cooperation. If détente was also a disaster, what would Nixon claim as his accomplishments in foreign policy?

The critical discussion took place in 1969 between President Nixon and Soviet Ambassador Dobrynin, who began by saying that Moscow thought that resolving the situation in Vietnam by force was unwise. Nixon commented that the U.S.S.R. had not made good its promise to be helpful during the year-long bombing pause and that perhaps it wanted the war to continue. Because "the humiliation of a defeat is absolutely unacceptable," Nixon told the Russians not once but many times, progress in improving American-Soviet relations would be difficult. "Does this mean there can be no progress?" Dobrynin asked. Here was the point of no return—if Nixon wanted to pursue a strategy that would have the Soviet Union lean on North Vietnam he had to say, "None." Instead, Nixon replied, "Progress is possible" but on a lower diplomatic level. At that time, Nixon remembers, Henry Kissinger cried, "It was extraordinary! No president has ever laid it on the line to them like that." Nixon tried to tantalize the Soviets by telling them that if they helped end the war "we might do something dramatic to improve our relations, indeed some-thing more dramatic than can now be imagined." Apparently, the Russians couldn't imagine it either because Nixon himself writes of the "apparent ineffectiveness" of this approach in 1969.

Enter the summit. By now it was the winter of 1972. Soviet arms poured into Hanoi; Nixon complained to the Soviets—they temporized. Same old story. But by now there was hope for a summit meeting with Soviet leaders ending in an agreement to limit strategic arms. The Soviet ambassador hinted the North Vietnamese would soon be more responsive, especially if Kissinger went secretly to Moscow to discuss items for the agenda at the summit. Here Nixon says his tactics differed from those of Kissinger. Nixon wanted Kissinger to refuse to discuss anything the Soviets wanted "until they specifically committed themselves to help end the war." Kissinger preferred a more flexible approach without preconditions. Meanwhile, back in Vietnam, there was a massive invasion of the South, and, back in Paris, the scheduled talks—about which the Soviets had hinted so pleasantly to Nixon—were cancelled by the North Vietnamese.

So Kissinger complained again to Ambassador Dobrynin, and Dobrynin again asked him to go to Moscow. Vietnam could be the first issue on the agenda, and, who knows, there was even a hint the ambassador of North Vietnam might also be in Moscow. What should be done? Nixon sent Kissinger to Moscow. What happened there? " . . . Brezhnev refused to promise to put any pressure on Hanoi to achieve either a deescalation or final settlement."

Reading over Kissinger's cables, Nixon reports he "felt that we might have missed the last opportunity to see how far the Soviets were willing to go to get the summit." Kissinger consoled Nixon with the thought that if the summit took place he would "be able to sign the most important arms control agreement ever concluded." Nixon was torn between the view that a harder line might have gotten Russian help on Vietnam or might have failed there and produced none of the benefits he hoped from a summit. Linkage may be a liability if there is more than a single issue of importance.

Linkage, in any event, chains Washington to Moscow as well as the other way. Before the summit Brezhnev sent a letter saying that the American stand in the Paris peace talks was harming a successful summit. But Nixon would not change his course in Vietnam even for a summit. When the North Vietnamese proved recalcitrant, Nixon believed he had to increase the bombing to get an acceptable settlement. The trouble with that, in an interconnected world, was that bombing the North might cause the Soviet Union to cancel the summit. And "that," as Nixon writes, "would be the worst possible outcome: A domestic outcry over the bombing and cancellation of the summit as well." What to do?

Treat weakness as strength. Instead of threatening to retreat from the summit, Nixon spoke of North Vietnam as a threat to it. Together, he had no doubt, the U.S. and the U.S.S.R. could bring about a peace without humiliation. In the meantime, he held his breath and went ahead with bombing Hanoi harbor. The Soviet Union did not cancel the summit. By taking a strong action, Nixon knew that going to the summit could not be called an act of weakness. That is how going to the summit became part of standing up to the Russians instead of lying supine before them.

As always, Kissinger knew how to put it to Nixon: "This has to be one of the great diplomatic coups of all times! Three weeks ago everyone predicted it would be called off and now we're on our way!" Toward what is the question? It will be some time before anyone can appraise the usefulness of the first SALT agreement and the ABM treaty. What is clear is that after so much effort and so many detours the trip to the summit had taken on a value in and of itself.

In the end, linkage neither added to nor detracted from the war in Vietnam, which was the ultimate test of President Nixon's foreign policy. Belief in the efficacy of linkage may have encouraged the illusion that it was possible to get the Soviet Union to do what the United States could not do for itself. But linkage abroad proved to be no substitute for unity at home.

Trading Timidity for Toughness

That a nation's foreign policy is only as strong as its domestic support is an adage accepted by everyone, including Richard Nixon. Despite claims that he would never give in to protesters, his record reveals otherwise. The difficulty in following the adage comes in estimating the interactive effects between foreign policy and domestic support. If it is true that few foreign policy ventures are worth significant internal opposition, it may also be true that allowing a situation to deteriorate abroad may cause trouble at home.

A good case in point is the EC-121 episode (named after a Navy reconnaissance plane that was shot down off the North Korean coast in the spring of 1969). President Nixon believed he was being tested (it was early in his administration) by a "deliberate affront to American honor" that questioned the ability of the United States to protect its military men abroad. Nixon wanted to meet force with force by bombing an airfield in North Korea. His secretaries of state and defense, however, felt that this provocation was isolated, like the Pueblo incident. National Security Adviser Kissinger is reported as saying that "If we strike back even though its a risk, they will say 'This guy is becoming irrational—we'd better settle with him.' But if we back down, they'll say, 'This guy is the same as his predecessor—and if we wait he'll come to the same end." For Kissinger it might have been High Noon but Nixon feared it might be the longest night if a war broke out in Korea. "As long as we were involved in Vietnam," he writes, "we simply did not have the resources or public support for another war in another place." The matter was decided by their common recognition that they "could ill afford a Cabinet insurrection at such an early date" and that "congressional and public opinion were not ready for the shock of a strong retaliation . . . ." Though Nixon later wondered whether he was right to avoid retaliation, his anticipation of domestic opinion, fortified by dissent within his own administration, did matter.

Indeed, it is at least arguable that public opinion was decisive in shaping the Nixon administration's strategic posture in Vietnam. Though opinion polls at the time indicated that most people would have liked military victory, Nixon realized they probably thought of it as "a knockout blow." But only two were possible. One was to bomb the dikes thereby killing several hundred thousand people. The other alternative was the use of small nuclear weapons. "The domestic and international opinion that would have accompanied the use of either of these knockout blows," as Nixon puts it with understatement, "would have got my Administration off to the worst possible start." The remaining decisive act, escalating conventional warfare, including invading North Vietnam, would have required months of fighting with severe losses. And, here we have Nixon's most important statement, " . . . there was no way that I could hold the country together for that period of time in view of the numbers of casualties we would be sustaining." Whatever followed may well have been determined more by the elimination of these strategic alternatives due to anticipation of opinion than by anything that followed. For if it was then a question not of directly defeating the North Vietnamese but of determining which side would outlast the other, the die was cast in favor of the side less constrained by domestic opinion.

As the war dragged on against the president's optimistic hopes that it could be quickly concluded, the question arose of how his administration was to treat domestic protests. Nixon was trying to end the war with a negotiated settlement. If it appeared that domestic pressure would force the United States to leave Vietnam, his efforts would come to nought because there would then be no need to make concessions. To protect his negotiation posture, the president said at a press conference that he knew there were protests but that " . . . under no circumstance will I be affected by it." And he followed this up with his "Silent Majority" speech on November 3, 1969, arguing essentially that since the dissenters were a small minority, the nation's foreign policy should not be determined by their behavior.

Thus Nixon placed himself in a paradoxical position; in order to make his policies credible, he felt he had to say that protest would not change them, though he knew their credibility could be undermined by protest. Truly, Nixon protested too much. The worse the war, the more important domestic opinion became, the less attention he felt he could afford to pay to it. While the protesters gained the impression the government paid them no heed, public and elite opinion grew in importance with every denial.

Of course the president understood the magnitude and importance of the protest movement, from his family, from his friends, from a society saturated with misgivings. But he had become locked into the logic of his own position: he couldn't carry on the war without public opinion and he couldn't placate this opinion if an immediate end to the war were demanded.

These considerations converged on Cambodia. Melvin Laird and William

Rogers argued that if the invasion would not end the war, which no one thought it would, the price in public opinion would be too high. The momentum of the peace movement had been slowed down by prior troop withdrawals and invading Cambodia would speed it up again. Nixon and Kissinger agreed there were good arguments on both sides: depriving the North Vietnamese of their sanctuary versus domestic disagreement. "I never had any illusions about the shattering effect a decision to go into Cambodia would have on public opinion at home," Nixon writes. " . . . I recognized it could mean personal and political catastrophe for me and my Administration." Why do it then? Because as Nixon told Kissinger, "defeat was simply not an option." But defeat is always possible, especially when you are losing. How, then, reconcile what must not happen with what is all too likely to happen? Claim defeat as victory.

Giving in Triumphantly

Stripped of the surrounding circumstance, the permanent pattern of the Vietnam negotiations was startingly simple: United States threatens, North Vietnam ignores, United States concedes. To see what happened, it is useful to present the stimulus and response in Nixon's own words, for he has no interest in making himself look bad.

Stimulus: "In March I confidently told the Cabinet that I expected the war to be over in a year. We had taken the initiative in Paris and proposed the restoration of the DMZ as a boundary between North and South Vietnam and advanced the possibility of a simultaneous withdrawal of American and North Vietnamese troops from the South."

Response: "But the North Vietnamese yielded nothing. They insisted that political and military issues were inseparable, that American troops must be withdrawn unilaterally, and that Thieu must be deposed as a precondition to serious talks."

Stimulus: "After weeks passed with no response, we decided to take the initiative once again. In a televised speech on May 14 I offered our first comprehensive peace plan for Vietnam. I proposed that the major part of all foreign troops—both U.S. and North Vietnamese—withdraw from South Vietnam within one year after an agreement had been signed."

Response: "There was no serious response from the North Vietnamese, either in Hanoi or Paris, to my May 14 proposal."

Stimulus: Kissinger to Nguyen van Thieu in Paris, August 1969. "I have been asked to tell you in all solemnity, that if by November 1 no major progress has been made toward a solution, we will be compelled—with great reluctance—to take masures of the greatest consequences." Nixon: "In the middle of September I announced the withdrawal of another 35,000 troops by December 15."

Response: "The North Vietnamese were not forthcoming."

Stimulus: "Despite the impasse in the secret talks and the worsening military situation in Cambodia, I decided to go ahead with the troop withdrawal scheduled for April 20. I discussed the issue at length with Kissinger, and we agreed that the time had come to drop a bombshell on the gathering spring storm of antiwar protest . . . Instead of announcing a smaller number over a shorter period, I would announce the withdrawal of 150,000 men over the next year . . . The withdrawal figure came as a dramatic surprise when I revealed it in a speech on April 20."

Response: "The only communist reaction was an escalation of the fighting."

Stimulus: "Kissinger's first secret meeting with the North Vietnamese since the Cambodian operation took place on September 7. Instead of the propaganda and vituperation he had expected, he found the friendliest atmosphere of any of the sessions so far. Summing up the meeting for me, he wrote, 'Not only did they change their tone, but they also indicated a readiness to move on substance. They in effect dropped their demand for a six-month "unconditional" withdrawal schedule, made no mention of the ten points, and indicated that they would reconsider their political proposals.'"

Response: "The meeting of September 27 dashed all hopes of a breakthrough. The North Vietnamese were argumentative and repetitive. They made it clear that their tactic would be to isolate Thieu as the man who stood in the way of peace."

Stimulus: " . . . a cease-fire in place throughout Indochina, . . . I presented this plan on television on Oct. 7. Five days later I announced that 40,000 troops would be withdrawn by Christmas. These two moves went so far toward removing the obstacles to a settlement that they effectively silenced the domestic antiwar movement by placing the burden squarely on the North Vietnamese to begin serious negotiations."

Response: " . . . But Hanoi stayed silent . . . . The optimistic days when I had envisioned ending the Vietnam war within a year were now long past. For more than a year the North Vietnamese had played a cynical game with the peace talks in Paris. Whenever Kissinger would make a substantial new proposal in one of the private sessions, they would either ignore or reject it. Then in the public sessions they would vehemently attack us for not showing any flexibility or interest in reaching an agreement. They would haggle about details, but on the bottom line they never wavered: they would not agree to a settlement unless we agreed to overthrow Thieu."

Stimulus: "On August 16, 1971 we offered the complete withdrawal of American and allied forces within nine months after an agreement."

Response: "On September 13 they rejected this proposal and continued to insist on the overthrow of Thieu as the *sine qua non* for reaching any agreement. In the meantime they used the public meetings in Paris to berate us for not wanting to negotiate seriously."

So much for tough talk.

Eventually, after continued agitation within the United States and the bombing of North Vietnam, the two sides achieved a written agreement. North Vietnam gave up its insistence on deposing President Thieu, and the United States no longer insisted that North Vietnamese troops leave South Vietnam. Instead, the parties agreed to put limits on reinforcing troops that were already there, though precisely how this was to be enforced was never entirely clear. Apparently, President Nixon expected to increase bombing to control violations. Optimism on enforcement is evident in the president's statement that the agreement "amounted to a complete capitulation by the enemy. They were accepting a settlement on our terms." The terms were indeed ours but whose capitulation they represented remains problematical.

When, after the last Christmas bombing, Congress effectively cut off funds, President Nixon claims this ruined any chance of enforcing the agreement and led to a massive invasion of the South by the North, which ended in conquest. But this effort to shift the blame, while understandable, will not withstand inquiry.

Once the United States withdrew troops it is difficult to imagine receiving congressional authorization to bring them back. Bombing alone was available for enforcement. And a multitude of difficulties awaited its use. Learning about violations would have been difficult, since they might have involved many movements of small groups, and since they would be denied. The United States would have found it hard to respond to each and every violation, because that would increase protests. And if North Vietnam was willing to take the punishment, nothing stopped it from sending in its main forces, which could be halted only be reintroducing American soldiers. Lack of congressional and popular support was not only the first but the final blow, because it would have defeated enforcement later just as it did earlier. Saying that a favorable settlement, leaving the government of South Vietnam intact, could have been obtained except for insufficient domestic support is like saying you lost because you did not win.

Being tough in one direction may be a cause of weakness in another. Being tough in Cambodia, for instance, had the effect of giving the North Vietnamese (and their Soviet allies) control over American ability to carry on the war. By refusing to negotiate a solution acceptable to Nixon, the Communist powers prevented him from gaining the one thing he needed to maintain his domestic position—a slowdown of the war. Instead of the outcome depending on what the United States did, it depended on what North Vietnam was willing to do. In the largest sense, however, the American ambivalence in Vietnam—staying was terrible and leaving was awful—merely mirrors the enduring dilemmas of U.S. foreign policy.

Dilemma of Defensiveness

To be tough is to hold your own: You don't take from others but keep what is yours. Being tough, in this usage, is tantamount to maintaining the status quo. But in foreign policy the ability to ward off blows, to keep things as they are, while superior to the opposite, leaves much to be desired. Why shouldn't anyone take a pot-shot at you if the worst that can happen to them is that you duck. Heads they win, as it were, and tails they don't lose.

Imagine a game in which each side has a thousand pieces, and the rules allow one side to try to grab them and the other side to hold on to them, but not to threaten the attacker. Sometimes, the defender holds on and loses nothing; othertimes the attacker gains. Ultimately, unless one or the other gets tired and gives up, the passive player will run out of pieces. He may be resolute, courageous perhaps, but not, I think, tough.

If it implies the possibility of turning the tables, toughness is symmetrical: What I try to do to you, you can try to do to me. Toughness becomes the rule of reciprocity: For every hoped-for gain there must be a feared loss. Toughness is not turning the other cheek; it is the other's cheek.

If symmetry is a synonym for toughness, there has been no reciprocity in recent times in American foreign relations. Not once—not one single time—did the Nixon administration engage in a resource-enhancing instead of a resource-depleting action. It may have stopped this or that depletion, ending up as before, but it undertook no actions that acquired resources formerly possessed by its opponents, thus leaving it in a stronger position. The one possible exception, the one that proves the rule, is taking over the Soviet place in Egypt after the October war. By saving Egypt's armies from annihilation, and perhaps Cairo from occupation, the United States restored itself in Egypt's good graces. The price of occupying this position, however, was abrogating the rule of reciprocity: There can be no symmetry if Egypt attacks Israel and Egypt is guaranteed against loss.

The defensive character of American foreign policy did not begin or end with President Nixon. It is inherent in the situation of a satisfied super power happy to hold on and unwilling to act except when provoked. Were the United States to do the opposite it would become offensive not only to its opponents but to itself. The U.S. really doesn't want what belongs to others and it cannot sustain the domestic support to make sacrifices for what seem to be surplus possessions. The truth must out. The United States acts like a defensive power because that is precisely what it is.

The question remains, however, whether defensiveness provides proper defense. Defensiveness is sustained by the belief that a rebuff here or there will make an opponent reluctant to try the same sort of thing elsewhere. Having intervened successfully in Greece in 1949, for example, it was only natural for President Truman to think of South Korea as "the Greece of the Far East." He told a White House assistant that "if we are tough enough now, there won't be any next step." As Bruce Kuniholm concluded, "Truman saw Korea as part of a sequence of aggressive moves by the Communist world which tested the United States. Each successful American effort he saw as persuading the Soviets to follow a more cautious policy. These analogies were not unique to Truman . . . . President Eisenhower in 1957 . . . Adlai Stevenson in 1964 . . ." on and on.

Why didn't this far from implausible theory—they advance-we resist, advance-resist, advance-resist, and then at last, no advance—work? Because there was no reciprocity.

If North Korea attempts to take over South Korea, and the North fails, symmetry suggests it must risk losing as much as it sought to gain—all or part of its own territory. If North Vietnam invades South Vietnam, the same symmetry applies. And so it does when Egypt and Syria invade Israel. Then there would be deterrence: The fear of losing as much or more as one hoped to gain. As things stand, however, an attack is just an invitation to do better next time.

Defensiveness is a dilemma. When all we do is react, we play a losing game—which one of our pieces shall we give up today? Rebuffing a threat here or an incursion there leaves a great deal to be desired by those in charge of making foreign policy. First of all, defensiveness is *perplexing*. A strain is put on intelligence to discover who is behind whatever is happening. The Soviets might be behind the North Vietnamese but so might the Chinese. Secondly, it is *enervating*. Individual decisions, involving different arrays of actors, have to be made about various parts of the world. Who wants to have to know whether Syria's motives in Jordan are directed toward Israel or Iraq or whether India is trying to get back at Pakistan or China? Third, defensiveness is *nerve-wracking* both to those worried about peace and about war. Numerous little episodes make it appear as if the United States is either at the brink of war or diverting itself from the main issues. For those concerned about war, it appears that either the United States is losing yet another engagement or is being distracted from the over-all hostile design. Critics on all sides agree, therefore, that United States foreign policy is incoherent.

Now one of the few propositions about social life that appears to have near-universal applicability is the more the complexity the greater the urge to impose simplicity. And the simplest theory is that there are not many causes, but only one: the Soviet Union is to be held responsible for whatever the United States doesn't like. Is this trick accomplished with mirrors? Almost, but not quite. By assuming what one wishes to be so, one may make it come true. Politicians are often held responsible for deeds not in the belief they can control themselves but in the hope they may learn how.

Holding the Soviet Union responsible certainly simplifies foreign policy. Why worry about who was responsible for what when Russia could take care of it? Why worry about distraction or perplexity when a call on the hot line would bring the required answer? Why, indeed, worry about domestic opinion or allied reaction, when all a president had to do was call Moscow?

Aside from its simplicity, and possibly its efficacy on single issues, however, one wonders whether growing addiction to the hot line is a favorable form of foreign policy. Is it in the interest of the United States to make the international arena into a more bipolar world than it is already?

Dilemma of Linkage

Until I read *The Memoirs* of Richard Milhouse Nixon, I had not realized how much of his foreign policy was dependent on Soviet cooperation. By now the litany is familiar: "Hey, Russia, why don't you get Syria out of Jordan?" "Hey Russia, why don't you get India out of (or prevent it from going into) Pakistan?" It was "Hey, Russia this" and "Hey, Russia that" until it came down to North Vietnam when no "Hey you's" (and there were plenty of them) were worth the breath with which they were uttered. No need to mine Hai-phong Harbor to stop Soviet supplies if the same purpose could have been accomplished by not sending them in the first place.

Having shown how deeply embedded the foreign policy of the Nixon administration was in its relationship to the Soviet Union, the often-uttered unwillingness of the American president to accept defeat in Vietnam takes on a larger significance. The policy, as in prior administrations, was, by throwing back incursions, to make it less advisable to try new ones. To this Nixon and Kissinger added a more explicit doctrine of linkage: You, Russia, cannot conflict in one place and expect cooperation in another. When the Soviets refused (or were unable) to respond in the required manner, as in Vietnam, it became all the more important to show that they could not gain by going it alone. If they could, then the whole house of cards would collapse. Hence when Nixon reiterated that " . . . whatever else happens we cannot lose this war," he was referring not only to Vietnam but to all of his foreign policy, to his web of reciprocal relations with Russia on which all depended.

How easy it would be to set all this aside as the wild or foolish ruminations of one man who history has discredited. Yet one cannot read *The Memoirs* without feeling there is more continuity than change in foreign policy. The *New York Times* printed this headline on July 14, 1978—"Carter's Quest:Line on Soviet"—then in smaller type—"He wants to Be Tough But Not Imperil Detente." The story says "One of his [Carter's] most persistent problems, underscored anew this week, has been to retain the benefits of détente and yet find strong enough countermeasures to show the Russians his toughness when

they are undermined by his public protests against Soviet policy and when they ignore his rising declarations that he will not let them 'push us around.'"
Déjà vu!

Linkage is a double dilemma: On one hand, the United States is not certain it has sufficient hold on the Soviet Union to make linkage work; if there are always things it wants from the Soviet Union the United States cannot insist on an all-or-nothing approach. On the other hand, linkage may prove so successful the United States may find itself tied to a tiger it cannot trust. A power that preaches pluralism might be better off to advocate it. The United States has independent allies; the Soviet Union does not. By blaming the Soviet Union, where it is not directly involved, it may be encouraged to acquire the influence it is assumed to have had.

Dilemma of Debate

To become like the Soviet Union in order to compete with it would be to make success the very definition of failure. Criticism must remain our sign of strength even as it inevitably conveys the appearance of discord. When we all do the same thing, then we're doing their thing.

Democracy thrives on debate. Our struggle is for, not against, diversity. Therefore we welcome rational discussion of differences. Suppose, however, that what is good for our domestic policy is bad for our foreign policy: i.e., that debate with opponents is often undesirable.

It is said that a major difficulty in following a long-term strategy is that democracies in general are tied to the electoral cycle, and that the United States in particular is composed of impatient people. Whether or not this is so, a belief in resolving differences by discussion is deeply ingrained. Our leaders have certainly shown a fondness for meetings, public and private, as a vehicle for resolving conflict, as if setting a time and place somehow speeded up the process of producing peace. Yet the Nixon-Kissinger negotiation process strongly suggests that thinking of meetings as places where issues are raised and resolved increased rather than decreased the level of violence.

How is it possible for direct negotiations to have anything but a good effect? Surely, the worst that can happen is continued disagreement. After all, how can conflicts be ended if the parties don't talk? Besides, if fighting is not to go on forever, there is no alternative to talking. Negative answers to all these questions would discomfort not the Right or the Left but all American policy.

In considering propositions that appear contrary to common understanding, it is wise to step back and think about different though related events. I refer to the famous SALT talks. By staging them periodically, it becomes necessary to build support with the military leadership of each country. To assuage their fears, it is necessary to promise increased spending on this or that force. Thus talks on limiting strategic arms may actually lead to production of more armaments than would have taken place in their absence. Of course, the possibility of a perverse outcome does not mean that no meetings should ever be held but only that careful thought should be given to the possibility that the process of making and signing agreements may be destabilizing.

Seeing how the negotiations actually increased the level of violence requires another look at the last days of the talks on Vietnam. On October 12, 1972 Nixon toasted the successful conclusion of the negotiations. Only minor matters remained. At a press conference on October 26, Kissinger said, ''Peace is at hand.'' A single decision would produce the final settlement. Alas, Nixon wrote, ''All our hopes were dashed on Monday. Le Duc Tho not only categorically rejected every change we had requested, but withdrew some that had already been agreed upon during the last round and introduced several new and unacceptable demands of his own.'' Since it appeared that the talks would be broken off, Kissinger suggested Nixon go on television and rally the people again. But Nixon thought (no doubt rightly) that telling the people we had been ''tricked again by the Communists . . . and that now we have to order resumption of the war with no end in sight and no hope is simply going to be a loser.''

By December 9, however, with only a single item in dispute, Nixon allowed himself ''to begin feeling optimistic'' for ''the roller coaster events of the past week . . . seemed to be ending with a settlement in sight.'' Yet ''at the meeting on December 11, the North Vietnamese were totally inflexible on the DMZ issue. Kissinger's report characterized their conduct as composed of ''equal parts of insolence, guile and stalling.'' All this (''Kissinger and I completely agreed on the cynicism and perfidy of the North Vietnamese'') led to a resumption of the bombing at a more explosive level.

But what was the alternative to all these meetings? One purpose of a direct negotiation is to ratify agreements already reached. This ratification function does not apply to Vietnam. Another purpose is to discover more about the position of the other so as to bargain through give and take. Early on, it should have been evident that all the giving was on one side and all the taking on the other. Thus the negotiations became part of the struggle. For meetings to serve this political purpose, each side must be able to use them either to strengthen its own forces or to weaken the other. Evidently, the United States was not in a good position to do this. Because domestic morale was a crucial consideration, the United States inevitably found itself saying one thing—talking tough—and doing another—acting weak.

Once the pattern of behavior emerges from the welter of events, both the temptation to talk tough and the inability to act tough are seen to stem from similar surroundings. If persuasion is to replace force as the main arbiter of international conduct, the parties must either agree on (or be able to convince one another about) how the struggle would have turned out if they had actually fought. Something must be shared, if not common values then a common view of the future. Peace rests on war in the imagination. It is to this sublimation of violence—living through it in theory so as not to have to experience it in practice—that tough talk is supposed to contribute. Toughness is the verbal test of violence.

Naturally, spliting hairs is prefered to cracking heads, especially in a nuclear era where one thing might well lead to another. But ability to make good the threats that are designed to deter war, calls for willingness to go to war. The danger of tough talk is that it might lead to the very thing it is supposed to prevent. When actions are both means and ends, valued for their substance and for what they indicate, there may be difficulty in distinguishing the two, so that one ends by acting without thinking. Apprehension about tough talk is amplified by the common practice of defending policies as indications of resolve until ultimately, as actions appear divorced from purposes, cynicism reigns supreme.

Does tough talk have a future? Since the basic situation has not changed, America's future foreign policy is likely to be like its past practices: Tough talk to avoid having to fight, and difficulty in mobilizing mass support behind strong action. Richard Nixon may have exacerbated the tendency, much like a display in a medical museum, but he did not invent it nor is he the last to be caught in its web of contradictions.

Was Nixon Tough?

Was Nixon tough? If toughness depends on working within constraints, he was sometimes and he wasn't others. But if toughness means challenging prevailing paradigms he didn't and he wasn't. If by being tough we mean triumphing over dilemmas, molding events instead of being shaped by them, President Nixon doesn't qualify. He never challenged the dilemma of defensiveness. No action went beyond containment, which, by the law of averages, cannot be wholly successful. The Cold War had become the cooperative conflict without discovering the missing link between avoiding losses and making gains.

Linkage was lacking. If everything had to be satisfactory for anything to be worthwhile, a reversion to the Cold War—opposition is the rule, cooperation the special case—would replace détente—cooperation the rule, opposition the exception. Yet if the Soviet Union ceased being the United States' main source of conflict and cooperation, America would need a new foreign policy.

Behind the dilemma of debate lies the deepest dilemma of all. If Nixon believed what he said to himself about the Soviet Union, debate was unlikely to be desirable, fostering, as it was bound to do, an image of Soviet reasonableness, of being people with whom it pays to talk things over, people, we think, like us. Maybe. Maybe not. If not, if the U.S. believed the U.S.S.R. was implacable, the most consistent course for American foreign policy might become transforming the Soviet system by making their political values similar enough to ours so as to make debate effective. Then the elements linking American foreign policy might run the other way round; instead of sacrificing dissidents to the hope of arms limitations, for example, arms would be secondary to dissent that might change Soviet politics. Containment would be replaced by punishment, seeking to find gains equivalent to losses. And debate would not be the search for solution but the manifestation of its achievement.

This dilemma is deep because no one wants to face up to the prospects for world peace if the Soviet Union and the United States become convinced that the survival of one requires the submission of the other. So far the Soviet Union has been satisfied to chip away and the United States has been content to limit its losses. The deepest dilemma is whether it is in our (or anyone's) interest to radically restructure all our other dilemmas.

By suggesting that the language of toughness is defective, I am not simultaneously saying that Nixon was ineffective in foreign policy. What I am saying is that thinking in terms of ''standing up,'' of being tough, while it may be better than being weak-kneed and taking things lying down, is too lumpy and too gross to guide foreign policy. The rhetoric risks mistaking personal consistency with public safety. It lacks the variety necessary to mesh well with the environment. The United States of America, not just Richard Nixon, has yet to find a foreign policy.

Carter Tries on the World for Size

Vincent Davis

The one most important actor to study and to emphasize in trying to understand U.S. foreign and defense policy is the president of the United States. In recent years Congress has attempted to assert a stronger role for itself, with some limited success. New forms of expression for public opinion are allowing specialized sets of citizens as well as the public at large (not merely the U.S. public, one should quickly add) to make stronger inputs to the policy-making process. For one thing, a wide variety of frequent opinion polls are carefully studied by most political figures. But, notwithstanding the changing nature and roles of Congress, and the enhanced opportunities for inputs from people who are not inside the decision-making community, the U.S. Constitution and the very nature of foreign policy put the president in the all-important central position.

Most observers understand this crucial central role of the president, and therefore most observers have been trying to figure out the nature of Jimmy Carter since he emerged as a leading candidate for the White House. The one word that most writers have seemed to use most frequently in describing this man is *enigmatic*. For example, the *Wall Street Journal* reported in September 1977: "All of us . . . still have a lot to learn about the man who has transfixed Washington, the enigmatic Jimmy Carter." The *Parade* Sunday supplement newspaper magazine in November 1977 featured a cover story by syndicated columnist Jack Anderson under the title: "What Is Jimmy Carter *Really* Like?" The opening sentence read: "The most publicized man in America, Jimmy Carter, still remains a mystery to millions of people." As late as April 1978, longtime foreign correspondent Robert A. Haeger was writing in *U.S. News & World Report* magazine that European allies of the United States remained "puzzled" and expressed "mystification" about Mr. Carter.

175

Based on my own experience working in Washington in the summer of 1977, in a combination of research and consultant-type duties, sometimes in close connection with staff activities of the National Security Council in the White House and Executive Office Building complex, sometimes in executive branch agencies elsewhere around town, and sometimes for legislative branch personnel on Capitol Hill, followed by fairly frequent follow-up contacts throughout the 1977-78 academic year, and reinforced by extensive commentaries published by respected journalists in many media, *enigmatic* is not the one word that comes most readily to my mind when I think of President Carter and his immediate entourage. Rather, the one word is *amateurish*.

James Reston reached essentially the same conclusion in his editorial column in the *New York Times* for September 25, 1977, except that he used the more tactful term *inexperienced*. Michael J. Robinson, in his "Learning by Doing" guest editorial in the Spring-Summer 1977 issue of *Presidential Studies Quarterly*, said basically the same thing. It has been a commonplace observation.

All of this is readily understandable. Mr. Carter, 54 years old as of early October 1978, has spent less than a dozen of those years in political life, and most of his staffers have spent considerably less time in government and politics. This contrasts to all other U.S. presidents since World War II, who were in one or another form of public service for virtually their entire adult lives. President Carter, one must remember, understood all of this very well, and advertised it as a virtue in his 1976 campaign. He was running as the outsider against the "old pros" in the political "establishment." Carter and his associates believed that the traditional ways of getting things done in the federal government were "bad." But he and his people have been unable to agree on—and to obtain a wide consensus on—a new set of groundrules. This factor, I think, accounts for at least some of the continuing confusion and uncertainty in Carter's Washington. For all of this and more, he has been exposed to a steadily stronger drumbeat of criticism from an ever wider array and range of sources.

In some respects, the situation is not as unique as current commentators might have suggested. Americans were typically rough critics of presidents throughout the nineteenth century. We did not think of them as poor beleaguered souls who needed our sympathy, nor did we deferentially treat them as if crowned heads of royal families. Very little that President Carter has attempted, and virtually none of the circumstances in which he has attempted it, is wholly unprecedented in the history of the American presidency. Almost all presidents have promised and perhaps genuinely attempted to deliver more "good things"—such as prosperity at home, peace internationally, and strong security against external threats. Almost all presidents have promised and perhaps genuinely attempted to prevent or at least to minimize "bad things"— such as inefficient government, a swollen bureaucracy, higher taxes, hard times, and war. Some presidents have used moralizing tones to lecture if not also hector their fellow Americans. Numerous presidents have encountered unruly obstreperous Congresses. Many presidents have experienced divided counsel, sometimes divided loyalties, and often contentious personal rivalries among and between their closest aides and advisors. None of these things is new. What may be relatively new, perhaps even unprecedented, in the case of the Carter administration, is a president who has promised so much, and at least initiated so much, with so little relevant experience and knowledge of national government and national problems as well as international affairs, with such a mixed bag of aides and advisors, in the face of so many massive and intractable problems at home and abroad.

Questionable Appointments

The president's amateurish inexperience was most immediately evident in the appointments process, and this in turn complicated and aggravated all of his subsequent problems. In the first place, he knew relatively few people personally, and therefore had to place heavy reliance on advice from strangers. Notwithstanding all of the press reports in late 1976 and early 1977 about an allegedly thorough and comprehensive talent search to find the very best people to staff the new administration, the process moved very slowly, and many key positions remained either unfilled or else filled by Ford administration holdovers for a year and more after Mr. Carter's inauguration. This resulted in inordinate delays in dealing with some policy issues, and in curious anomalies in other areas. For example, the policy on Reserve and Guard forces that was incorporated in President Carter's first defense budget, presented to Congress in early 1978 for the 1979 fiscal year, was based on a recommendation from Defense Secretary Harold Brown which Brown had routinely received from the Assistant Secretary of Defense for Manpower and Reserve Affairs William Brehm—who in turn was a Ford administration holdover who gave Secretary Brown precisely the same recommendation on this matter that Brehm and former Defense Secretary Donald Rumsfeld had packaged for President Ford's final defense budget. Not until the spring of 1978 was Harold W. Chase appointed to serve as deputy assistant secretary of defense for reserve affairs.

More serious than delays in filling some jobs, however, was the uneven procedure followed in filling those for whom appointees were found relatively early. Criteria were seldom obvious or, if evident, were difficult to accept. In the debacle in finding a person to become the director of Central Intelligence, for example, many newspaper editorials in various papers around the nation said, in effect: We do not know whether Theodore Sorenson or Admiral Stansfield Turner would be the best man for this position, but the men are so starkly different in backgrounds and perspectives that it's hard to understand what criteria were utilized in picking either one. That was in the spring of 1977.

One year later, in the spring of 1978, Mr. Carter made the critically important appointment of the man to become the new chairman of the Joint Chiefs of Staff: Air Force General David C. Jones. The *New York Times* suggested that one important factor in selecting General Jones was the president's pleasure in being able to discuss religion with this military officer, and that Mr. Carter had in fact included General Jones in presidential "prayer breakfasts" at the White House.

Certainly, as one source of appointees, Mr. Carter was drawn to some new acquaintances because of this kind of feeling of close personal affinity based on shared values not directly relevant to the jobs in question. Second, and at the start, he obviously turned to many people whom he had known in some context in his native Georgia. The "Who's Who in the Carter Administration" regular feature in the September 1977 issue of *The Washington Monthly* magazine reported: "There are now 51 Georgians on the White House staff and 18 more at OMB [Office of Management and Budget]." Third, Mr. Carter turned to people with whom he had enjoyed some contact, no matter how limited, such as many he had come to know to some extent in the meetings of the Trilateral Commission, and his old Naval Academy classmate Stansfield Turner (although he had not known Turner at the Academy, and had met him on only a few occasions while Mr. Carter was governor of Georgia). A fourth source was people urged on him by leaders of various Democratic party groups and factions—a traditional technique for unifying a party behind its new representative in the White House after a divisive election. President Carter apparently relied most heavily on Vice-President Mondale in this context, and many "Mondale people" sprinkle the Carter administration. Fifth, in keeping with his pledge to move back toward strong "cabinet government," including considerable autonomy for cabinet officers, Mr. Carter allowed many cabinet people to recruit their own key subordinates. As a result, some cabinet officers rejected appointees urged on them by the White House; this was particularly true for Defense Secretary Harold Brown who rejected at least two people whose appointments to high Defense positions had already been announced in the press, although these two salvaged attractive positions on the National Security Council (NSC) staff and preferred to say that they had turned down Secretary Brown rather than the other way around. Sixth, some holdovers from the Ford era were invited to remain indefinitely, particularly in areas of technical specialization, such as Navy Captain Gary Sick who remained as one of the two key Middle East specialists on the NSC staff.

Top presidential appointees drawn from widely diverse sources are not an unusual situation and would not be debilitating for the Carter administration if the president were capable of welding them into a unified team. Mr. Carter has not revealed this capability, however, for reasons based partly on some of his own characteristics, and for other reasons deriving from major policy disputes crashing around him like mountainous tidal waves.

Decision-making Style

One of his characteristics has been a tendency to immerse himself in reading massively detailed documents while in isolation from staffers for prolonged periods. He prefers receiving information and recommendations in these written forms rather than in face-to-face briefings and discussions. In the face-to-face situations, I am told from several knowledgeable sources, he often provides little or no feedback comments or even indicative gestures or facial expressions, such that staffers feel deprived of instructive interaction. Decisions have often been made by the president in a mechanical style that he likes, checking ''yes'' or ''no'' boxes on long lists of written options prepared for him by key aides. These and other important aspects of Carter's decision-making style were comprehensively covered by noted reporter Hedrick Smith under the title,'' Problems of a Problem Solver,'' in the *New York Times Magazine*, January 8, 1978.

More importantly, a second characteristic of Carter's style was revealed in this same Hedrick Smith profile, summarized in the subheading under the title: ''At the end of President Carter's first year, it is clear that he has chosen to rush into decision making at the cost of projecting a clear vision of the American future.'' The critical question here is whether Mr. Carter in fact has any such vision. The previously mentioned article in the *Wall Street Journal*, based on interviews with almost everybody who had ever known the president, reported that the following query was addressed to all interviewees: ''Does he have any vision?'' The reply: ''Almost without exception, the answer is no.''

A third Carter characteristic is a tendency to work closely with only a very few people on his immediate staff and treating these intimates with great loyalty. This was evident enough when Bert Lance, Hamilton Jordan, and others seriously injured the president's authority and integrity but were treated most gently. But, even more generally, Mr. Carter has appeared very reluctant to ''knock heads'' or to apply punitive pressures against *any* wayward appointees or congressional adversaries. To the extent that he was aware of actions by such people which could damage him politically, he was nevertheless remarkably tolerant and permissive.

Soviet Union

The problems associated with the extraordinarily mixed bag of aides, advisors, and key appointees, in conjunction with the three characteristics of Mr. Carter suggested immediately above, have become all the more serious in view of the one most fundamental and momentous issue confronting him and all others associated with foreign policy and defense policy for the United States. This issue, quite starkly, is to what extent the Soviet Union is the enemy of the

United States, and how serious is the threat that the U.S.S.R. might pose to U.S. security?

This same question was of fundamental importance in the years immediately after World War II. After raging debate within Truman's cabinet and in many other quarters from late 1945 until the fall of 1946, the decision was gradually reached—yes—the U.S.S.R. was *the* prime enemy of the United States and did pose a serious threat. Although Truman did not state this decision in public to the American people until March 1948, U.S. foreign and defense policies for a quarter of a century following World War II were premised on this basic tenet. Given the preoccupation with the Vietnam War in the later 1960s, and some signs of a growing thaw in American-Soviet relations, the question of the Soviet Union along the friend-enemy continuum in American thinking was put in abeyance. Concepts such as peaceful coexistence and detente, along with some evidence to support them, caused a continuation of a moratorium on the basic question into the mid-1970s. As of the beginning of the Carter administration, however, this dominant old question once again was pushed to the forefront (although not always immediately visible in the forefront, because of an occasional rhetorical smokescreen) of debate. Morton Kondracke, in an article entitled "Is There a Present Danger?" in the January 29, 1977, issue of *The New Republic* magazine, summarized some of the key dimensions of this most basic of all basic questions at the outset of the Carter administration's tenure. The fate of this administration—and, without sounding excessively melodramatic, the fate of the nation and indeed the world—could well hinge on how Mr. Carter ultimately answers the question.

Thus far, the results have been anything but reassuring, not so much because the question has not been answered, but because it probably has not been squarely faced. If it has been faced, it has been answered in many contradictory and incompatible ways at different points over remarkably short spans of time. It is precisely because of this circumstance that Mr. Carter has increasingly been accused of "vacillation" and "indecisiveness" if not worse. The heat began to build with a major cover story in the August 8, 1977, issue of *Time* magazine under the title "Carter's Foreign Policy: Jimmy in the Lion's Den." Earlier, on stylistic issues, *U.S. News & World Report* under the title "Foreign Policy By Committee—Can It Really Work?" in its issue for February 21, 1977, was raising procedural issues, but by the fall of that year the doubts and debates focused on the alleged mishandling of substantive problems. Jack Anderson and Les Whitten, in their syndicated column for August 19, 1977, were reinforcing the argument that the president tended to immerse himself in trivia and minutiae at the expense of American long-range goals, a point also raised in the February 21 issue of *U.S. News* (". . . allies and foes are wondering who's in charge of Carter diplomacy—and what American goals really are."). Charles Mohr, evaluating the president's first nine months in office, said on the front page of the *New York Times* of October 23, 1977, that growing numbers of leading politicians and government executives were raising serious questions about Mr. Carter's "competence." A Harris Poll widely reported in the final week of November 1977 indicated that 57 percent of the public were questioning the president's "competence" too.

In the field of foreign policy and military policy, the clear evidence has pointed to a bewildering array of zigs and zags on almost every significant issue. Often even the speeches and the rhetoric have been inconsistent but, where some thread of continuity could be seen in verbal declarations, the talk was often at substantial—sometimes diametric—variance with the actions. Sometimes it appeared to be merely bungled planning, as in the case of the major presidential trip abroad that was announced early in the fall of 1977, then soon thereafter was postponed on the grounds that Mr. Carter could not leave the country until he had got Congress to enact his energy bill, and then was eventually rescheduled (although omitting several key countries that had been on the original itinerary) notwithstanding that no progress had been achieved on the energy bill and a major coal strike was pending. But bungled planning was a minor matter in comparison to far more serious difficulties on substantive policy issues of great significance. Joseph Fromm, for almost 30 years the chief of European correspondents for *U.S. News & World Report* but by summer 1977 back at Washington headquarters as the No. 2 person in charge of that magazine (with the title deputy editor), said in a report of the March 6, 1978, issue of his magazine that the Soviets no less than the Americans were "baffled" by Carter foreign policy. Fromm suggested that, over the first 15 months of the Carter tenure, this foreign policy had moved through three phases particularly with regard to the U.S.S.R. The first phase was "uncompromising in condemning human-rights violations in Russia, pressing for drastic reductions in nuclear arsenals and expressing determination to challenge Russia in the Horn of Africa." The second phase was marked by a sharp shift almost around to the opposite direction, emphasizing "conciliation and cooperation with the Kremlin." Now in the spring of 1978, said Fromm, Carter's détente policy was entering a third phase that "reflects growing concern inside the administration about Soviet behavior and controversy over what to do about it."

Two articles in the April 8, 1978 issue of *The New Republic*—a magazine that has moved some distance away from its earlier ritualistic and automatic antimilitary posture, but is still not quite yet being published in the Pentagon basement—expressed amazement over recent zig-zags in Carter's foreign and defense policy statements and actions. In the first of these pieces, by highly respected and long-time White House correspondent John Osborne, the story reported on the role of Zbigniew Brzezinski, Samuel P. Huntington, and Secretary Harold Brown in "toughening up" the president's by-now famous

Wake Forest speech in Winston-Salem on March 17. But, reflecting back on the Notre Dame speech on May 22, 1977, and even earlier campaign speeches by Mr. Carter, John Osborne concluded: ''The record testifies that the speech represents yet another shift in the Carter rhetoric of foreign and defense policy and little if anything more.'' Morton Kondracke, author of the second of these pieces, reinforced the same point by noting that the president's well-publicized visit to a substantial U.S. naval force steaming in the Atlantic Ocean off the Carolina coast, during which an array of dazzling naval weaponry was displayed at considerable cost, came on the afternoon before Mr. Carter's Wake Forest speech. The two events together—the naval display, and the speech—seemed to signal a very stern message to the Kremlin. But then, Kondracke noted, the Navy budget will be sharply cut in the recommendations recently sent to Congress by Mr. Carter, thus undermining whatever message of tough resolve that the president might have wanted Moscow to perceive. Similarly, Kondracke reported, Brzezinski was saying that progress on SALT II might well hinge on a reduction of Soviet involvement in the Horn of Africa while Mr. Carter was telling syndicated and prominent columnists that he wanted to press ahead on SALT II without mentioning Africa or any other coupled problems.

Morton Kondracke, writing again in the following week's issue of *The New Republic*, dated April 15, 1978, observed that there is ''a growing feeling in this country that the U.S. is weak and getting dangerously weaker. It is reflected in public opinion polls, in high intellectual discourse about nuclear strategy and in a new respect being accorded to panicky time-is-running-out pronouncements that previously were dismissed as so much new missile-gappery. This infectious perception of U.S. weakness has spread widely in Congress.'' Kondracke ably summarized Mr. Carter's role in creating this new perception of American military weakness among Americans:

> ... President Carter must restore confidence in the country's military and political strength. But repeatedly he has done exactly the opposite. He has created a strong impression that he lacks any geopolitical vision or strategic sense, any understanding of how moves in one part of the globe affect events and judgments in other parts. He appears to have come to office with a set of vague themes in his head for making the world good—''human rights,'' ''disarmament,'' ''nuclear nonproliferation,'' ''North-South dialogue''—but without any notion of how to put them into effect, or how they might affect the East-West power balance. He has been forced to back down and shift course repeatedly, creating doubts about his resolve and judgment.

The neutron bomb issue was merely the latest to provoke new waves of doubt and anxiety about President Carter's competence, both at home and abroad. James Reston in his regular column in the *New York Times*, April 7, 1978, did his best to put a good face on the president's actions and decisions, offering a variety of reasons to support Mr. Carter at that point in time. But, the day before the *Times* used its lead editorial space to mount one of its harshest attacks against the president under the headline "The Mishandled Bomb." The editorial writer zeroed in on both the procedural and substantive aspects of the presidential action on this issue in the immediately prior week. Then, on April 8, Hedrick Smith reporting from Washington and Flora Lewis reporting from Europe candidly stated that Mr. Carter's performance on the neutron bomb issue had deepened the already serious reservations about his leadership abilities both within the United States and abroad.

My own impressions verify President Carter's eroding stature in Washington. On numerous research trips to Washington during 1977-78, including more than a month in each of those summers, I concluded that civilian and military officials in a variety of major departments and agencies felt that the nation was virtually leaderless. Pessimism was deep. Faith and trust in presidential leadership was lower than I had personally ever seen it. Even at the depths of the Johnson presidency in the summer of 1968, and at the nadir of the Nixon presidency in the summer of 1974, there was more respect for and confidence in presidential leadership than I could observe during my 1977-78 research year in and out of Washington.

Camp David

This overall picture of faltering presidential leadership was momentarily brightened in mid-September 1978 when Mr. Carter, with the help of two distinguished visitors from Cairo and Tel Aviv, produced a marvelously Rafshoonian television spectacular complete with an Arab straightman, a Jewish stand-up comic, and a Bible verse in recognition of the Sunday night occasion—although there was an almost-instant replay one night later for another audience on Capitol Hill. Without for a moment disparaging the noble intentions of at least most of the key principals, several things might be said to help put all of that into context. First, for many reasons too complex to elaborate here, the United States, Israel, and Egypt had nowhere else to turn except further into each other's embrace, while other key players in that game—most notably the Palestinians—were not represented at Camp David although they held powerful trump cards. Second, while Mr. Carter would doubtless claim—and would surely deserve—some political credit if he could help to advance even a partial peace in the Middle East, the major credit would redound to the record of Henry Kissinger who would finally have begun to earn the Nobel Peace Prize that he fraudulently accepted for other circumstances which earlier endured for only a few months elsewhere in the world. Third, while there was a modest upsurge in poll results supporting Mr. Carter on several questions in the aftermath of the Camp David peace initiative starting in September 1978, an increasingly sophisticated public did not readily convert credit in one area to an overall endorsement. No obvious foreign policy for Asia remained a serious problem stretching back over a decade. New turmoil in Iran was a kettle that could boil over at any moment, but few if any senior officials in Washington wanted to believe it, or to prepare for possible adverse contingencies. The Carter administration was attempting some imaginatively delicate diplomacy in Africa in the fall of 1978 but with few indications of what it could do if it could not make its best-possible-case aspirations come to fruition. Perhaps most seriously, massive economic problems nationwide and worldwide received occasional band-aid attention from the Carter administration, but with no sign of confident vigorous leadership equal to the magnitude of the problems. Bruce Nussbaum, reporting in *Business Week* magazine on October 23, 1978, on Mr. Carter's efforts to halt the massive international erosion of the dollar and related economic woes, flatly summarized: "The biggest factor in the international confusion over U.S. intentions and actions is President Carter." In overall conclusion, the Camp David initiatives in the fall of 1978 were welcome, like a tiny ray of sunshine on a stormy day, but not sunny enough to cause people to put away their umbrellas, or to decide that the Carter White House had suddenly been successfully immunized against the Peter Principle.

Battling Agencies

If faltering presidential leadership is the dominant impression that one gained on every hand when observing the Washington scene, one possible ray of hope could conceivably be found for foreign policy and defense matters if somehow strong and able leaders were visibly taking up some of the slack in the key agencies. While some bright spots could be discerned here and there, the scene within each of the key agencies and components did not offer much encouragement. The official party line that one could hear around Washington from various sources is that interdepartmental relations are relatively cordial. But a closer probing revealed that not to be the case. Press reports indicated growing tensions and disagreements among main participants. "Hawk" and "dove" groups have emerged on the fundamental question of how to perceive and behave toward the Soviet Union. Vice-President Mondale and some of the so-called "Mondale people," many of whom should more accurately have been called the "McGovern people" or the "McCarthy people" because they supported those presidential candidates in 1972 and 1968 respectively, rank among the 1978 doves. These include David Aaron in his role as deputy director of the NSC staff (immediately under Brzezinski), and Richard Holbrooke, Anthony Lake, and Richard Moose working generally at the assistant secretary level in the Department of State, plus certainly Ambassador Andrew Young and his deputy Ambassador Donald McHenry at the United Nations. Chief dove, needless to add, was Paul Warnke as director of the Arms Control and Disarmament Agency (ACDA). (Until Mr. Warnke jumped, or was shoved, out of that job in mid-October 1978, it was fairly clear that Warnke was a victim of a purge provoked by Senate hawks, led by Henry Jackson and his hatchet man Richard Perle, just as Gerard Smith and other ACDA stalwarts had been earlier victims when Jackson & Co. told President Nixon that those "softies" had to go as the price of their Senate support for SALT I. In the more recent case, Warnke had to go as the price and their *possible* support for SALT II. Yet, it was a questionable bureaucratic ploy on the part of Mr. Carter, shoving Warnke out and thus making him an independent agent free to roam the nation, building strong rebuttals against any Jackson & Co. efforts to emasculate SALT II treaties.) On the hawkish side are Brzezinski and, until late summer 1978, his *de facto* surrogate, Samuel Huntington, on the NSC staff. (Huntington returned to his Harvard faculty position in fall semester 1978, and was more or less replaced by Fritz Ermarth—an extremely talented Soviet specialist whose career had featured a shuttle back and forth between RAND and the CIA, and who was not likely to be any softer than Huntington, although perhaps more bureaucratically skilled.) Harold Brown at Defense sounded hawkish whenever he thought his White House master wanted to hear it, and the senior professional military officers sounded hawkish whenever they thought they could get away with it (which was less and less frequently) without serious risk of being *Singlaubed*. Trying to be "objective"—calling the shots as they see them on particular issues—are Cyrus Vance at State and Admiral Stansfield Turner at the CIA.

Players are fragmented and factionalized on issues other than perceptions of the U.S.S.R. One of the most divisive issues is the reorganization of the U.S. intelligence system, and the ill will generated in this ongoing dispute can be expected to color intrabureaucratic perceptions and postures on a variety of other matters. Admiral Stansfield Turner, believing that he had a clear initial mandate from the president to take charge of the overall intelligence system in his position as director of Central Intelligence, proceeded to do that starting in the early spring of 1977 just after taking office. He was quickly perceived by Brown at Defense, however, as a serious threat, because Defense controlled something well in excess of 90 percent of U.S. total intelligence assets; thus, any centralizing under Turner was almost certain to mean some losses for Defense, and Brown was never one to surrender turf graciously. Moreover, he had the full weight of professional military opinion behind him. Vance at State, with relatively little to lose and perhaps something to gain if the overall intelligence product could be improved and made available to him (Defense had always been reluctant to share what it gathered), often sided with Turner additionally because logic and the president seemed behind the admiral. Brzezinski was a different story, however. With relatively little actually to manage in terms of people and budgets outside of his reduced and streamlined

NSC staff, and knowing something about the old "knowledge is power" adage, he made a major effort at one point in 1977 to rejigger the U.S. intelligence system so that he could manage it from the White House.

Therefore, it is relatively easy to forecast that a running gun battle on a three-cornered field, with Brown and Turner and Brzezinski at the corners, will continue into the indefinite future in the Carter administration as to who will have precisely how much power over what parts and stages of the intelligence system and process. This battle can and probably will relate to battles over substantive policy issues from time to time as Brzezinski and Brown and Turner color themselves different shades of hawk depending on the issues in hand. An alert and perceptive reader might have had suspicions that some of this had already occurred in 1977 and early 1978 as major "turfing" disputes erupted throughout the Carter administration including but not confined to foreign and defense policy bureaucracies. A major front-page story in the *New York Times* for January 23, 1978, written by a team of reporters, analyzed some of these intrabureaucratic struggles for money and authority within the Carter administration. According to this *Times* analysis, critics were calling these bureaucratic wars merely more evidence of weak presidential leadership, some scholars were saying that these were routine and expectable events in government, and President Carter was saying that they were not only expectable but a positively good thing because they represented a healthy form of "bureaucratic democracy."

Weak Leadership

President Carter is in fact a weak leader, and may have been permanently injured beyond the possibility for full recovery by all of the apparent zigzags in foreign and defense policy matters thus far. He reads a lot, absorbing many details, but he understands very little, particularly in foreign policy and defense policy matters. At the same time, he has a sublime kind of self-assurance in his knowledge and his abilities, which he perceives to be far greater than almost anybody else will ever again perceive them to be. This terrifying sense of being right is not much mitigated by an inclination to think that he may in fact be wrong from time to time. If and when Mr. Carter thinks that he has been wrong, it will be because some perceived inner voice—not the voices of others—will have told him so.

For these reasons, it really does not much matter, in terms of overall grand policy decisions, that bureaucratic wars will erupt and flare up and occasionally rage from time to time among and between and within the various components of the foreign and defense policies apparatus. The president will want and will study the structured information and recommendations provided to him by the components of this apparatus, but he will eventually hear whatever he wants to hear from whatever sources—and his wants in these matters will be determined by a complex personal value structure not easy to pinpoint and describe. He will thus notice the bureaucratic wars, but he will not be overly concerned by these matters because he will not perceive that they have that much significance for him either in terms of his policy preferences or his own political future. Therefore, he will intervene to dampen down bureaucratic wars in his family only if the noise and furor become a nuisance, and not because of governmental reasons—only to remove an annoyance, not an impediment.

All of the above also implies that Mr. Carter will be more concerned with making policy than with monitoring its implementation. He will discover only too late, if ever, that many of his policies will have been undermined by bureaucratic warriors to whom he paid too little attention.

If he has a vision, it is an engineer's vision of efficiency in government, and one important bottom line will be a balanced budget. For this kind of reason, and not because he also made an issue of these matters in his 1976 campaign promises, he will indeed continue struggling to hold down the size of the federal budget, the federal debt, and the federal bureaucracy. A McNamara-style "body count" showing a smaller number of people in federal service at the end of his presidency than at the beginning would surely be pleasing to him, regardless of any other unpleasant consequences associated with such a reduction.

Mr. Carter will be particularly attracted to cutting down the defense budget, because it is an attractively large target, and because—notwithstanding his Naval Academy education—he has little or no understanding of the diplomatic or hostile uses of armed forces in any case. Lawrence J. Korb, in a briefing for the press in Washington on "Changing Defense Priorities: The FY 1979-83 Defense Program" held on February 1, 1978, said the following things about Mr. Carter's defense budget:

- The Carter Administration gives less priority to defense than any post-World War II administration. For the first time since fiscal year 1950, defense outlays will fall below 5 percent of GNP as of FY 1981. The figure was 10 percent, for example, in 1967, and Secretary McNamara was bragging about that.

- The FY 1979 defense budget is at best level in constant dollars, and would be a declining budget if the Congress should cut the presidential request by more than 1.8 percent.

- The emphasis will be on fighting a short intensive war in Europe, with a bit more money for the Army and a bit less for the Air Force and Navy, but enough less particularly for the Navy that its capabilities will be severely reduced as of FY 1983—indeed, so reduced that even the Army is worrying on it, because the Army needs the Navy to take it wherever the Army could be asked to fight overseas.

Mr. Carter will undertake even unilateral disarmament measures in the nuclear weapons category, blocking new weapons developments and slowing down or halting the procurement of more older weapons, if the SALT negotiations should fail—although he will be prepared to make almost any concession so that SALT negotiations do not fail. Many in Congress will be alarmed, and will threaten and attempt to take many actions and sanctions against Mr. Carter, but they will ultimately fail because when public opinion is ultimately confronted with the costs either in inflation or new higher explicit taxes required to support the new military items desired by some in Congress, the public will opt against the military items. In short, in the face of a growing taxpayers' revolt nationwide, and the increasing public anxieties about inflation, butter will win over guns. Many instinctive hawks will choke on the butter, but butter it will be.

A favorite and traditional American solution will try to disguise some unpleasant consequences. In contrast to the advice of Theodore Roosevelt, President Carter and many Americans of bellicose inclinations will speak "stickly" while carrying a big "soft." Rhetoric will heat up as capabilities cool down. But it will be only rhetoric. The *New Republic*'s distinguished longtime White House correspondent John Osborne was right when he reported in the April 8, 1978 issue of that magazine that Mr. Carter's tough-talking Wake Forest speech of March 17 raised "a question whether the defense speech represents the 'shift in emphasis in American foreign policy' that an angry Moscow response said it did." Osborne continued: "The gaps between Carter's fiscal 1979-80 defense budget projections and the scope of responsibility defined at Winston-Salem [i.e., the Wake Forest speech] raise the same question." Osborne's answer to the question, quite correctly in my judgment: "The record testifies that the speech represents yet another shift in the Carter rhetoric of foreign and defense policy and little if anything more." In short, the tough talk was all fluff and bluff. The reality is a weaker and weaker United States.

Contributors

GRAHAM ALLISON, dean of the John F. Kennedy School of Government, Harvard University, is the author of *Remaking Foreign Policy* and numerous other books and shorter works. He is a frequent consultant to many top U.S. executive branch officials.

THOMAS E. CRONIN is professor of political science at the University of Delaware and director of the Direct Democracy Research Project. He is the author of *The State of the Presidency* and co-author of several books, including *The Presidency Reappraised*, *Government By the People*, and *State and Local Politics*. A former White House fellow, Cronin has served on the staff of the Brookings Institution and been a visiting fellow at the Center for the Study of Democratic Institutions. Cronin also serves as associate editor of *Presidential Studies Quarterly*.

VINCENT DAVIS is director and the Patterson Chair Professor of International Studies at the Patterson School of Diplomacy and International Commerce, University of Kentucky. He is the author of several books, including *The Admirals Lobby*, and many articles. He has consulted and/or lectured extensively for U.S. agencies and schools concerned with foreign and defense policy.

LAWRENCE C. DODD is associate professor in the Department of Government at the University of Texas at Austin. He is the president-elect of the Southwestern Political Science Association, and a former congressional fellow (1974-75). He is the author of *Coalitions in Parliamentary Government*, and co-editor (with Bruce Oppenheimer) of *Congress Reconsidered*.

MALCOLM E. JEWELL, professor and former chairman of the Department of Political Science, University of Kentucky, simultaneously served in 1979 as the vice-president and president-elect for the Southern Political Science Association, and as president of the Midwest Political Science Association (for which he previously had served as the editor of the MPSA's journal). A leader in many other professional contexts, one of the most recent of his prolific publications is *The Legislative Process in the United States* (co-authored with Samuel C. Patterson).

LAWRENCE J. KORB, professor of management, U.S. Naval War College, is the author of *The Joint Chiefs of Staff* and numerous shorter works. A longtime active leader in the International Studies Association, he has for several years been the primary author-editor of the annual analysis of the U.S. defense budget for the *AEI Defense Review* magazine.

RONALD A. KRIEGER, vice-president for International Economics Research and Publications for Chase Manhattan Bank, has previously been an officer with The World Bank and with First National City Bank (Citicorp), as well as earlier service in the position of Economics Editor for *Business Week* magazine. His academic positions have included professorships at the Graduate School of International Studies in Denver, and at Goucher College where he was also chairman of the Department of Economics.

MARTIN A. LEVIN has taught at the University of California, Berkeley, and is associate professor of political science at Brandeis University and director of the James Gordon Urban Policy Program. He is the author of *Urban Politics and the Criminal Courts*, and the forthcoming, *The Political Dilemmas of Social Policymaking*.

GEORGE E. REEDY, Nieman Professor of Journalism at Marquette University, is the author of *Twilight of the Presidency*, and *The Presidency in Flux*, among numerous other works. He spent a number of years as a reporter in Washington for the United Press (later UPI), and another extended period as a staff member for congressional committees, before his work as special assistant to Vice-President Lyndon B. Johnson and later as press secretary to then-President Johnson.

RICHARD ROSE is director of the Center for the Study of Public Policy at the University of Strathclyde, Glasgow. His most recent books are *What is Governing: Purpose and Policy in Washington*, and with B. Guy Peters, *Can Government Go Bankrupt?* He also analyzes elections as a psephologist for *The Times* and *The Telegraph* in London, and for British television companies.

AARON WILDAVSKY, professor of political science at the University of California, is the author of numerous books and articles on politics and public policy including the forthcoming *Speaking Truth to Power: The Art and Craft of Policy Analysis* and *Planning and Budgeting in Poor Countries* (Transaction Books, 1980).